Palgrave Politics of Identity and
Citizenship Series

Aim of the series

The politics of identity and citizenship has assumed increasing importance as our polities have become significantly more culturally, ethnically and religiously diverse. Different types of scholars, including philosophers, sociologists, political scientists and historians make contributions to this field and this series showcases a variety of innovative contributions to it. Focusing on a range of different countries, and utilizing the insights of different disciplines, the series helps to illuminate an increasingly controversial area of research and titles in it will be of interest to a number of audiences including scholars, students and other interested individuals.

More information about this series at
http://www.springer.com/series/14670

Tania Saeed

Islamophobia and Securitization

Religion, Ethnicity and the Female Voice

Tania Saeed
Lahore University of Management Sciences
Lahore, Pakistan

Palgrave Politics of Identity and Citizenship Series
ISBN 978-3-319-81346-2   ISBN 978-3-319-32680-1   (eBook)
DOI 10.1007/978-3-319-32680-1

© The Editor(s) (if applicable) and The Author(s) 2016
Softcover reprint of the hardcover 1st edition 2016
This work is subject to copyright. All rights are solely and exclusively licensed by the Publisher, whether the whole or part of the material is concerned, specifically the rights of translation, reprinting, reuse of illustrations, recitation, broadcasting, reproduction on microfilms or in any other physical way, and transmission or information storage and retrieval, electronic adaptation, computer software, or by similar or dissimilar methodology now known or hereafter developed.
The use of general descriptive names, registered names, trademarks, service marks, etc. in this publication does not imply, even in the absence of a specific statement, that such names are exempt from the relevant protective laws and regulations and therefore free for general use.
The publisher, the authors and the editors are safe to assume that the advice and information in this book are believed to be true and accurate at the date of publication. Neither the publisher nor the authors or the editors give a warranty, express or implied, with respect to the material contained herein or for any errors or omissions that may have been made.

Cover illustration © Eduardo Huelin / Alamy Stock Photo
Cover design by Jenny Vong

Printed on acid-free paper

This Palgrave Macmillan imprint is published by Springer Nature
The registered company is Springer International Publishing AG Switzerland

For
Ama and Abu

Acknowledgements

This book is a result of over half a decade of hard work and procrastination that went into my doctorate at the University of Oxford, which could not have been possible without the love and support of friends, colleagues and my family. I would like to take this opportunity to thank them, for their patience, their love and guidance.

My thanks go to my courageous participants, who welcomed me into their lives and trusted me with their narratives. I only hope I have done justice to their accounts and will be eternally grateful for their generosity.

I am forever grateful to my supervisor, Dr David Johnson, for his support and encouragement, helping me grow as a researcher and an academic. He patiently listened to my ramblings, guided me when I got lost and, in equal measure, rejoiced when I succeeded.

I cannot thank Dr Nasar Meer enough for his support and for taking a chance on a complete stranger. He not only gave me the opportunity to publish in this series, but has also been a guiding light as I tread the murky terrain of modern day academia.

Professor Jonathan Githens-Mazer and Dr Mohammad Talib, such insightful examiners of my doctoral work, challenged me, and made me recognize my strengths and weaknesses. I thank them for their in-depth exploration of my work, which contributed to the further development of my ideas for this book.

I am further grateful to Professor Tariq Modood, Professor Tariq Ramadan and Professor Anthony Glees for taking the time to talk to a student when she was just beginning her research. Their insights were instrumental in guiding the direction of my study.

Professor Ingrid Lunt has been a source of inspiration throughout my research, teaching me how to succeed in getting my 'licence to do research'. I hope I can live up to her expectations in the future and will always be thankful for her encouragement and support.

I extend my gratitude to Dr David Tyrer, Professor Marie Lall, Dr Katherine E. Brown, and Dr Serena Hussain, all of whom shared their experiences and were a constant source of encouragement.

I was honoured to have received the Higher Education Commission of Pakistan's PhD scholarship for my initial years as a PhD student; I have also been supported by the Harold Hyam Wingate Foundation as their Wingate scholar in finishing my thesis, and the Al Charitable Fund and the Carr and Stahl Fund, which further supported my field trips. I will always be grateful for their generosity. Another person without whom this book would not have been possible is my editor, Amelia Derkatsch. I thank her for her patience during this publishing process.

I am also grateful to the wonderful people of St Antony's College, especially Karin Leighton and Mastan Ebtehaj, our one-off warden Professor Margaret MacMillan, and the most supportive porters in Oxford, especially Mick, Neil and John. I thank the most generous and caring housemates of the Convent of the Sacred Heart and its Sisters, especially the late Sr Sue Acheson—I can imagine her looking down from Heaven with a smile, saying 'Well done'.

The fact that I emerged from the doctoral experience having retained my sanity and managed to write this book is due to the support of my incredible friends; they tolerated my rants, accompanied me to midnight sessions at G&Ds, fed me chocolate when I was desperate and, despite everything, never gave up on me. Bipana Bantawa, Nahal Khabbazbashi, Pegah Zohouri Hagian, Remzi Cej and Muneera Al Khalifa who started this journey with me, I thank them for always being there no matter what, especially in the final months of my doctorate. I am grateful to Usha Kanagaratnam, Amoghavarsha Mahadevegowda, Navneet Vasistha, Sanchita Bakshi and Gunnar Langfah for being such great friends, for looking after me in the House, for feeding me and letting me hide in my room (or theirs) and, of course, Helen Pickford especially, for introducing me to *Doctor Who*. I thank Maria Repnikova, Roham Alvandi, Farida Makar, Eliza Gheorghe, Arthur Vissing, Şeyma Afacan, Nadiya Kravets, Fatemeh Shams, Ricardo Borges de Castro, Richard Stanley, Matteo Legrenzi and Farid Boussaid, for their support and for making St Antony's unforgettable. I thank Sara Chaudhry for encouraging me through her wisdom and experience but, most importantly, for letting me crash at her place during the field work—without her, this research would not have been possible. Sakina Jafri and Asma Niaz I thank for their phone calls and messages, especially when I was writing this book; Kashmali Khan and Izza Farrakh, for being so understanding and giving me time off from my 'real world' job to work on my book. Another friend who stood by me from the beginning, helped with my thesis and gave feedback and his critique is Ahad Ali. I am forever grateful for his encouragement and generosity. Finally, to all those colleagues who silently kept me going—a huge thank you.

While I have been very fortunate to have such supportive friends, I have been equally blessed with the most understanding and encouraging family. I am grateful to my nephew Abdullah Haroon, and my niece Daneen Haroon, to my brothers Haroon Saeed and Shahid Saeed, to my sisters-in-law Zainab Haroon and Ayesha Amin, *naani ama* and *daadi ama* (and her *dum wala paani*), for reminding me that anything is possible.

However, the two people who have made this book possible, made my work possible, everything I have achieved a reality, to whom I dedicate this piece of work, are my parents Zareena Saeed and Saeed uz Zaman. I feel blessed to have such selfless and loving parents, who have always encouraged me to follow my passion and never let anyone or anything get in my way. I thank my father for making sure I always had everything I needed and more. I could not have made it this far without his constant support and belief in me. There are not enough words to express my gratitude to my mother. She has been my inspiration. As a child, I enjoyed reading and learning because of her encouragement and her love for knowledge and books. She supported me throughout my doctorate, staying up nights proof-reading, editing and calming my nerves. For this book, she discussed all the latest developments and continued to edit my chapters, giving constant feedback. She has been my biggest and most constructive critic, and my strongest supporter. I thank her for making this book possible.

Contents

1 Introduction: Gender, Islamophobia and
  the Security Discourse   1

2 Muslims, South Asians and the Pakistani Community
  in Britain: Intersecting Security, Identity and Belonging   25

3 Securitizing the Muslim Female: Islamophobia
  and the Hidden Terrorist   57

4 Securitizing the Educated Muslim: Islamophobia,
  Radicalization and the Muslim Female Student   85

5 Securitizing the Ethno-Religious Identity(s): Exploring
  Islamophobia as Pakophobia   117

6 Challenging Islamophobia and the Security
  Discourse: Dialogue and the Muslim Activist   147

7 Conclusion: Gender, Islamophobia and the Security
  Discourse—Future Challenges   169

Appendix 1A   183

Appendix 1B   191

Index   231

List of Abbreviations and Acronyms

ACLU	American Civil Liberties Union
BBCD	British Born Confused Desis
BNP	British National Party
CSC	Centre for Social Cohesion
FOSIS	Federation of Student Islamic Societies
ISocs	Islamic student societies
J4NW10	Justice for North West 10
NUS	National Union of Students
NYPD	New York Police Department
Paksocs	Pakistani student societies

1
Introduction: Gender, Islamophobia and the Security Discourse

In February 2016, Tareena Shakil became the first British Muslim female to be found guilty in a British court of law for joining the terrorist organization Daish, also known as the Islamic State of Iraq or the Levant (Isil or Isis). In his ruling, the judge presiding over Shakil's case observed, '[y]our role as a woman in Isis was different to that of a man but you embraced it and were willing to support those in Raqqa, and potentially those outside, to come and play their role in providing fighters of the future and were willing, shamelessly, to allow your son to be photographed in terms that could only be taken as a fighter of the future' (Morris 2016). Shakil's case, like the fifty or more British Muslim women dubbed the 'jihadi brides' who have fled to join Isis, has shocked the British public, with experts and policy makers struggling to understand how and why British Muslim women are joining terrorist organizations (Sanghani 2015). As noted by the judge in Shakil's case, these women are providing a supportive role as wives of existing Isis members, or mothers to future terrorists. British Muslim men like 'Jihadi John', on the other hand, are a direct physical threat who are violent, as evident in Isis' video of Jihadi John beheading fellow British citizens, and later threatening to unleash terror on his

© The Author(s) 2016
T. Saeed, *Islamophobia and Securitization*, Palgrave Politics of Identity and Citizenship Series, DOI 10.1007/978-3-319-32680-1_1

return to Britain (Sawer 2015; BBC News 2016). While the reasons why Muslim men and women join such terrorist causes continue to be investigated (Hoyle et al. 2015; Saltman and Smith 2015), where radicalization is no doubt a problem that needs to be carefully tackled, the response of media and political actors in Britain and across Europe has resulted in a sensationalized narrative that implicates all Muslims as potential terrorists, hidden in plain sight. The security agenda has crept into the mundane and the ordinary with families, school teachers, universities and other social institutions all carrying the burden of preventing the radicalization of young Muslims (see HM Government 2015a). While the Isis phenomenon is more recent, the Muslim community has been submerged in a discourse of (in)security and terrorism since 9/11 and 7 July 2005.

The radicalized Muslim female first emerged in 2007, when Samina Malik was tried and found guilty under the Terrorism Act 2000 for possessing material 'useful' for terrorists (Bowcott 2007). Media and political actors responded with a sense of heightened insecurity and paranoia about the Muslim community, with the Muslim woman located within an oxymoronic spectrum of the vulnerable-fanatic, one susceptible to radicalization and therefore in need of being rescued. The Muslim male, however, continued to be perceived as dangerous, posing a more direct physical threat, with examples of terrorists such as Umar Farouk Abdulmutallab (BBC News 2011b), who attempted to blow up a plane bound for the USA. This paranoia led to counter terrorism policies that, since 2005, have increasingly brought social institutions within the ambit of security, often at the expense of human rights and freedoms—which, ironically, are what these policies aim to protect as 'British values'. The entire Muslim community of 2.7 million Muslims have been 'securitized' (Croft 2012; Office for National Statistics 2012) and made to take responsibility for the actions of self-defined 'Islamist terrorists', who are as much a threat to the Muslim community as they are to the British public at large. This securitization has further increased suspicion and discrimination of the Muslim community in the form of Islamophobia, resulting in physical and verbal assaults, direct and indirect, where Muslim men and women have constantly to prove their innocence, against a wider socio-political discourse that labels them as would-be terrorists.

This book enters this conversation by exploring the 'everyday,' mundane realities of British Muslim women that are submerged within this wider discourse of insecurity and paranoia. Forty British Muslim and non-British Muslim women living across England share biographical narratives highlighting their experiences of securitization and Islamophobia. These women express different 'degrees of religiosity' from those who wear the niqab, hijab or jilbab,[1] to practising Muslims without any religious signifiers, highlighting how the level of acceptability of a Muslim in modern day Britain is determined by a non-Muslim host community, where Muslim acceptability fluctuates within an extremist/moderate spectrum.

These Muslim women are educated, either studying in universities or, on graduation, entering the labour market. Media and political stereotypes of the Muslim terrorist also evoke the 'educated' 'alienated' Muslim citizen, vulnerable to radicalization within educational institutions. This is evident particularly in the Counter Terrorism and Security Act 2015, which has made it legally incumbent on universities and other educational institutions to report on any student in danger of 'being drawn into terrorism' (HM Government 2015a, sect. 26(1)). Police officials and anti-terrorism experts have also been working with universities in attempts to provide student 'welfare' by countering radicalization on campuses (Association of Chief Police Officers 2012). Between the tragedy of 7 July 2005 and the Counter-Terrorism and Security Act 2015, a period of ten years, the Muslim student identity has been subject to 'surveillance' and a discourse of constant (in)security (Home Affairs Committee 2012; Saeed and Johnson 2016). As educational spaces—not just in Britain, but also Europe and the USA—become implicated in the security discourse of the state, the experiential narratives in this study provide insights into the realities of Muslim female students, who become vulnerable targets of hate, ignorance and surveillance as a consequence of such counter terrorism measures. Islamic student societies (ISocs) and the ISoc sisters, placed within the vulnerable and 'at risk' category are further implicated in the

---

[1] A burqa/niqab covers the face (Allen 2010a) with only the eyes showing and is often worn with a jilbab. A hijab is a 'headscarf' (Droogsma 2007). A jilbab is 'a cloak covering most of the body' (Vakulenko 2007).

security discourse, having to defend their innocence against accusations of radicalization and extremism (Home Affairs Committee 2012; HM Government 2011c).

While the exploration of Islamophobia and securitization highlights the racialized religion and gendered identity(s) of the 'educated' Muslim, the book further unpacks the category 'Muslim' to examine how other categories of identity, such as 'ethnicity', play a role in experiences of hyper-securitization and Islamophobia. For the sample presented in this book, the ethnic identity is Pakistani; both British Muslim women with a Pakistani heritage and Pakistani Muslim female nationals living in England are part of the sample. Their experiences highlight how the dominant 'security' discourse related to terrorism, Islam and Pakistan creates paranoia about the Muslim and the equally dangerous Pakistani. Islamophobia often takes the form of a 'Pakophobia', where both identities become problematic in the socio-political imagination. The religio-ethnic conflation is important in highlighting diversity in experiences amongst the Muslim community, which is often overlooked when Muslims are treated as a homogenous group, or a single category. These differences are not only important in developing an in-depth theoretical understanding of Islamophobia informed by lived experiences, but has further policy implications for Muslim communities who, at particular points in the socio-political narrative, may be at greater risk of discrimination because of the hyper-securitization of not only their religious identities, but also their ethnic identities. A case in point is the Syrian connection in a post-Isis socio-political context, where either Muslims from Syria, or those travelling to Syria and the region, are more likely to be viewed as suspect.

The narratives further reveal how young Muslims are not simply passive victims of discrimination and securitization, but are also playing their part in resisting the dominant stereotype about their identities as potential terrorists, by the simple act of *resistance through dialogue.* They are attempting to 'normalize' their presence in universities and across communities to counter the hatred and insecurity that results from sensationalist accounts of their identity in media or political rhetoric. By presenting biographical narratives of (in)security and Islamophobia, the book focuses on individuals who get lost in sensationalized reports about Islam and terrorism. The representation of Muslims, their 'otherization' 'racialization' and 'securitization' (Said 1994; Meer and Modood 2010; Croft 2012) primarily focuses on the male; women are reduced to a physical embodiment of the quintessential 'victim'. Muslim women are more likely to be talked about rather than included in a conversation about their lives as Muslim women in Britain.

The Context: Islamophobia, Orientalism and the Security Discourse

In understanding the experiences of Muslim women in this book, one needs, first, to examine the nature of Islamophobia that Muslims confront in their day-to-day lives. In attempting to define such a controversial contemporary phenomenon, it is crucial to investigate the historical context that contributed to its inception, and the existing realities that continue to mould and define its meaning (see Abbas 2004; Fekete 2009; Malik 2009; Allen 2010a). As Kumar (2012: 9) observes, 'the history of "Islam and the West," as it is commonly termed, is a story not of religious conflict but rather of conflict born of political rivalries and competing imperial agendas'. Drawing on Britain's Imperialist history, Islamophobia is situated within an ideological Orientalist struggle, where '[a]t the heart of Islamophobia is [...] the maintenance of the "violent hierarchy" between the idea of the West (and all that it can be articulated to represent) and Islam (and all that it can be articulated to represent)' (Sayyid 2010: 15). This ideological struggle has resulted in what Fekete (2009) describes as 'European Orientalism', where 'the Orient' is 'not [...] a separate geographical region but [...] a problem located [...] within the boundaries of Europe (the Occident) itself' (2009: 193).

Such agendas as outlined during the Crusades and Europe's Imperialist ventures are important historical points of intersection between the West and Islam, encounters that led to exaggerated stereotypes and caricatures of a violent Islam (see Esposito 1999; Gottschalk and Greenberg 2008; Fekete 2009; Allen 2010a; Sayyid 2010; Zebiri 2011; Kumar 2012; Lyons 2012; Sardar and Ahmad 2012: 2–3). These stereotypes gained further meaning in the context of the war against Al Qa'ida and its affiliates, and the more recent war against Isis, often projected as a war against violent 'Islamist' ideology by media and political actors (see Frost 2008; Gottschalk and Greenberg 2008; Saeed 2008; Esposito and Kalin 2011; Greenberg and Miazhevich 2012; Meer 2012). Therefore, in exploring Islamophobia, especially within Britain, it is important to explore both a historical overview and the present day socio-political context.

The term 'Islamophobia' has been traced as far back as the early twentieth century in a French article 'by Etienne Dinet and Slima Ben Ibrahim' who wrote 'accès de délire islamophobe', though the meaning of the term was different from the present day reference to discrimination (Allen 2010b: 15; Taras 2012). However, modern day Islamophobia as understood in the UK may have 'grassroots in the "London Borough of Brent in the early 1980s, where a distinct anti-Muslim prejudice was first being identified almost simultaneously with the emergence of a distinct 'British Muslim' identity"' (Allen 2010b: 16). The term Islamophobia gained institutional importance as a result of the Runnymede Trust, which defined Islamophobia as 'unfounded hostility towards Islam', the result of certain 'closed views' about Islam (Runnymede Trust 1997: 4–5). While the Runnymede Trust report was ground-breaking in providing an institutionalized definition of Islamophobia, it was limited to the extent that it gave a generic guidance for 'practitioners working with Muslims' (Tyrer 2003: 56). It further failed to take into consideration the complexities of Islamophobia, where discrimination may not be as straightforward as problems in gaining employment, or experiencing direct verbal or physical abuse. It overlooked the historical context of colonialism and imperialism, which located the Muslim within Britain's imperialist conquest—a fact that further problematizes a historical narrative around the British Muslim subject and belonging, post-Empire. Examples not just from Britain, but also other countries around Europe and the USA, testify to the relevance of this historical narrative.

In September 2012, for instance, ten New York subways displayed an advertisement stating 'In Any War Between the Civilized Man and the Savage, Support the Civilized Man. Support Israel Defeat Jihad' (Beaumont 2012; Dabashi 2012). This advertisement caused an outrage for its Islamophobic implications, with Muslims depicted as 'savages' but, more importantly, it highlighted precisely the ideological battle that

Sayyid (2010) and others (Fekete 2009; Allen 2010a; Cesari 2010b; Tyrer 2010; Zebiri 2011; Kumar 2012; Lyons 2012) link to the phenomenon of Islamophobia, where the Orientalist 'tropes' of 'civilized' and 'savage' continue to shape the debate on Muslims and the West (see Dabashi 2012). Similar rhetoric has been used by the Republican party candidate Donald Trump in his election campaign for the party's presidential candidacy for 2016, which includes banning Muslims from entering the USA, to sharing and almost promoting an anecdote about 'Islamic terrorists' being killed 'with bullets dipped in the blood of pigs'. His malicious political propaganda is being linked to increased Islamophobia across the USA (Miller 2015). This Orientalist imagery was also repeated with the 'Ground Zero mosque' controversy, when a 'Muslim group' planning to build a 'cultural centre and mosque near Ground Zero' encountered opposition, with 'Pastor Terry Jones' announcing a plan to burn the Quran, the Muslim holy book, in protest (Rohrer 2010; see also Lambert and Githens-Mazer 2011). However, the USA is not alone in perpetuating this 'clash of civilization' narrative. Isis, in its attacks on Paris in November 2015 that killed 127 people, declared that the attacks were meant '[t]o teach France, and all nations following its path, that they will remain at the top of Islamic State's list of targets, and that the smell of death won't leave their noses as long as they partake in their crusader campaign' (Knecht 2015). Isis, in its attempts to establish an 'Islamic State', also uses the rhetoric of a 'clash of civilizations' where the Crusades continue. It is the innocent, both Muslim and non-Muslim, who become victims of these attacks, with peaceful Muslim citizens held responsible for 'the growing jihadist cancer' (*The Guardian* 2015).

As Muslims and Islam continue to be situated within this Orientalist narrative of the Crusades and Imperialism, the imagery of a backward and repressive Islam, of violent Muslims, continues to be invoked (see Fekete 2009; Gest 2010; Maira 2011: 110). The antithetical nature of Islam and the West is highlighted time and again in tragedies such as the Charlie Hebdo attacks in Paris, an attempt to avenge the Prophet of Islam in response to a depiction of the Prophet that was offensive to Muslims (Hopper 2015). These tragedies, like the 9/11 attacks, reinforce the violent stereotypes, where the 'fear and hostility' that was evoked by 'the earliest European scholars of Islam' continues 'both in scholarly and non-scholarly attention to an Islam viewed as belonging to a part of the world—the Orient—counterposed imaginatively, geographically, and historically against Europe and the West' (Said 2003: 344). The Muslim community, therefore, in its appearance and mannerisms, physically manifests an alien presence in the West, perceived as a challenge to Western values of liberalism and enlightenment. The 'niqab ban' in France and Belgium further testifies to the fear of a 'foreign' culture invading the landscape of modernity. Carrying the civilizing mission further, the niqab in France was banned in public in order to protect its '"republican values" of secularism in the public space', with Muslims forced to 'accept French norms', while the non-Muslim host society was protecting 'Muslim women from religious extremism' by giving 'them freedom of choice, rather than taking it away' (Erlanger and Camus 2012; see also Wieviorka 1996; Freedman 2004; Jouili 2009). The niqab, in this instance, was not considered part of that choice; a woman wearing a niqab is instantly identified with an extremist religion, in need of being protected and saved. Belgium also suffers from this saviour complex; the niqab is perceived as 'a symbol of the oppression of women' (BBC News 2011c). In Switzerland, the ban on minarets in 2009 echoed similar Orientalist sentiments, with the Swiss People's Party representative Martin Baltisser observing that '[t]his was a vote against minarets as symbols of Islamic power' (BBC News 2009b). In Germany, the attitude of the public towards Muslims could be gauged by the response to a 2010 book by the 'then-Bundesbank member Thilo Sarrazin [...] in which he accused Muslim immigrants of lowering the intelligence of German society' (Bowen 2012: 22). While the book was criticized and Sarrazin was 'dismissed from his central bank position, the book proved popular', with 'one poll' showing 'a third of Germans believed that the country was "overrun by foreigners"' (ibid: 22–23), a sentiment that may be reinforced with the arrival of Syrian refugees in Germany and the Cologne attacks on women who were sexually assaulted on New Year's Eve 2016 by 'men of Arab and North African backgrounds' (Schmidt and Graham-Harrison 2016).

Said, in an interview with Eleanor Wachtel (2001: 238), observed 'the rather stubborn continuity between European views of Islam in the twelfth century and European views of Islam in the eighteenth, nineteenth, and twentieth centuries: they simply don't change', views that have continued into the twenty-first century. The would-be terrorist continues to be framed within such an Orientalist imagination, drawing on an essentialized narrative of Muslims, discrimination and racism that moves beyond the 'colour' of the skin, and targets 'culture', leading to a form of 'cultural racism' (Modood 2005:27 discussing Barker 1981, Gordon and Klug 1986 and Gilroy 1987). As Ali (2004: 79) observes, 'the 'new racism' of the late 1980s was as likely to be based on ethnic and cultural differences as it was on skin color, and the work of academics was to understand the ways in which ethnicities themselves became racialized'. The changing nature of racism illustrates how the concept is not merely a static phenomenon, but also changes with time.

Rana (2007) provides an exploration of anti-Muslim racism in the USA, demonstrating how the present day notion of racism that privileges 'biological difference as natural difference without including religion' was a result of what is termed 'modern racism', that displaced religion (ibid.: 153). Religion continued to be a factor in the Otherization process of the 'White' masters and Muslim 'African' slaves as early as the 'fifteenth and sixteenth century', and continued in the twentieth century with movements such as the 'Nation of Islam' under 'Elijah Muhammad', who believed that 'the very nature of the black man is a Muslim' (ibid: 155–156). Whether it is the 'Moors' or 'Arabs' of the Crusades, or the slaves of the Americas, religion, historically, has been a factor in the development of a narrative on racism. Therefore, in understanding Islamophobia in the contemporary socio-political Western context, Sayyid's (2010: 13) observation is important in revealing how '[r]acialised bodies were never exclusively biological; they were marked at the same time as religion, culture, history, and territories were marked and used to group socially fabricated distinctions between Europeanness and non-Europeanness' (see also Amin 2009, 2010). This particularly holds true in situations where white converts who stand out because of their Muslim appearance experience Islamophobia (Franks 2000; Afshar et al. 2005; Allen 2010a).

An exploration of Islamophobia therefore requires a two-way process that overcomes this restrictive understanding of race by incorporating not only biology, but also culture and religion, where cultural tropes of Islam are racialized in a similar mode as biological characteristics of non-White races. Drawing on a form of 'cultural racism', especially within Europe, the nature of 'antipathy' to Muslims is not just the result of the assumption of their inferiority but also the perception that they represent 'an alien culture' or belief system (Modood 2005: 11). Such '[r]acialisation does not depend on biology to produce "races"; rather it sees the construction of collective identities as a product of social processes' (Sayyid 2010: 14). With symbols such as the 'hijab' and 'niqab' reduced to a form of oppression, where agency and choice are removed from the purview of the Muslim woman, where a bearded man who prays five times in a mosque is reduced to the category of a fundamentalist, Muslims, through sociologically gendered traits in place of mere biology, are reduced to a 'racialized' group. Such categories of the fundamentalist/moderate encourage a form of 'racialised governance' (Tyrer 2010), where Muslims are confined to artificial categories by the state and media.

While Islamophobia draws on such binary constructions, it may also operate in other less direct ways, through what Tyrer (2010) calls 'degrees of alterity'. Building on Deleuze and Guattari (2004) he argues that while one cannot 'deny the persistence, recoding and recirculation of older modes of racist discourse, it is the dominant form taken by Islamophobia' that 'locates Muslims as indeterminate people, racializing them on the basis of degrees of difference from the white male universal self, and even racializing them as incompletely racialised—that is, as purely religious—subjects' (Tyrer 2010: 104; see also Tyrer and Sayyid 2012). Therefore, racism does not simply function in clear opposition to the 'White-Man' but, rather, is determined in line with a 'degree of deviance' which may be tolerated 'at given places under given conditions, in a given ghetto', while at other points simply being erased, again dependent on the 'White-Man' who controls how other groups are defined at different points in time (Deleuze and Guattari 2004: 197–198, as cited by Tyrer 2010: 105). However, while Tyrer's observation is important in understanding how racism operates, particularly with respect to Islamophobia, the old 'tropes' of 'civilized' versus barbaric are just as relevant in today's context as demonstrated in the New York subway advertisement campaign against Jihad (Beaumont 2012; Dabashi 2012), or the media narratives about Isis. When and how they are invoked determines the level of what

Tyrer (2010) calls 'alterity', but the jargon of media and state actors continue to regurgitate the age-old imperialist rhetoric.

Further, the Orientalist Other and the potential for violence that they possess fall within a 'securitized' discourse. 'Security' as a term carries social and 'political' credence, whereby an invocation to security—an act or action in the name of security—is often deemed acceptable for the social conscience (Laustsen and Wæver 2000; Booth 2007). The urgency that is evoked through inferences to homeland 'security' is important, particularly in the aftermath of a major attack (such as the attack on 7 July 2005), where the public, out of fear of a similar potential attack, is more readily supportive of counter terrorism measures (Huddy et al. 2007; Nacos et al. 2011), even when these measures curtail individual rights and freedoms. Booth (2007) captures the fundamental acceptance of such a security narrative when he observes how 'people understand what security is by knowing how insecurity feels' (Booth 2007: 101). It is precisely the sense of human insecurity in the aftermath of 7/7 in Britain that resulted in support for counter terrorism measures that curtailed civil and individual liberties, as well as a retaliation against the enemy— the Muslim community or those who looked Muslim—through acts of discrimination or Islamophobia.

Defining security as a concept, however, is not a straightforward task, as it can have different meanings in different contexts. The *Oxford English Dictionary* (2013) defines security as 'the state of being free from danger or threat'. What is this 'danger or threat'? Who defines it? At what point?; these are all questions crucial in understanding this concept. Within International Relations and the question of state and security, the 'traditional' approach 'assumes that nation-states have one driving goal in their relations with other states—their own survival' (Steele 2008: 2). This definition in particular was credible during the Cold War era of inter-state rivalry, yet the events of 9/11 brought insecurity within the nation-state, especially where the threat was no longer from a tangible external entity but, rather, was more internal or 'home-grown' through an ideology that transcended material boundaries, recruiting ones own citizens for a transnational cause. With the changing nature of insecurity and warfare, the more traditional means of understanding security are also changing (Tibi 2007), resulting in the normalization of the security agenda through a form of 'securitization' (Buzan and Wæver 2009; Croft 2012: 76–77). This 'securitization' involves identifying 'an existential threat to a valued referent object' and justifies 'exceptional measures' in countering that threat (Buzan and Wæver 2009: 257). In Croft's conception of securitization in Britain following the incidents of 7/7, the security threat is created in the form of an Other that is both radically different and 'inferior' from the British Self—what Croft calls both 'the Radical' and the 'Orientalized Other' (2012: 246–247). This is the Muslim 'Other' who is perceived as a potential threat and continues to be placed within a security framework, where their family life, education, employment or interaction in the public sphere are all 'securitized.' This Orientalist form of securitizing results in greater suspicion and distrust of the Muslim community, leading to experiences of Islamophobia, as highlighted in this book.

The Research Method

The narratives in this book were collected between 2010 and 2012 at a time when the Pakistani Muslim identity was highly securitized because of the "Af-Pak problem," i.e. the "war on terror" that was at its height in Afghanistan and Pakistan, and the eventual killing of Osama bin Laden in Pakistan. The 'educated' Muslim was also perceived as a problem with the discoveries of Umar Farouq Abdulmuttalab, Roshonara Choudhry—a student who stabbed a British MP to avenge the people of Iraq (BBC News 2010b), and the case of Pakistani students arrested and acquitted on charges of terrorism. The Justice for North West 10 campaign was only launched in response to the government's plan to deport the students. In order to identify the sample for this study, the focus was placed on universities located across England, primarily in London, West Yorkshire, North and South West England, North and South East England, and the West Midlands. The dataset was further supplemented through an overview of existing literature on ethnic student choice and participation in higher education (see Egerton and Halsey 1993; Ahmad 2001; Reay et al. 2001; Dale et al. 2002; Gayle et al. 2002; Shiner and Modood 2002; Archer 2003; Archer and Leathwood 2003; Connor et al. 2004; Gorard and Smith

2006; Tyrer and Ahmad 2006; Bagguley and Hussain 2007; Gittoes and Thompson 2007; Bhopal 2008; Broecke and Hamed 2008; Brooks 2008; Richardson 2008; Thompson 2008; Office for Public Management and Hussain 2009). A profile of the university location was further studied to gain insights into the composition of the population of the specific town in terms of its ethnic and religious diversity. This was done to ensure participation from young Muslims in towns where they were in a minority, as well as places where they were a majority, and to explore difference in experiences (a detailed profile of each university is given in Appendix 1A). By using purposive sampling and 'snowballing' (Creswell 2009: 178, Denscombe 2010: 37), young Muslim women were identified through Islamic student societies (ISocs) and Pakistani student societies (Paksocs). The women were between the ages of 19 and 28, either studying in university or, on graduation, working in the UK (a detailed profile of each participant is given in Appendix 1B).

A narrative approach was adopted in collecting data, with a focus on dialogue in order to capture the biographical narratives of Muslim women. The dialogues highlighted experiences of the 'everyday' and the mundane. For this study, the 'everyday' is defined within a Bakhtinian framework of 'discourse' that places language as a central feature, where words and human experience are historically and socio-politically positioned, where meanings are not static but are, instead, the result of an ongoing 'intersubjective' exchange between social beings and their 'material' environment (Holquist, in Bakhtin 1990: xxxi; see also Bernard-Donals 1994). Hence, a Bakhtinian understanding of reality highlights the ability of individuals to influence their environment, and each other, through a 'dialectic' where a multiplicity of 'voices' and 'meanings' are constantly in circulation, communicated across various groups and individuals; yet, these voices are also constrained by their evolving 'material' circumstances and surroundings (Bakhtin 1986; Bernard-Donals 1994). The realities that influence the student narratives in this research include the 'historical' that place the British-Muslim-Pakistani-female identity within a narrative of race and racism, further informing their experiences of Islamophobia (see also Meer and Modood 2010). It also consists of the contemporary 'security' realm that 'securitizes' the British-Muslim-Pakistani-female identity (Croft 2012). Such a wider discourse intersects at different points, informing the 'everyday' realities of Muslim women in Britain. These narratives further have implications for a socio-political context where the security discourse has become even more pervasive, implicating Muslim families and social institutions within a security framework.

The participants were also provided the protection of anonymity through the use of pseudonyms. The researcher followed the University of Oxford's code of ethics in conducting the research, ensuring that the participants had time to understand the research and to ask questions, and that they provided 'informed consent' for the research. The narrative analysis included a thematic approach to identify dominant themes of securitization, related to nationality, gender, ethnicity, education and activism, as divided across the chapters in this book.

Structure of the Book

In exploring the narratives of securitization and Islamophobia as described by young Muslim women, the book begins with an exploration of the Muslim community in Britain, illustrating a diversity of religiosity based on ethnicity, sect and culture, often overlooked when Muslims are homogenized as a single category in media and political rhetoric. Chapter 2 further focuses on the British South Asian and, in particular, the British Pakistani identity. It traces the evolution of the 'Pakistani immigrant' who, categorized by the host state as 'South Asian', emerges in the 1980s as a politicized 'British Muslim' citizen. While the male is portrayed as a physical threat, the Pakistani Muslim female is viewed as a victim of a patriarchal culture, either 'forced' into marriage, or forced to carry the burden of community 'honour'. However, the tragedies of 9/11 and 7/7 securitize the problematic British Muslim Pakistani, as explored in the counter terrorism policies of Britain. Given this context, the second part of the chapter engages with participant narratives of young British Muslims with a Pakistani heritage, exploring what it means to be British, Muslim and Pakistani in a context where their 'Britishness'—and, in particular, their loyalty—is questioned by media and political actors. The narratives of young women in this study have similarities with Muslim men (as discussed in existing literature), carrying forward a struggle against an official discourse that categorizes them differently based on ethnicity, and places their religious beliefs against nationalist loyalties.

Chapter 3, in exploring this securitization of identity, focuses on the securitized female and her experiences of Islamophobia. The chapter highlights how the Muslim female identity oscillates between the oppressed victim and the hidden radical. The chapter begins with a discussion of media accounts of Muslim women and the emergence of individuals such as Samina Malik, the 'lyrical terrorist'; Roshonara Chaudhry, who attacked an MP to avenge the 'people of Iraq'; and the more recent 'jihadi brides'. These women, some of whom have been educated in British institutions, lend credence to the belief that Muslim women, like Muslim men, can be a potential threat, oxymoronically hiding in plain sight. Within this backdrop, the chapter explores participant narratives about their Muslim female identity, as portrayed in media and political rhetoric, and how it influences their 'everyday' lives. The focus of the discussion is on 'Muslimness' and its link to Islamophobia and securitization, where both veiled and non-veiled Muslim participants are caught within external categories of the moderate/extremist that determines their interaction with other people. The chapter therefore explores how 'degrees of religiosity' determined by physical signifiers impacts on how Islamophobia is experienced.

The fear of the 'vulnerable' Muslim female also implicates the 'educated' Muslim; individuals such as Roshonara Chaudhry, Umar Farouk Abdulmutallab and Jihadi John were all educated at British universities and were later implicated in acts of terrorism. Chapter 4 therefore focuses on the 'securitized' Muslim student—typically, an intelligent yet vulnerable young individual, susceptible to radical ideologies of extremist groups. This susceptibility has drawn universities into an Orwellian framework of monitoring and surveillance, as evident in legislation such as the Counter Terrorism and Security Act 2015, which places a 'statutory' responsibility on universities to inform on students at risk of radicalization. Such a fear of the potential Muslim terrorist has resulted in greater insecurity for and about Muslim students within educational institutions, leading to experiences of Islamophobia. The chapter undertakes a two-part exploration, beginning with participant narratives about how the language of radicalization, which confines Muslim students within artificial categories of the radical and moderate, is a problem in their everyday lives. The second part of the chapter highlights how this fear of radicalization has resulted in insecurity about the educated Muslim identity, by exploring the narratives of ISocs—in particular, the female wings of ISocs (also known as the ISoc sisters). Their accounts reveal how Muslim students are constantly under suspicion, especially the ISoc sisters, with reports of being watched, spied on, or feared by fellow students.

Chapter 5 unpacks the securitized Muslim identity by focusing on the problematic ethno-religious juxtaposition in the form of the Pakistani-Muslim connection. This chapter explores such hyper-securitization, illustrating how experiences of Islamophobia differ across Muslim communities, determined by the prevailing security discourse that implicates not just the religious identity, but also different ethnic identities. It therefore examines the phenomenon of Pakophobia as a form of Islamophobia experienced by Pakistani Muslim females—especially between 2010 and 2012, a point when the AfPak problem was at its peak—and the Pakistani identity particularly prominent after the killing of Osama bin Laden in Pakistan. The chapter further discusses Pakophobia in relation to student activism, particularly in the case of the J4NW10 campaign, and campaigns for Palestine, where the securitized ethnic identity is more prominent and is perceived as a greater problem. These narratives reveal how the nature of Islamophobia is linked to a securitizing socio-political discourse that often implicates different Muslim communities. With the present day threat of the Islamic State, and the ongoing war in Syria that has attracted British Muslims from different ethnic backgrounds, the experiences of Islamophobia may differ, based on such a hyper-securitization that focuses on not just the Muslim identity, but also other ethnic identities.

While the first four chapters examine the securitized experiences of Muslim women, Chapter 6 refocuses the lens on Muslim women challenging the dominant discourse about Islam and terrorism by engaging in *resistance through dialogue*. Taking forward the Bakhtinian notion of a dialogue, the chapter explores how both Muslim individuals and student societies are attempting to take control of the meta-narrative about their identities by raising awareness about Islam and Muslims. Within the university, the chapter explores how Islamic student societies are attempting to 'normalize' Muslim student presence by promoting student activism beyond the Islamic society; how Paksocs are also providing an alternative narrative about Pakistan. The chapter further highlights the strategies of 'dialogue' and communication that are being employed at the individual level both by young women and by young men to challenge this securitized discourse that limits their expressions of being British, Muslim and Pakistani in contemporary Britain.

Chapter 7 concludes this volume by exploring the implications of the discussion in the book for Muslims in Britain and other countries in the West. While it is important to counter the threat of Muslims, both men and women, joining terrorist groups such as Isis, the narratives in this book reveal how the existing policy of counter terrorism is counterproductive, breeding greater insecurity and suspicion. The Conclusion, in exploring future challenges, also highlights the experiences of Muslim communities across Europe and the USA where similar policies of surveillance and insecurity continue to implicate innocent Muslims. The 'everyday' accounts in this study are linked to narratives of Islamophobia that have emerged elsewhere in the West, revealing the limitations of securitizing entire Muslim communities. In summarizing the discussion in the book in light of recent developments across Britain, Europe and the USA, the Conclusion illustrates how, as a consequence of securitization, Islamophobia is increasingly becoming an unchallenged and acceptable part of the British and Western social psyche.

Bibliography

Abbas, T. (2004) After 9/11: British South Asian Muslims, Islamophobia, multiculturalism, and the state. *American Journal of Islamic Social Sciences*, 21 (3), pp. 26–38.

Afshar, H., Aitken, R. and Franks, M. (2005) Feminisms, Islamophobia and identities. *Political Studies*, 53 (2), pp. 262–283.

Ahmad, F. (2001) Modern traditions? British Muslim women and academic achievement. *Gender and Education*, 13 (2), pp. 137–152.

Ali, S. (2004) Reading Racialized Bodies: Learning to See Difference. In *Cultural bodies: Ethnography and theory*, eds. H. Thomas and J. Ahmed, Malden, MA: Blackwell Pub, pp. 76–97.

Allen, C. (2010a) *Islamophobia*. England: Ashgate Publishing Limited.
Allen, C. (2010b) Contemporary Islamophobia before 9/11: A brief history. *Arches Quarterly Islamophobia and Anti Muslim Hatred: Causes & Remedies*, 4 (7), pp. 14–23.
Amin, A. (2009) The Racialisation of Everything. In *Thinking About Almost Everything: New Ideas to Light Up Minds*, eds. A. Amin, M. O'Neill, D. Brown and S. Daya, London: Profile Books Ltd, pp. 43–46.
Amin, A. (2010) The remainders of race. *Theory, Culture & Society*, 27 (1), pp. 1–23.
Archer, L. (2003) Social Class and Higher Education. In *Higher Education and Social Class. Issues of Exclusion and Inclusion*, eds. L. Archer, M. Hutchings and A. Ross, London: Routledge Falmer, pp. 5–20.
Archer, L. and Leathwood, C. (2003) Identities, Inequalities and Higher Education. In *Higher Education and Social Class. Issues of Exclusion and Inclusion*, eds. L. Archer, M. Hutchings and A. Ross, London: Routledge Falmer, pp. 175–192.
Association of Chief Police Officers. (2012) *Prevent, Police and Universities Guidance for Police Officers and Police Staff to Help Higher Education Institutions Contribute to the Prevention of Terrorism*. UK: Office of National Coordinator Prevent.
Bagguley, P. and Hussain, Y. (2007) *The Role of Higher Education in Providing Opportunities for South Asian women*. Bristol, UK: Policy Press, Joseph Rowntree Foundation.
Bakhtin, M. (1986) *Speech Genres and Other Late Essays*. C. Emerson and M. Holquist (eds.), Translated by V.E. McGhee. Austin: University of Texas Press.
Bakhtin, M.M. (1990) *Art and Answerability: Early Philosophical Essays*. Austin: University of Texas Press.
BBC News. (26/02/2016) Who are Britain's jihadists? Available from: http://www.bbc.com/news/uk-32026985 (Accessed 03/01, 2016).
BBC News. (23/07/2011b) *Belgian ban on full veils comes into force*. Accessed from BBC News. [Online]. Available from: http://www.bbc.co.uk/news/world-europe-14261921 (Accessed 09/15, 2012).
BBC News. (02/05/2011c) *Osama Bin Laden, al-Qaeda leader, dead—Barack Obama*. BBC News. [Online]. Available from: http://www.bbc.co.uk/news/world-us-canada-13256676 (Accessed 11/09, 2012).
BBC News. (22/04/2009b) *No charges after anti terror raid*. BBC News. [Online]. Available from: http://news.bbc.co.uk/1/hi/uk/8011341.stm (Accessed 12/15, 2009).

Beaumont, P. (26/09/2012) *Activist arrested in New York for defacing anti-Muslim poster.* The Guardian. [Online]. Available from: http://www.guardian.co.uk/world/2012/sep/26/activist-new-york-anti-muslim-poster (Accessed 11/09, 2012).

Bernard-Donals, M.F. (1994) *Mikhail Bakhtin Between Phenomenology and Marxism.* Cambridge: Cambridge University Press.

Bhopal, K. (2008) Shared communities and shared understandings: The experiences of Asian women in a British university. *International Studies in Sociology of Education*, 18 (3–4), pp. 185–197.

Booth, K. (2007) *Theory of World Security.* Cambridge: Cambridge University Press.

Bowcott, W. (11/09/2007) *Woman called 'lyrical terrorist' celebrated act of beheading.* The Guardian. [Online]. Available from: http://www.theguardian.com/uk/2007/nov/09/terrorism.ukcrime (Accessed 02/19, 2013).

Bowen, J.R. (2012) *Blaming Islam.* USA: MIT.

Broecke, S. and Hamed, J. (2008) Gender Gaps in Higher Education Participation. An Analysis of the Relationship between Prior Attainment and Young Participation by Gender, Socio-Economic Class and Ethnicity. *Department of Innovations, Universities and Skills.*

Brooks, R. (2008) Accessing higher education: The influence of cultural and social capital on university choice. *Sociology Compass*, 2 (4), pp. 1355–1371.

Buzan, B. and Wæver, O. (2009) Macrosecuritisation and security constellations: Reconsidering scale in securitisation theory. *Review of International Studies*, 35 (02), pp. 253–276.

Cesari, J. (2010b) Securitization of Islam in Europe. In *Muslims in the West after 9/11 Religion, Politics and Law*, ed. J. Cesari, London: Routledge, pp. 9–27.

Connor H., Tyers C, Modood T. and Hillage J. (2004) *Why the Difference? A Closer Look at Higher Education Minority Ethnic Students and Graduates.* London: Institute for Employment Studies.

Creswell, J.W. (2009) *Research Design Qualitative, Quantitative, and Mixed Methods Approaches.* Third ed. London: SAGE Publications Ltd.

Croft, S. (2012) *Securitizing Islam Identity and the Search for Security.* Cambridge: Cambridge University Press.

Dabashi, H. (24/09/2012) *The war between the civilised man and the savage.* Al Jazeera. [Online]. Available from: http://www.aljazeera.com/indepth/opinion/2012/09/201292464012781613.html (Accessed 03/01, 2013).

Dale, A., Shaheen, N., Kalra, V. and Fieldhouse, E. (2002) Routes into education and employment for young Pakistani and Bangladeshi women in the UK. *Ethnic and Racial Studies*, 25 (6), pp. 942–968.

Denscombe, M. (2010) *The Good Research Guide for Small-Scale Social Research Projects.* Fourth ed. England: Open University Press.

Droogsma, R.A. (2007) Redefining Hijab: American Muslim women's standpoints on veiling. *Journal of Applied Communication Research,* 35 (3), pp. 294–319.

Egerton, M. and Halsey, A. (1993) Trends by Social Class and Gender in Access to Higher Education in Britain. *Oxford Review of Education,* 19 (2), pp. 183–196.

Erlanger, S. and Camus, E. (01/09/2012) *In a Ban, a Measure of European Tolerance.* The New York Times. [Online]. Available from: http://www.nytimes.com/2012/09/02/world/europe/tolerance-eases-impact-of-french-ban-on-full-face-veils.html?pagewanted=all (Accessed 09/15, 2012).

Esposito, J.L. (1999) *The Islamic Threat: Myth or Reality?* USA; Oxford: Oxford University Press.

Esposito, J.L. and Kalin, I. (2011) *Islamophobia: the Challenge of Pluralism in the 21st Century.* Oxford & New York: Oxford University Press.

Fekete, L. (2009) *A Suitable Enemy Racism, Migration and Islamophobia in Europe.* London: Pluto Press.

Franks, M. (2000) Crossing the borders of whiteness? White Muslim women who wear the hijab in Britain today. *Ethnic and Racial Studies,* 23 (5), pp. 917–929.

Freedman, J. (2004) Secularism as a Barrier to Integration? The French Dilemma. *International Migration,* 42 (3), pp. 5–27.

Frost, D. (2008) Islamophobia: Examining causal links between the media and "race hate" from "below". *International Journal of Sociology and Social Policy,* 28 (11/12), pp. 564–578.

Gayle, V., Berridge, D. and Davies, R. (2002) Young people's entry into higher education: quantifying influential factors. *Oxford Review of Education,* 28 (1), pp. 5–20.

Gest, J. (2010) *APART Alienated and Engaged Muslims in the West.* London: Hurst & Co. (Publishers) Ltd.

Gilroy, P. (1987) *"There Ain't No Black in the Union Jack": The Cultural Politics of Race and Nation.* London: Hutchinson.

Gittoes, M. and Thompson, J. (2007) Admissions to higher education: Are there biases against or in favour of ethnic minorities? *Teaching in Higher Education,* 12 (3), pp. 419–424.

Gorard, S. and Smith, E. (2006) *Review of widening participation research: addressing the barriers to participation in higher education. A report to HEFCE by the University of York, Higher Education Academy and Institute for Access Studies.*

Gottschalk, P. and Greenberg, G. (2008) *Islamophobia Making Muslims the Enemy.* USA: Rowman & Littlefield Publishers, Inc.

Greenberg, D. and Miazhevich, G. (2012) Assimilationism vs. multiculturalism: US identity and media representations of British Muslims over a 12-year span. *Communication, Culture & Critique*, 5 (1), pp. 75–98.

Her Majesty's Government (HM Government). (2015a) *Counter-Terrorism and Security Act 2015.* Available from: http://www.legislation.gov.uk/ukpga/2015/6/notes/contents (Accessed 03/28, 2015).

Her Majesty's Government (HM Government). (2011c) *Report to the Home Secretary of Independent Oversight of Prevent Review and Strategy by Lord Carlile of Berriew Q.C.* UK: Crown.

Home Affairs Committee. (2012) *Roots of Violent Radicalisation. Nineteenth Report of Session 2010–12, Volume 1.* London: The Stationery Office Limited.

Hopper, B. (16/01/2015a) *Should All Muslims Be Held Responsible For The Charlie Hebdo Attack?* The Huffington Post. Available from: http://www.huffingtonpost.co.uk/becky-hopper/charlie-hebdo_b_6482962.html (Accesed 03/02, 2015).

Hoyle, C., Bradford, A. and Frenett, R. (2015) *Becoming Mulan? Female Western Migrants to ISIS.* Institute for Strategic Dialogue.

Huddy, L., Feldman, S. and Weber, C. (2007) The political consequences of perceived threat and felt insecurity. *The Annals of the American Academy of Political and Social Science*, 614 (1), pp. 131–153.

Jouili, J. (2009) Negotiating secular boundaries: Pious micro-practices of Muslim women in French and German public spheres. *Social Anthropology*, 17 (4), pp. 455–470.

Knecht, E. (14/11/2015) *Islamic State says France remains top target.* Reuters. Available from: http://www.reuters.com/article/us-france-shooting-claim-idUSKCN0T30LL20151114 (Accessed 01/19, 2016).

Kumar, D. (2012) *Islamophobia and the Politics of Empire.* Haymarket Books.

Lambert, B. and Githens-Mazer, J. (2011) Islamophobia and Anti-Muslim Hate Crime: UK Case Studies 2010–An Introduction to a Ten Year Europe-Wide Research Project.

Laustsen, C.B. and Wæver, O. (2000) In defence of religion: Sacred referent objects for securitization. *Millennium-Journal of International Studies*, 29 (3), pp. 705–739.

Lyons, J. (2012) *Islam Through Western Eyes.* New York: Columbia University Press.

Maira, S. (2011) Islamophobia and the War on Terror: Youth, Citizenship, and Dissent. In *Islamophobia The Challenge of Pluralism in the 21st Century*, eds. J.L. Esposito and I. Kalin, Oxford: Oxford University Press, pp. 109–126.

Malik, M. (2009) Anti-Muslim prejudice in the West, past and present: An introduction. *Patterns of Prejudice*, 43 (3–4), pp. 207–212.

Meer, N. (2012) Complicating 'radicalism'—Counter-terrorism and Muslim identity in Britain. *Arches Quarterly Terrorism and Counter Terrorism: Spotlight on Strategies and Approaches*, 5 (9), pp. 10–19.

Meer, N. and Modood, T. (2010) The Racialisation of Muslims. In *Thinking through Islamophobia: Global Perspectives*, eds. S. Sayyid and A. Vakil, London: Hurst and Co. (Publishers) Ltd., pp. 69–84.

Miller, M.E. (10/12/2015) *Attacks on Muslims across the country as Trump rhetoric puts them in 'the line of fire,' congressman says*. The Washington Post. Available from: https://www.washingtonpost.com/news/morning-mix/wp/2015/12/10/attacks-on-muslims-across-the-country-as-trump-rhetoric-puts-them-in-the-line-of-fire-congressman-says/ (Accessed 01/03, 2016).

Modood, T. (2005) *Multicultural Politics Racism, Ethnicity, and Muslims in Britain*. Minneapolis: University of Minnesota Press.

Morris S. (01/02/2016) *British woman who joined Isis is jailed for six years*. The Guardian. Available from: http://www.theguardian.com/uk-news/2016/feb/01/british-woman-tareena-shakil-convicted-being-isis-member-jailed-xx-years (Accessed 03/23, 2016).

Nacos, B.L., Bloch-Elkon, Y. and Shapiro, R.Y. (2011) *Selling Fear Counterterrorism, the Media, and Public Opinion*. Chicago: University of Chicago Press.

Office for National Statistics. (2012) *Religion in England and Wales 2011*. UK: Crown.

Office for Public Management and Hussain, S. (2009) *The Experiences of Muslim Students in Further and Higher Education in London*. London: Greater London Authority.

Oxford Dictionary. (2013) *Oxford Dictionary*. Oxford University Press. [Online]. Available from: http://oxforddictionaries.com/definition/english/security (Accessed 02/02, 2013).

Rana, J. (2007) The Story of Islamophobia. *Souls: A Critical Journal of Black Politics, Culture, and Society*, 9 (2), pp. 148–161.

Reay, D., Davies, J., David, M. and Ball, S.J. (2001) Choices of degree or degrees of choice? Class, race and the higher education choice process. *Sociology*, 35 (4), pp. 855–874.

Richardson, J.T.E. (2008) *The Attainment of Ethnic Minority Students in UK Higher Education*. Abingdon, Oxfordshire: Carfax International Publishers.

Rohrer, F. (25/08/2010) *Is 'Ground Zero mosque' debate fanning the flames?* BBC News. [Online]. Available from: http://www.bbc.co.uk/news/world-us-canada-11076846 (Accessed 03/25, 2013).

Saeed, T. and Johnson, D. (2016) Intelligence, global terrorism and higher education: Neutralising threats or alienating allies? *British Journal of Educational Studies*, 64(1), pp.37–51.

Saeed, A. (2008) Teaching and learning guide for: Media, racism and Islamophobia: The representation of Islam and Muslims in the media. *Sociology Compass*, 2 (6), pp. 2041–2047.

Said, E. (2003) *Orientalism*. London: Penguin Books.

Said, E. (1994) *Culture and Imperialism*. London: Vintage Books.

Saltman, E.M. and Smith, M. (2015) *'Till Martyrdom Do Us Part' Gender and the ISIS Phenomenon*. Institute for Strategic Dialogue.

Sanghani, R. (28/05/2015) *AK47s, heart emoji and feminism: How jihadi brides are luring British girls to join Isil*. The Telegraph. [Online]. Available from: http://www.telegraph.co.uk/women/womens-politics/11635643/How-Isil-jihadi-brides-lure-British-girls-AK47s-emoji-and-feminism.html (Accessed 07/20, 2015).

Sardar, Z. and Ahmad, W.I.U. (2012) Introduction. In *Muslims in Britain: Making Social and Political Space*, eds. W.I.U. Ahmad and Z. Sardar, USA: Routledge, pp. 1–16.

Sawer, P. (13/11/2015) *Who is Jihadi John? How did Mohammed Emwazi, a quiet football fan, become the symbol of Isil?* The Telegraph. Available from: http://www.telegraph.co.uk/news/worldnews/islamic-state/11992681/Jihadi-John-profile-how-did-Mohammed-Emwazi-a-quiet-football-fan-become-the-symbol-of-Isil.html (Accessed 02/03, 2016).

Sayyid, S. (2010) Out of the Devil's Dictionary. In *Thinking Through Islamophobia: Global Perspectives*, eds. S. Sayyid and A. Vakil, London: Hurst & Co. (Publishers) Ltd, pp. 5–18.

Schmidt, J. and Graham-Harrison, E. (16/01/2016) *'If we want Germans to accept Arabs, Arabs must also learn to accept them'*. The Guardian. Available from: http://www.theguardian.com/world/2016/jan/16/germans-accept-arabs (Accessed 02/05, 2016).

Shiner, M. and Modood, T. (2002) Help or hindrance? Higher education and the route to ethnic equality. *British Journal of Sociology of Education*, 23 (2), pp. 209–232.

Steele, B.J. (2008) *Ontological Security in International Relations. Self-identity and the IR State*. New York: Routledge.

Taras, R. (2012) 'Islamophobia never stands still': Race, religion, and culture. *Ethnic and Racial Studies*, (ahead-of-print), pp. 1–17.

The Guardian (10/01/2015) Murdoch says Muslims must be held responsible for France terror attacks. Available from: http://www.theguardian.com/

world/2015/jan/10/rupert-murdoch-muslims-must-be-held-responsible-for-france-terror-attacks (Accessed 03/01, 2016).

The Runnymede Trust. (1997) *Islamophobia A Challenge for Us All. Commission on British Muslims and Islamophobia.* London.

Thompson, D.W. (2008) Widening participation and higher education. Students, systems and other paradoxes. *London Review of Education*, 6 (2), pp. 137–147.

Tibi, S. (2007) Jihadism and Intercivilisational Conflict. Conflicting Images of the Self and the Other. In *Islam and Political Violence. Muslim Diaspora and Radicalism in the West*, eds. S. Akbarzadeh and F. Mansouri, London: Tauris Academic Studies, pp. 39–64.

Tyrer, D. (2010) 'Flooding the Embankments': Race, Bio-Politics and Sovereignty. In *Thinking through Islamophobia: Global Perspectives*, eds. S. Sayyid and A. Vakil, London: Hurst & Co. (Publishers) Ltd, pp. 93–110.

Tyrer, D. (2003) *Institutionalized Islamophobia in British Universities. Degree of Doctor of Philosophy.* Institute of Social Research, University of Salford.

Tyrer, D. and Ahmad, F. (2006) *Muslim Women and Higher Education: Identities, Experiences and Prospects. A Summary Report. Liverpool John Moores University and European Social Fund.* Oxford: Oxuniprint.

Tyrer, D. and Sayyid, S. (2012) Governing ghosts: Race, incorporeality and difference in post-political times. *Current Sociology*, 60 (3), pp. 353–367.

Vakulenko, A. (2007) Islamic Dress in Human Rights Jurisprudence: A critique of current trends. *Human Rights Law Review*, 7 (4), pp. 717–739.

Wachtel, E. (2001) Edward Said: Between Two Cultures. In *Power, Politics and Culture Interviews with Edward W. Said*, ed. G. Viswanathan, London: Bloomsbury Publishing, pp. 233–247.

Wieviorka, M. (1996) *Identity and difference: Reflections on the French non-debate on multiculturalism.* Clayton, Australia: Thesis Eleven.

Zebiri, K. (2011) Orientalist Themes in Contemporary British Islamophobia. In *Islamophobia: The Challenge of Pluralism in the 21st Century: The Challenge of Pluralism in the 21st Century*, eds. J.L. Esposito and I. Kalin, USA: Oxford University Press, pp. 173–190.

2

Muslims, South Asians and the Pakistani Community in Britain: Intersecting Security, Identity and Belonging

A community's identity is located within the particularities of a socio-historical context, but is by no means confined by it. Tariq Ramadan's exploration of the Muslim identity in the West highlights how 'new kinds of citizens' have emerged who 'are increasingly "integrated" into society', who are 'visible through their color, their dress, and their differences, but they speak the country's language' (Ramadan 2010: 25). Their identity has evolved from the immigrant to that of a citizen, with all its differences and similarities, where the notion of what it means to be a citizen of a particular country also evolves over time. The nature of that evolution is dependent on not just the immigrant community, but also the host society's interaction with what they define as an 'outsider' in their midst. The extent to which the 'outsider' is given a space to belong, without being consumed by the dominant status quo (read: assimilated), is a testament to that society's evolutionary capability.

In Britain, policies of different British governments towards immigrants have varied from 'assimilation […] to integration in the 1970s, which in turn was replaced by multicultural pluralism in the 1980s, leading to the celebration of difference and diversity under New Labour in the 1990s' (Sardar and Ahmad 2012: 2). 'Assimilation' had called for the immigrant community adopting and adapting to the host society, with little 'change' within the host society, whereas integration concerned 'equal opportunity', accompanied 'by cultural diversity in an atmosphere of mutual tolerance' (Modood 2013: 42–43, is discussing Jenkins 1967: 267). This recognition of diversity had become especially important by the 1980s, when the 'multi-racial character' of British social life was an 'irreversible' fact, with the 'black and Asian' communities increasing from '1.2 million' in 1971 to '2.1 million' within a decade (Addison 2010: 365–367). The gradual focus of government policies on 'British multiculturalism', then, was 'not just about positive minority identities but a positive vision of the whole remade so as to include the previously excluded or marginalised on the basis of equality and belonging' (Modood 2013: 46; see also Taylor 1994; Parekh 2010; Modood and Dobbernack 2011; Triandafyllidou et al. 2012). It represented a form of 'dialogical citizenship', the result of 'repeatedly negotiating differences' located within 'the context of national and international conflicts, often beyond the control of actors involved' (Werbner 2005c: 764; see also Bakhtin 1981, 1986).

This process is especially evident when situated within the historical encounter with Commonwealth immigrants entering the 'Imperialist Centre', thus visibly altering the social make-up of British society. 'Belonging' in this context moves beyond a recognition to an acceptance of the minority community where, as the writer Hanif Kureshi (2011: 239) observes, a feeling of 'not having to notice where you are, and, more importantly, not being seen as different, would happen'. There is a sense of 'commitment' and 'mutual trust', as well as 'a spirit of relaxed tolerance' (Parekh 2011: 68). However, for the Muslims in Britain the problem with 'not being seen as different' is that Muslims in their religious demands, in their dress and in their habits are often perceived as different; the right to practise Islam is often portrayed as antithetical to Britishness.

The Muslim community forms '4.8 % of the population in England and Wales', with 47 % born in the UK (Office for National Statistics 2012; MCB 2015: 16). The Muslim identity includes a diversity of race, ethnicity, culture, sect and tradition. The majority is from South Asia, while others are from 'parts of Africa, Cyprus, Malaysia, the Middle East and […] Eastern Europe' (Ansari 2002: 6; see also MCB 2015). For 73 %

of Muslims, 'their only national identity is British (or other UK identity only)' (MCB 2015: 17). Yet, in media and political rhetoric, Muslims are predominantly perceived as a homogenous group, to be distinguished within an artificial spectrum of 'extremist' and 'moderate', where their nationalist loyalties are always suspect as a result of their religious affiliation. However, the ethnic affiliations are, on occasion, flagged within the socio-political imagination, when considered especially conspicuous, as has been witnessed in the case of the Pakistani ethnicity. It may be reflected in relation to the 'grooming scandal', where men of Pakistani origin were caught running 'a child exploitation ring' (Akwagyiram 2012; BBC News 2012c; Pearson 2014); or other domestic and international incidents directly related to terrorism, including Osama Bin Laden's killing in Pakistan in May 2011 (BBC News 2011b); or the link between British Pakistanis frequenting terrorist training camps in Pakistan (BBC News 2012a). According to Prevent 2011, 'almost 25 %' of 'Islamist terrorism-related' convictions between 2001 and 2011 had involved 'links to Pakistan—either as British nationals with Pakistani heritage or Pakistani nationals' (HM Government 2011a: 19).

In examining such a religio-ethnic identity, and its place within Britain's socio-political imagination, the chapter explores the evolution of a politicized Muslim community in the UK, with a particular focus on the South Asian population and, in particular, the British Pakistani identity. The chapter argues that the 'Pakistani immigrant' was categorized by the host state as 'South Asian', by the anti-racist as 'Black', and, instead, emerged as a politicized 'British Muslim' citizen in the 1980s. The 'Paki' male continues to be a problem, even in the 1990s and 2000s, being involved in sporadic rioting, only to become a prime suspect in the aftermath of 9/11 and 7 July 2005. While the male is portrayed as a troublemaker, the British Pakistani Muslim female is viewed as a victim of a patriarchal culture, either 'forced' into marriage, or forced to carry the burden of community 'honour'. However, the chapter further explores narratives of young British Muslim women with a Pakistani heritage who discuss their different identities to reveal a range of responses to the question of Britishness, where the stereotype of the British Muslim Pakistani is nothing more than an Orientalist image of a dynamic community reduced to the 'alien' within.

British and Muslim: A Politicized Identity

The British Muslim identity became prominent in media and political discourse in 1988–1989 when riots broke out in Britain against Salman Rushdie's book *The Satanic Verses*, which included offensive 'passages relating to Prophet Muhammad, his wives, and the Qur'an' (Modood 2005: 214). The book further resulted in Ayatollah Khomeini of Iran issuing a 'fatwa'[1] condoning the killing of the author for committing blasphemy (Allen 2010a; see also Asad 1990; Modood 2005; Githens-Mazer et al. 2010). The 'Rushdie affair' was, however, not the first time that the Muslim communities in Britain had organized around their Muslim identity. As early as 1938, a small number of Muslims living in Britain and others across the colonies protested against the book *A Short History of the World* by H.G. Wells (Piscatori 1990). The book portrayed 'an unflattering portrait of the Prophet' that resulted in protests 'in Kenya […] Uganda […] and London', with the British Imperialist authority fearful of riots spreading to the Indian subcontinent, which were only avoided because of the limited distribution of the book (Piscatori 1990: 767–768). The event is important in demonstrating the potential of arousing a Muslim political conscience, particularly when a reverent figure such as the Prophet is attacked or ridiculed. However, the politicization of the Muslim identity in the Rushdie affair did not happen overnight. Addison (2010) observes how Muslims in Britain were gradually becoming more publicly religious, with the number of mosques growing from 13 in 1963 to 338 in 1985 and 'more than' a 'thousand' in 1997 (Addison 2010: 374). These statistics provide an important backdrop in understanding the Muslim identity in Britain, where British Muslims, while not politically active, were publicly becoming more religiously conscious. The first time the 'host' society became aware of a Muslim presence in Britain was in the 1970s after the OPEC crisis, when 'all "Muslims" became "Arabs", and all "Arabs" were shifty, dangerous people determined to undermine civilization' (Sardar and Ahmad 2012: 2), thereby evoking an Orientalist perception of the Muslim community living at the centre of the old Empire.

---

[1] A religious edict.

Despite the visibility of the Muslim population, and the awareness of a Muslim presence, the Rushdie affair was important in 'politicizing' the Muslim identity. It problematized the narrative of the British Self as it questioned the identity of the British Muslim, believed to have gone against the 'liberal values' of 'freedom of speech and expression' (Addison 2010: 376). With Ayatollah Khomeini's fatwa, and British Muslim protests against Rushdie, this incident was perceived to be emblematic of a clash between religion and Western liberalism (ibid: 375–76; see also Samad 1992). For the first time, the British public became aware of 'the presence of minorities' who not only 'subscribed […] to a national' and regional 'identity', but also to a 'universal Muslim identity', which was reinforced by British Muslims themselves in their 'public' demands (Meer and Noorani 2008: 203). Hence, the politicized Muslim identity highlighted what Hall (1996: 442), discussing the changing black identity, had called a shift 'from a struggle over the relations of representation to a politics of representation itself'.

South Asian Communities and the 'Politics' of (Re)presentation

Muslims from South Asia were at the forefront in the anti-Rushdie riots (Modood 2005). Institutionally and within political and media rhetoric, Muslims from the subcontinent—particularly Pakistan—were often located within the 'regional' South Asian category; in formal documents, whether 'equal opportunities questionnaires' or the 'census', South Asians were grouped together (Panayi 2010: 138; see also Modood and Salt 2013: 9). Their respective ethnic and religious identities were often overlooked or conflated within the 'South Asian' identity. While ethnicity often draws on 'language, culture, religion, nationality and a shared heritage' (Bagguley and Hussain 2005: 216), ignoring the dynamics of the ethnic and religious aspects of the Pakistani identity, the 'early Muslim communities thus became part of the hegemonic collective that was known as the "Asian" community' (Hussain 2008; Allen 2010a: 8). Homogenizing 'people who trace their origins either directly to the Indian subcontinent

(Indian, Pakistan, Sri Lanka, Bangladesh), or else indirectly through their ancestors who migrated to East and South Africa, Fiji, East and South-East Asia, the Caribbean and elsewhere', in the category of South Asian was problematic, as it failed to take into account the diversity that encompassed South Asia (Sahoo and Maharaj 2007: 13). Yet, depending on the context, certain problematic ethnicities would, nonetheless, be conveniently flagged, as seen in the example of Enoch Powell. Hanif Kureshi shares the example of a speech made by Enoch Powell in the 1960s in which he 'quoted a constituent of his as saying that because of the Pakistanis "this country will not be worth living in for our children"' (Kureshi 2011: 6). The racist attitude towards Pakistanis was particularly evident in the use of terms such as 'Paki' (discussed in detail in Chap. 5), which became synonymous with 'loathed aliens', directed towards the Pakistani and South Asian communities, further normalized through the media—'television comics' had started using 'Pakistanis as the butt of their humour' (Kureshi 2011: 6).

In relation to civil rights and anti-racism movements, the 'South Asian' community was also mostly invisible, viewed within the 'coloured' lens of 'black power' and politics. 'Anti-racism in the seventies was only fought and only resisted in the community, in the localities, behind the slogan of a Black politics and the Black experience' (Hall 2000: 151; see also Gilroy 1987). The problem with such slogans was that they excluded the experiences of Asians, which did not always fall in line with the Black anti-racism movement (Modood 2005). The nature of racism, with Britain becoming 'multiracial', also became more complex, as '[t]he "No-Coloreds" racism was not unitary: racists always distinguished between the groups they rejected'; 'the culturally constructed grounds of rejection varied depending on the immigrant group' (Modood 2005: 34). Echoing Shah, such categorization served the objective of assisting the host state and community to 'imagine' and create groups for the practical purpose of 'managing' them (1998: 51), with identity not just negotiated internally by a group, but also externally with the host. The 'Asian' identity was therefore part of this struggle between self-definition and state management. However, second- and third-generation South Asians moved more towards a 'Muslim' identity, being unable to identify completely with their ancestral home in South Asia, with the Rushdie affair acting as a catalyst. The problem the British Muslim community—in particular, the British Pakistani community—would encounter is the general perception after the Rushdie affair that, even though 'new kinds of citizens' (Ramadan 2010) had emerged, their religio-cultural values and beliefs were against 'British values'. Hanif Kureshi captures this conflict in an anecdote of a Muslim waiter at an Indian restaurant in England whom he met at the time of the Rushdie affair. The waiter 'mentioned his fear that rather than embodying the "immigrant dream" of wealth, individuality and respect, they would become the permanent scapegoats of British society, as the black' became 'in the US' (Kureshi 2011: 102).

While the British Muslims became politicized around their Muslim identity, the reaction of the 'white' host state and community reinforced the 'alien' status of this politicized discourse. Furthermore, the second- and third-generation British Pakistani Muslims started looking more towards Islam outside their cultural prisms, realizing the distinctions between 'culture' and 'religion' (Jacobson 1997: 242). As Parekh noted, '[w]hile the parents would have said that they were Muslims, their offspring say that they have a Muslim or Islamic *identity*', adding 'the difference is deep and striking' (Parekh 2006, as cited in Allen 2010b: 16). The expression of such a religious identity proved problematic within the Western notion of citizenship and belonging. It further brought into question the parameters of the Race Relations legislation which, after 1983,[2] included 'Sikh minorities' in the definition of an identity protected against 'discrimination' by virtue of their 'ethno-religious' identity, but not Muslims (O'Toole et al. 2013: 30). Ironically, it was the heterogeneous nature of the Muslim religious identity that prevented the same level of legal protection against racism as was guaranteed to the Sikh and Jewish communities (ibid.).

Events such as the publication of Kalim Siddiqui's *The Muslim Manifesto: A Strategy for Survival*, which aimed to provide guidelines for a united 'Muslim identity' in Britain; the subsequent establishing of the Muslim Parliament, though it did not survive (Allen 2010b: 18); the

---

[2] A consequence of the ruling in *Mandla* v. *Dowell Lee*, a case that involved 'a Sikh' student's right to wear 'a turban' to school, a part of his 'ethnic' identity (Banton 1991: 119; see also Meer 2008: 69–71; Modood 2005: 20).

opposition to the Gulf War in 1991; and the 'race riots' in Bradford, Burnley and Oldham in 2001 reinforced the position that the differences between Muslims and Britishness were irreconcilable. Bagguley and Hussain (2005) note how 'the official reports into the riots' of 2001 focused 'on issues of segregation and social cohesion within a discourse that' constructed 'the segregated communities as "the problem"' (2005: 210), without examining the issues of structural of socio-economic inequality that led to such segregation and isolation in the first place. Modood and Dobbernack further notice 'the knee-jerk exclusion from the public sphere' reaction that such protests encounter, 'which, in turn, makes minorities that protest [...] seem like trouble-makers' (2011: 56). What the British state overlooked in this politicized Muslim identity was how second- and third-generation British Muslims were acting within the boundaries of British citizenship through the assertion of their religious identity, which for them was never viewed as antithetical to their British identity. As Modood notes, what such a narrative around the British Muslim failed to recognize was that 'Muslim assertiveness' as 'triggered and intensified by what' were 'seen as attacks on Muslims' were 'derived not from Islam or Islamism but from contemporary Western ideas about equality and multiculturalism' (2006: 46, see also Yaqoob 2007). Hence, the kind of disruptions that erupted prior to the events of 9/11 brought about by Muslims and those with a Pakistani heritage in Britain were an expression of British Muslims exercising their rights as British citizens through peaceful protest which, in certain instances, turned violent.

While the Muslim identity was politicized, the ethnic element cannot be overlooked. Both Modood (1990) and Jacobson (2006) highlight how the majority of Muslims who took part in the protests against Rushdie were from Pakistan and followed a particular version of Sunni Islam; i.e. either Barelvi or Deobandi (Modood 1990: 150–151, 154; Jacobson 2006: 27).[3] While the Deobandis in Britain are 'apolitical' exploring their religion 'in-depth' and spreading Islam, the Barelvis are not as 'apolitical', having a strong 'reverence' towards the 'Prophet' which exceeds 'the orthodox' (Modood 1990: 150–151). The version of Islam that was

---

[3] Both schools trace their origins in South Asia to the teachings of Shah Wali Ullah (Modood 1990).

being followed in the Pakistani community was mostly non-political. However, *The Satanic Verses*, perceived as an assault on the Prophet of Islam, resulted in a response from the Barelvi Pakistani community, the result of their 'sensitivity' and 'excessive' reverence towards the Prophet of Islam[4] (Modood 2005: 106; see also Modood 1990: 156). The response was exacerbated by international events, mainly Khomeini's fatwa against Salman Rushdie (Modood 2005: 107; Addison 2010: 375–376). A Shia leader, Khomeini's message nonetheless resonated with the Sunni Pakistani population who had felt insulted by Rushdie's book. The reaction triggered by this event in both media and policy circles resulted in the British Muslim identity being further politicized, their religio-ethnic identity again occupying a problematic place in the socio-political imagination of a 'white' British populace.

Securing the Self: Understanding the 'Home-Grown' Muslim Threat

The politicized British Muslim identity became 'securitized' after the events of 9/11 and 7/7. As discussed in the Introduction, this securitization (Croft 2012) framed every aspect of the Muslim existence within a narrative of insecurity and suspicion. Jackson (2015) discusses the extent to which the 'everyday' was securitized, ordinary members of the public becoming actors of a security agenda having been asked to inform on 'suspicious' individuals in their day-to-day lives. What defined 'suspicious' behaviour was left to a socio-political imagination, 'rooted in' a form of a 'what-if' scenario based on the 'epistemological premise that we cannot know who, when, where, why and how terrorists might strike and that terrorists are sophisticated, adaptive, and always creatively

---

[4] While the response to the Rushdie affair grouped all Muslims together as reactionary, without identifying the different schools of thought they belonged to, the response in the Indian subcontinent also varied amongst different Muslim groups. For instance, the Tablighi Jamaat in India called for a show of 'compassion' towards Salman Rushdie, and a *dawat* (invitation) to Islam, in following the example of 'the Prophet' (Talib 1997: 33–34, discussing the reaction of Mr Anwar Ahmad). While the Tablighi Jamaat is 'apolitical' and does not represent the mainstream view, its reaction is nonetheless crucial in illustrating how Muslim responses varied, depending on different schools of thought or movements within Islam.

evolving their tactics—there are therefore no clear signs of terror to be identified' (Jackson 2015: 34, 39). Hence, operating on the 'Rumsfeldian "unknown unknown"', the Muslim community is a persistent threat, if not today then tomorrow in the form of the would-be terrorist (Jackson 2015: 41). The counter terrorism policy has evolved in the past decade between 2006 and 2016, after 7/7, following the logic of the 'unknown unknown' where even non-violent extremism is considered an offence.

The British Terrorism Act 2000 had defined 'terrorism' as 'the use or threat of action where' '(2) [a]ction […] (a) involves serious violence against a person, (b) involves serious damage to property, (c) endangers a person's life, other than that of the person committing the action, (d) creates a serious risk to the health or safety of the public or a section of the public, or (e) is designed seriously to interfere with or seriously to disrupt an electronic system' (HM Government 2000). The definition[5] had been criticized for being 'too wide', implicating non-violent social and political activists with no links to terrorism (Carlile 2007: 21, discussing the University of Exeter report 'The Rules of the Game'). While in his independent review of defining terrorism Lord Carlile suggested minor amendments to this definition,[6] it continues to be the guiding definition for UK counter-terrorism policy. The definition becomes further problematic when linked to Islam, or what is defined as 'Islamism'—considered a violent strand of Islam, where phrases such as 'Islamist terrorism' can create greater confusion and misunderstanding about Muslims and their religion (see Jackson 2007; Meer 2010).

The 2006 Counter Terrorism Act detailed the Operation Contest strategy through a four-pronged approach of 'PREVENT, PURSUE, PROTECT and PREPARE', where 'the core elements of prevention' included the need to address '"structural problems" such as inequality and discrimination, changing "the environment" to deter radicalization and "engaging in the battle of ideas"' (HM Government 2006; Klausen 2009: 406). Such measures also brought immigration under a counter terrorism lens through the introduction of the Immigration, Asylum and

---

[5] This definition has been updated to further specify terrorist activity yet, despite the amendment, it still remains 'too wide' (Terrorism Act 2000, as updated on http://www.legislation.gov.uk/ukpga/2000/11/part/I#commentary-c1675655).

[6] See Carlile (2007), in particular his main conclusion, clauses (8) to (16) (2007: 47–48).

Nationality Act 2006, which placed 'security as its guiding principle, introducing a "good character" test, and lowering the threshold required to deprive rights of abode and citizenship on the basis of national security' (Brown 2010: 173). Further amendments to the Terrorism Act were put forward in 2008 with 'stronger asset-freezing powers, post-charge questioning of terrorist suspects, additional powers of entry over "controlled" individuals, restrictions on those who have been convicted of terrorism-related offences after they've served their criminal sentences, and powers to direct financial institutions to act against terrorism' (Brown 2010: 173, citing HM Government 2009: 67; see also Ansari 2006). The 2009 counter terrorism strategy CONTEST further securitized the Muslim community by framing community projects on integration within a counter terrorism lens. Projects under the 'Commission on Integration and Cohesion [...] became quickly entangled in the Prevent strategies [...] viewed as identifying the wrong problems' (O'Toole et al. 2013: 37).

CONTEST 2011 continued to build on the four-pronged agenda: 'Pursue' to 'stop terrorist attacks'; 'Prevent' to 'stop people from becoming terrorists or supporting terrorism'; 'Protect' to 'strengthen' the country's 'protection against a terrorist attack'; and 'Prepare' to 'mitigate the impact of a terrorist attack' (HM Government 2011b: 10), all against not only the 'known' danger, but also the 'unknown unknown' danger (Jackson 2015). The Conservative government's 'active muscular liberalism' therefore aimed at challenging both 'violent' and 'nonviolent' extremism (Cameron 2011; O' Toole et al. 2015: 3–10). In preventing such 'nonviolent' extremism in a context where the 'unknown unknown' threat still existed, more innocent Muslims were implicated.

Qureshi (2015) highlights how the existing counter terrorism policy of the British government follows the same colonialist logic as that of the British Raj after the Indian war of independence in 1857. At this point Muslim grievances and resistance were attributed to a primitive religion, rather than an outcome of material conditions, where the only kind of Islam allowed was one 'palatable' to the British 'value' system (Qureshi 2015: 183). The Counter Terrorism and Security Act 2015 also reinforces such a set of 'British values', seeking to challenge not just violent extremists, but also those with 'intolerant ideas [...] ideas which are hostile to basic liberal values such as democracy, freedom and sexual equality [...]

which actively promote discrimination, sectarianism and segregation', or those that ascribe to 'conspiracy theories' (Cameron 2015). This piece of legislation is akin to an Orwellian thought police, and has further drawn educational institutions within the security fold, placing a statutory duty on these institutions to inform on 'vulnerable' students 'at risk' of being radicalized (see HM Government 2015a; Saeed and Johnson 2016). These vulnerable students are predominantly Muslim students in schools and universities, with their teachers reduced to 'mere informants' for the government (see Saeed forthcoming). This has resulted in innocent Muslim students being accused of terrorism, as in the example of a 14-year-old student in a school in London suspected of being radicalized because he used the term 'L'ecoterrorisme' in a discussion about 'violence and the environment' (Dodd 2015). The child was taken to what is termed an 'inclusion centre' for an interview to determine whether he was radical, or had links to Isis (Dodd 2015). This overreaction on the part of the school authorities is just one example amongst many reported and unreported events which further isolate young Muslims (see Hooper 2015).

As Qureshi (2015) notes, 'terrorism convictions in the UK that involve actual plots are relatively low, only accounting for 66 (Qureshi 2014) out of the 838 individuals charged (Home Office 2013a, 2013b) with terrorism offences', where 'other offences are largely made up of the parts of counterterrorism legislation that seek to criminalise thought and belief, such as articles relating to possession and glorification of material considered to be "extremist"' (2015: 185). Qureshi, in his article, goes on to describe the case of Umm Ahmed who was wrongly convicted of possession of terrorism material, where the judge in her case acknowledged the 'lack of any intention' on her part, but still handed out a 12-month prison sentence since he was 'unsure' if she was 'pretending to be something' she was not (2015: 186), thereby invoking the fear of the 'unknown unknown'. According to the counter terrorism policy of Prevent, a 12-month sentence brought Umm Ahmed under its CHANNEL program (Qureshi 2015: 186). The Channel program 'uses a multi-agency approach to protect vulnerable people', 'identifying' the individual 'at risk', 'assessing the nature of the vulnerability of that risk' while 'developing' a 'support plan' that is 'appropriate' for the concerned 'individual' (HM Government 2015b: 5). Umm Ahmed, as so many other Muslims, became 'another terrorism statistic' (Qureshi 2015: 186) proving the (in)effectiveness of the existing counter terrorism policy promoted in media and political discourse.

As young Muslims continue to be framed within such a securitized context, their British Muslim identity, their thoughts and beliefs are constantly suspect. With David Cameron having declared 'multiculturalism' a failure, because of its inability to integrate Muslims into British society, his 'muscular liberalism' has increasingly gained strength. Cameron's government has repeatedly emphasized the importance of 'British values' where, despite the emphasis on rights and freedoms, the rights of British Muslims continue to be violated. The British Muslim female, in particular, embodies this contradiction of values through her physical appearance and modest demeanour. The Muslim female needs to be 'empowered'; the language of empowerment ironically is cloaked within the rhetoric of counter terrorism, as demonstrated in the 'English language policy'. The Conservative government has dedicated '£20 million' to 'language classes' in order 'to teach' English to 'the 190,000 Muslim women in England' who do not speak English (Payton 2016). 'Migrants', especially 'Muslim women' or 'spouses on migrant visas', are to be given 'two and a half years' to learn English, or else be 'forced to leave' if they 'fail' English 'language tests' (Mason and Sherwood 2016a, 2016b). This requirement, while linked to integration, was incorporated into a counter terrorism strategy to ensure that Muslim women do not fall victim to extremism, and are also more aware of the activities of their children, protecting them against extremism and radicalization (Mason and Sherwood 2016a). The irony of this policy is that it means to integrate newly arrived Muslim immigrants into British society, yet ends up further securitizing their existence within a counter terrorism framework. It further highlights how lessons of history remain unlearnt, as this policy is similar to the policy of David Blunkett, the Home Secretary during the 2001 riots, regarding 'new immigrants' passing 'tests in English and British citizenship', where his 'primary concern was […] not the individual's right to choose […] but the collective good of the "community"' (Werbner 2005c: 746–748). It also seems illogical, given that the cases of British Muslims who are part of the 'terrorist statistics' are English-speaking individuals, many of whom are educated. Hence, by simplifying a highly complex problem of radicalization (discussed in detail in Chap. 4), the British government has brought a population of 2.7 million Muslims within an insecure discourse of security, where regular, law abiding Muslims are constantly under pressure to prove their innocence and their right to belong to Britain. Present day policies of the Conservative government—especially in the aftermath of Isis, the war in Syria and the exodus of refugees fleeing the war—is bringing Britain back to where it started from, a country promoting assimilation instead of celebrating the diversity, the 'multi-ethnic' and 'multi-racial' character of its new citizens.

The Female Problem: Being British, Muslim and Pakistani

The British Muslim female with a Pakistani heritage is also viewed through an Orientalist lens—considered oppressed, a victim of a backward culture and religion. The British Muslim aspect of the female's identity was first highlighted in media and political rhetoric during the English 'scarf affair' in 1989, which 'began when two teenage Muslim girls (the Alwi sisters)' were suspended for wearing 'headscarves to school' (Werbner 2005b: 35). While the school board eventually allowed the girls to wear scarves, the narrative that permeated media accounts about Muslims varied from the 'oppressed' to the 'fanatic' (Werbner 2005b: 36; see also Werbner 2007).

While the British Muslim female in her appearance was a visible (re)presentation of Islam, the British Pakistani female was a victim of an oppressive, patriarchal culture—barely able to speak English and subjected to forced marriages, or honour killings. Sondy, for instance, highlights the struggle of first-generation Pakistani women who followed their husbands to Britain in the 1960s, and attempted to preserve their Pakistani culture while living in Britain, unable to speak the language or assimilate to a 'foreign' culture (2013: 264). The British Pakistani female therefore remained largely invisible; the focus during the Rushdie affair was on the male troublemaker, with the female perceived to be a victim of a primitive religio-ethnic belief system. The Muslim female was also mostly invisible in the 2001 riots. Yet, the Muslim identity carried a different type of significance for the British Pakistani female. It provided her with an 'authentic' voice to challenge patriarchal cultural practices such as 'forced marriages', and the concept of 'izzat' (honour). Mellor (2011), in examining issues of class and social mobility for Muslim women, highlights how Islam was instrumental in 'empowering' women to challenge such cultural practices, yet this empowerment was dependent on how accommodating individual families were of their daughters' ambitions. Access to education—and, in particular, higher education—further equipped British Pakistani women with the tools to negotiate their identities as British, Muslim and Pakistani women. Higher education for second- or third-generation British Pakistani women resulted in a sense of security as a middle-class or working-class British citizen, yet this security, unlike the white middle class, did not translate into individual mobility; rather, it allowed women to stay and contribute within their community. It also gave them greater 'bargaining power' in choosing their future husbands (Mellor 2011). The conflict between individual ambitions and familial restrictions nonetheless remained a problem, and continued to be a dominant theme in the depiction and perceptions about British Pakistani women (Dale et al. 2002). The second- and third-generation British Pakistani female was seen as negotiating two lives: one as a Pakistani daughter, and the second as a British citizen (Dale et al. 2006; see also Abbas 2003; Archer 2003; Rizvi 2007; Coles 2008; Hussain 2008; Bhopal 2009; Change Institute 2009; Khattab 2009; Ijaz and Abbas 2010; Ahmad 2012).

The primitiveness of the Pakistani identity was also highlighted in cases of honour killings or forced marriages. The British Pakistani female's identity fluctuated within a narrative of oppression and agency, where the backwardness of her culture conspicuously stood out in individual cases of honour killings or forced marriages. In 2012, for instance, the case of Shafilea Ahmed caught the attention of the British public when her parents killed her in the name of 'honour' as she was considered too 'Westernized', thereby dishonouring the family (Carter 2012). Media, especially the tabloid press, portrayed this killing as a Pakistani problem, implicating the entire Pakistani population, who were once again viewed as oppressive, with the British Pakistani woman falling victim to the primitive Pakistani mind-set (see also Tyrer and Ahmad 2006; Sanghera and Thapar-Björkert 2007; Bhimji 2009; Shirazi and Mishra 2010; Thapar-Björkert and Sanghera 2010; Williamson and Khiabany 2010; Siraj 2011). This oppression, when placed against the 'grooming scandal' that projected a hyper-sexualized abusive Pakistani male (see Pearson 2014), further reinforced a simplistic yet dangerous Orientalist view of the British Pakistani Muslim, with the female reduced to the mercy of an exploitative Pakistani male in media and political (re)presentations of the Pakistani community in Britain.

Yet, these antagonistic characteristics that are ascribed to the British Pakistani and Muslim identity, for both Muslim men and women, are often projected onto individuals by a predominantly 'white' and non-Muslim host society. The accounts of young British Muslim women with a Pakistani heritage in this study highlights how there is no single dominant narrative about Britishness, Muslimness, or Pakistaniat, where individuals associate differently with their diverse identities. Far from a conflictual process, young Muslim women are able to *balance* these different identities, while being productive members of British society. Kiran, a Muslim who wears the hijab, highlights this balancing act—which is often overlooked in sensationalized accounts of Britain and its non-white 'citizens':

> I think that I am British, I have some British aspects to me, I am Muslim because I have Muslim aspects, and I am Pakistani I have Pakistani aspects. I think religion, culture and national identity are all different sections. You can't put them in boxes and pair them against each other. They are there in different areas of life. If someone was to ask about being Muslim and Christian at the same time that is different. I can be Pakistani British and Muslim at the same time. I don't see why people have to argue with that. I find it really easy to be all at once. At the moment I feel like some kind of super woman.
> —Kiran, London1, 22, Graduate (Science), British

For Kiran, there is no conflict between the different aspects of her identity; being British is not contradictory to her practising her religion, or negotiating the cultural requirements of her ethnicity. However, Kiran's expression of her identity may or may not be similar for other British

Muslim women with a Pakistani heritage, who may prioritize one part of their identity over another; yet, such prioritizing does not translate into disloyalty towards being British. Far from it, the negotiation is part of the freedom that comes with being British in the twenty-first century.

Tehmina highlights this problem in her narrative:

> Since 9/11 the whole identity question has become more focused on Muslims especially with Pakistani background, and Indian. I see myself as British [...]. This is my own country and you are telling me that I am not part of it because I am not white [...] my mother was born here, my father was born in Pakistan [...] for me I am British, I am a British Muslim. I think the Asian bit comes at the end of the equation. But for some people it is different. Being Pakistani is very important to them [...] for myself as British I don't need to, and then obviously my faith is important to me, I am Muslim [...] I don't think it needs justification [...] being English is something different [...] being British does not mean it's white. If you look at the British flag it's not like it is made up of one colour [...] again for different people it is different. I know people who were born here, their parents were born and bred here but they do not see themselves as British at all. And they would argue that you will never be British you never can be. You're a Pakistani.
> —Tehmina, West Midlands1, 19, Undergraduate (Social Sciences), British

Tehmina's narrative encapsulates the overarching discourse about immigrant communities and citizenship in Britain. Brown (2006), in a discussion on Britishness before the arrival of the 'colored' immigrant in the 1950s, highlighted how 'being British' was still premised on 'being ethnically Caucasian, having roots in one of the regions of the country [...] sharing a Christian, and mainly Protestant, culture [...] and bearing a proud political heritage symbolised by the monarchy' (Brown 2006: 119). While Britain now has a population of 2.7 million Muslims, with British citizens who look different because they are 'visible through their color, their dress, and their differences' (Ramadan 2010: 25), there remains an overarching discourse of Britishness being linked to the ethnically 'white'. Young British Muslims such as Tehmina and Kiran have, no doubt, created a place for themselves where they belong on their own terms; yet, the space given by the 'host' community to the non-white citizenry continues to be a problem, highlighted in racial slurs such as 'Paki' or attacks on Islam, considered violent and against 'British values'.

As Tehmina observes:

> But I think the whole thing about identity and justifying I don't think we need to justify, and I'm sick of it, personally I'm sick of it of justifying that I'm not like this. You know I had a whole thing with Black minority ethnic wording. I am not keen on calling me a minority. I am not keen with that word made popular by middle class politicians that we have in this country [...] just because I am not white
> —Tehmina, West Midlands1, 19, Undergraduate (Social Sciences), British

The fact that second- and third-generation Pakistani immigrants still need to defend and define their identity, where being considered a 'minority' places them in a different 'box' or category, reveals a negotiation that is ongoing with the host society's perception of Britishness, rather than simply an identity crisis within the community. Tehmina further echoes Homi Bhabha's observation of 'a danger' associated with 'the very title of the "minority"' that 'creates a hasty equivalence between public spheres, normalising forms of social difference, and "moralising" divergent strategies of subordination, oppression, or resistance into a hasty and homogenous interpellation of shared victimage' (Bhabha 1998: 123). This homogeneity of the minority category, especially for the British Muslim Pakistani, is one that is imposed as much from the outside as it is negotiated within the community. The sentiment 'you will never be British', as highlighted in Tehmina's narrative about other British Muslim Pakistanis, is the result of a 'majority' discourse on Britishness, where the minority community situated in a socio-historical context is constantly reminded of its status as an outsider (see also Abbas 2005; Fekete 2009; Allen 2010a; Virdee 2014). However, as Tehmina's narrative reveals, the danger of a 'hasty and homogenous interpellation of shared victimage' around an imposed 'minority' category may not be that straightforward where the negotiation of identity, of Britishness, varies across the minority community, with different British Muslim Pakistanis identifying differently with their various identities—some accepting their minority position, while others like Tehmina refusing to give in.

Farzana captures this conflict in her narrative:

Personally I don't think that I have been like oo I have to prove that I am Muslim and be this way and have to prove that I am British and be this […] I am me and I am quite happy being me. But if you have to define me, like you know if I have to fill a form, I am not ticking the White box, now am I? I am ticking British Pakistani or whatever?
—Farzana, South West1, 20, Undergraduate (Medicine), British

The space available for British Muslims with a Pakistani heritage to express these identities is therefore dependent on external factors, including what Shah (1998: 51) describes as the host state imagining and creating categories for the practical purposes of 'managing' immigrant communities. Hussain (2008) notes how the categorization of individuals in such a way is 'political'. Discussing Skerry's (2001) work, Hussain highlights how 'every category in the Census or in official surveys is the result of political judgements even if such judgements are not narrowly self-interested' (Hussain 2008: xix). These boxes that define Farzana or Tehmina's identity might be there out of the practical necessity of identifying the ethnic make-up of modern day Britain, or reinforcing the 'minority' status of communities; but the perception that being white is the predominant characteristic of being British remains, one that is constantly felt by young Muslims, especially the diverse group of Muslim women in this study.

As Farzana goes on to explain:

Farzana: Well I am British and I do actually think I am British but I will feel stupid saying that to a white person because there has to be a way to differentiate them from me because we are not the same.
Interviewer: What makes you different?
Farzana: Look at me. Helloooooo.
—Farzana, South West1, 20, Undergraduate (Medicine), British

Farzana, like the other participants, is placed in a Fanonian context, where the validity of identity is ascribed against the legitimacy of the 'white' Self; where the internalization of what it means to be British continues to be determined in 'proximity' to the discourse on whitenesss (Fanon 1967; see also Bhabha 1998; Tyrer 2010).

These degrees of proximity and legitimacy of being British are also evident in Faiza's narrative, where she further brings in the metaphor of cricket as a testament to loyalty and Britishness:

> I count myself as a total British person. If someone said to me what are you first British or Pakistani, I would say British. But I have to say that in the cricket world cup I supported Pakistan not England, I don't know why [...] everyone else in my family, two of my sisters were rooting for Pakistan but [...] my father is for England [...] I've come across Pakistani people whose ethnicity is Pakistani but nationality is British. They are the most British people you can come across but in international competitions they would always be rooting for Pakistan. So I don't know. But I think in things like you hold dear to you, small bits of like stuff Pakistan is actually good at, I think the Pakistani in you comes out at that time. But you know with the upcoming royal wedding [...] I like the British royal family, I appreciate the monarchy, my parents pay taxes, I appreciate being British. But I don't know what does it take to be British, but I think to be white, to be white British is what it takes to be a complete British [...] I think again supporting Pakistan just shows you can never be a full British person sort of feeling.
> —Faiza, West Yorkshire2, 22, Undergraduate (Humanities), British

Faiza's observation about the cricket match echoes the 'infamous Tebbit test' that questioned the loyalty and Britishness of 'minority communities' for 'harking back' to the country they or their parents left by not supporting England in cricket (Burdsey 2007: 616). Criticized for being 'racist' and exclusionary, the Tebbit test reinforced artificial measures of loyalty for the migrant community. However, in the case of Faiza, with her father a first-generation immigrant supporting England, and a family divided in their support, the Tebbit test proves to be nothing more than a divisive mechanism that sensationalizes the 'outsider' status of the 'minority' community, undermining individual choice and agency which should be the celebrated part of being British. Ironically, the discrimination and racism that embodies the Tebbit test is what encouraged Faiza, a Muslim British Pakistani who wears a niqab, to support a 'South Asian' team, as she explains:

> To be quite honest I thought if Pakistan get out I'd still not want England to win, I'd rather have a South Asian team. Because sometimes you know the attitude of ignorant white people, gets to you and you think [...] this British country wouldn't have been what it is right now [...] had it not been for you know Pakistani and Indian forefathers you know what I mean [...] The British Raj you know, the gold and everything, they have stolen it, that doesn't belong to them. It has come from the backs and the blood of Indian and Pakistani men. I think that's where this whole thing comes from, you still have that Pakistani in you that wants to prove to British people that we might have come from back home, still you wouldn't have been here if it weren't for our forefathers.
> —Faiza, West Yorkshire2, 22, Undergraduate (Humanities), British

Faiza's support for Pakistan or any other South Asian country playing against England is not a consequence of 'feeling' like an outsider, as she clearly feels British, but, rather, it is a consequence of being made 'to feel' like one through her experiences of Islamophobia. Faiza would have failed the racist Tebbit test but the fact that a 'Conservative MP' could propose such a 'test' in 1990 which, to this day is considered worthy of debate or discussion, reflects how racism and xenophobia have become acceptable (Burdsey 2007). Far from challenging the racism that Faiza describes, the 'host' community instead reinforces the 'outsider' status of law abiding British citizens, who continue to be perceived as 'minorities' and second- or third-generation immigrants. Yet, Faiza's narrative is informed by a socio-historical context that Werbner highlights in her discussion on loyalty and Britishness. For Werbner, '[t]he Rushdie affair, the Gulf war, the Israel-Palestinian conflict, September 11, Bosnia, Chechnya, Kashmir, Afghanistan, the war with Iraq and July 7 have all led to a process of spiralling progressive alienation of Muslims in Britain', that sets 'Pakistanis in Britain apart from other South Asian groups', where the act of British Pakistanis supporting Pakistan in a cricket match is viewed as 'serious moral breaches of the national consensus' (Werbner 2005c: 762–763). Ironically, for the British Pakistani this questioning of loyalties, and being forced into the position of an 'outsider', is also a problem faced in Pakistan:

> When we go to Pakistan where there is a term called '*walaity*'[7] and they keep saying the *walaity* are here and I was like okay I just found out I'm a foreigner [...] but when I am here they call me Paki and I am not British. What is British, I don't understand what it is? The Romans have invaded it, the Vikings have invaded it, the Normandy everyone has invaded Britain [...] I think a lot of that pride [...] the key difference is that with people coming in I don't think they can handle that society is changing [...]
>
> I am so British first and I will give back to England because they have offered me something that if my parents were in Pakistan I wouldn't be offered that [...] the education level in England is far more higher than it is in Pakistan partly because we have the means to afford it [...] I will be British first [...] then I will be Pakistani because that is where my parents are from. And everything else [...] I am a Muslim first than any other identity but then after British I will be Pakistani because of my culture.
> —Tamana, West Yorkshire2, 19, Undergraduate (Social Sciences), British

For Tamana, just like the other participants, being Muslim is not antithetical to being British. However, the Pakistani side of her identity is also not in conflict, despite being made to feel like an outsider not only by the 'white' population in the UK, but also by Pakistanis in Pakistan. Yet, while these differences might be imposed on her, Tamana is clear about her association with the diverse identities that reflect her identity—which are far from being irreconcilable, as painted in media and political rhetoric.

Yet, in Britain today, in a post 7/7 context, that space to express such a diversity of Britishness is shrinking:

> There has been such pressure on the Muslim community to fit in. Our loyalties are being questioned. Our idea of whether we have got British values before being Muslim, that idea of whether we accept British values.

---

[7] *Walaity* means 'foreigner' in Punjabi.

Therefore, you don't want to sound like you are angry [...] I feel this is my country, this is my government, this is my taxpaying money, I have an opinion on how this country is run [...] If you feel like you are under threat, and if you feel like you are not welcomed, then you are less likely to have an opinion or voice your opinion.
—Lyyla, North West1, Alumna, Activist, British

Placed within the socio-historical context of the South Asian and Pakistani identity is the securitization of that identity, which has an impact on both men and women. Muslims have become not just 'outsiders', but also an active threat to the British way of life. Lyyla's description of Muslims who stay silent out of fear of being considered disloyal reflects how the idea of 'multiculturalism' as respecting and valuing other 'ethnic and religious identities' (Modood and Dobbernack 2011: 56) is being compromised in the current Islamophobic and xenophobic environment.

Mehnaz in her narrative, however, recognizes not only the problems within the Pakistani community related to cultural practices that make her less likely to connect with the Pakistani identity, but also the problematic securitization of the Muslim Pakistani:

If someone asks me my ethnicity I would say British, I will not say Pakistani because I am born and bred in the UK [...] I think being Pakistanis are making us more vulnerable, because we have certain practices that are wrong, culturally yeah acceptable, Islamically not acceptable. I think with those practices we have made ourselves more vulnerable. 7/7 is actually like a fuse of problems, and with that fuse being blown up we have made ourselves more vulnerable [...] With Pakistanis we keep ourselves to ourselves, we don't like socializing that much. The Indians have accepted the culture of Britain much more happily than Pakistanis. Indians are okay with marriages outside your communities, Pakistanis we've even got caste systems we don't want to get out of that caste system to get married. So like I think with those ideas and those cultural practices I think that is why many people are looking at Pakistanis and are saying you know what, I am sure they have something going on there. I am sure they are planning something. They don't know as Pakistanis we can't keep our mouths shut. That is our problem. If we were terrorists we would be the most horrendous terrorists in the universe. Do you know how much problem we have of keeping our mouth shut?
—Mehnaz, West Yorkshire2, 22, Undergraduate (Law), British

Mehnaz's narrative highlights different aspects of the securitized British Muslim Pakistani identity. On the one hand, she echoes Mellor (2011) and Ahmad's (2012) assertion that Islam is considered more empowering for Muslim Pakistani women, against patriarchal 'cultural' beliefs. But she also highlights the nature of self-segregation that has created greater suspicion around the Pakistani community, compared with other South Asian communities, such as the Indians, who are better integrated. Yet, the self-segregation, while problematic, does not translate into the 'security threat' that these communities are perceived to present, as Mehnaz evoked the South Asian stereotype about Pakistanis as being loud and talkative. While self-segregation is a problem, the narratives in this chapter reveal how that segregation is also reinforced by the 'white' non-Muslim community that constantly challenges and questions the loyalty of the British Pakistani community. The British Pakistanis might be more inward looking, as described by Mehnaz, especially in relation to marriage and cultural beliefs, yet this chapter reveals how such inwardness entails a process of negotiation, which is overlooked where the diverse identities of the British Muslim Pakistanis are perceived as a single, problematic category of troublemakers, thereby removing agency from the purview of the British Muslim Pakistani citizen.

British Muslim Pakistanis: Between (In)security and Britishness

The British Muslim Pakistani identity is located within a socio-historical context of colonialism and the Commonwealth, where second- or third-generation British Muslims are perceived to be part of a minority community, as defined by a predominantly white British majority. The community has repeatedly faced problems of acceptability and adaptability in the British socio-political imagination. An invocation to the religious political identity in the case of the Rushdie affair, or in defence of Kashmir or Palestine, and in opposition to the invasion of Iraq and Afghanistan in 2001, is perceived as a challenge to Britishness. What is lost in this brown and white depiction of Britishness is how political dissent in the form of protests or campaigns against British foreign policy is an integral part of being British, of living in a free and multicultural society where assimilation should not be the norm.

Such a discourse is also evident in addressing local issues in relation to the British Muslim Pakistani community. The 2001 riots, for instance, were blamed on the community for not having integrated; instead, there should have been recognition of the 'structural issues' related to socio-economic discrimination that pushed young people onto the streets of Bradford, Oldham and Burnley (Cantle 2001; Ouseley 2001; Hussain and Bagguley 2005; Macey 2007: 166–168; Meer 2010). The stereotype of the ghettoized British Pakistani community leading 'parallel lives' (Cantle 2001) inundated media and political accounts of the troublesome British Muslim Pakistani (Meer 2010). British Pakistani women, however, continued to be depicted as victims of a patriarchal socio-cultural belief system—either killed in the name of honour, or forcefully married off to cousins or relatives in Pakistan. The possibility of agency and choice was completely removed from the purview of the British Muslim Pakistani woman.

The events of 9/11 and 7/7 further securitized the British Muslim Pakistani identity, especially on discovering the Pakistani connection of the 7/7 home-grown terrorists. The resultant fear of the unknown living amidst the mundane, the 'unknown unknown' terrorist attack that can happen anywhere, at any time, and come from any Muslim securitized the entire Muslim community. British Muslim men were considered more dangerous because of their ability to be physically violent, while British Muslim women, as Chap. 3 illustrates, fluctuated between a potential threat and a victim to be rescued. Despite this overarching discourse about the British Muslim Pakistan identity, the narratives in this chapter have illustrated how Britishness continues to be negotiated against the dominant 'white' discourse of identity in Britain. Young Muslims, far from being in a 'state of crisis', are able to balance the different parts of their identity in a variety of ways, despite the constraints imposed on them by a predominantly white discourse on Britishness. However, the extent to which different identities become significant is linked to material conditions and experiences, where racism and Islamophobia can be a catalyst towards disenfranchisement.

Bibliography

Abbas, T. (ed.) (2005) *Muslim Britain. Communities Under Pressure*. London: Zed Books Ltd.

Abbas, T. (2003) *The Impact of Religio-Cultural Norms and Values on the Education of Young South Asian Women*. Oxford: Carfax Pub. Co.

Addison, P. (2010) *No Turning Back: The Peacetime Revolutions of Post-war Britain*. Oxford & New York: Oxford University Press.

Ahmad, F. (2012) Graduating towards marriage? Attitudes towards marriage and relationships among university-educated British Muslim women. *Culture and Religion*, 13 (2), pp. 193–210.

Akwagyiram, A. (09/05/2012) *Grooming and race—What do we know?* BBC News. Available from: http://www.bbc.com/news/uk-18004153 (Accessed 06/09, 2015).

Allen, C. (2010a) *Islamophobia*. England: Ashgate Publishing Limited.

Allen, C. (2010b) Contemporary Islamophobia before 9/11: A brief history. *Arches Quarterly Islamophobia and Anti Muslim Hatred: Causes & Remedies*, 4 (7), pp. 14–23.

Ansari, H. (2002) *Muslims in Britain*. UK: Minority Rights Group International.

Ansari, F. (2006) *British Anti-terrorism: A Modern Day Witch-hunt*. Islamic Human Rights Commission.

Archer, L. (2003) Social Class and Higher Education. In *Higher Education and Social Class. Issues of Exclusion and Inclusion*, eds. L. Archer, M. Hutchings and A. Ross, London: Routledge Falmer, pp. 5–20.

Asad, T. (1990) Multiculturalism and British identity in the wake of the Rushdie affair. *Politics & Society*, 18 (4), pp. 455–480.

Bagguley, P. and Hussain, Y. (2005) Flying the Flag for England? Citizenship, Religion and Cultural Identity among British Pakistani Muslims. In *Muslim Britain: Communities Under Pressure*, ed. T. Abbas, London: Zed Books Ltd, pp. 208–221.

Bakhtin, M. (1986) *Speech Genres and Other Late Essays. C. Emerson and M. Holquist (eds.), Translated by V.E. McGhee*. Austin: University of Texas Press.

Bakhtin, M. (1981) *The Dialogic Imagination Four Essays. M. Holquist (ed.), Translated by C. Emerson and M. Holquist*. Austin: University of Texas Press.

Banton, M. (1991) The race relations problematic. *British Journal of Sociology*, 42 (1), pp. 115–130.

BBC News. (08/05/2012a) Rochdale grooming trial: Nine found guilty of child sex charges. Available from: http://www.bbc.com/news/uk-england-17989463 (Accessed 05/06, 2015).

BBC News. (17/07/2012c) *Oldham wife Shasta Khan guilty of Jewish jihad plan.* BBC News. [Online]. Available from: http://www.bbc.co.uk/news/uk-england-manchester-18882619 (Accessed 19/11, 2012).

BBC News. (23/07/2011b) *Belgian ban on full veils comes into force.* Accessed from BBC News. [Online]. Available from: http://www.bbc.co.uk/news/world-europe-14261921 (Accessed 09/15, 2012).

Bhabha, H.K. (1998) Anxiety in the Midst of Difference. APLA Distinguished Lecture 1996, *PoLAR*, 21(1), pp. 123–137.

Bhimji, F. (2009) Identities and agency in religious spheres: A study of British Muslim women's experience. *Gender, Place and Culture*, 16 (4), pp. 365–380.

Bhopal, K. (2009) Identity, empathy and 'otherness': Asian women, education and dowries in the UK. *Race Ethnicity and Education*, 12 (1), pp. 27–39.

Brown, K.E. (2010) Contesting the securitization of British Muslims: Citizenship and resistance. *Interventions*, 12 (2), pp. 171–182.

Brown, J.M. (2006) *Global South Asians: Introducing the Modern Diaspora.* Cambridge: Cambridge University Press.

Burdsey, D. (2007) Role with the punches: The construction and representation of Amir Khan as a role model for multiethnic Britain, *The Sociological Review.* 55(3), pp. 611–631.

Cameron, D. (2015) *Extremism: PM speech. Her Majesty's Government.* [Online]. Available from: https://www.gov.uk/government/speeches/extremism-pm-speech (Accessed 28/07, 2015).

Cameron, D. (2011) *PM's Speech at Munich Security Conference.* Her Majesty's Government. [Online]. Available from: http://www.number10.gov.uk/news/pms-speech-at-munich-security-conference (Accessed 09/08, 2012).

Cantle, T. (2001) Community cohesion: A report of the independent review team.

Carlile, A. (2007) *The Definition of Terrorism. A Report by Lord Carlile of Berriew Q.C. Independent Reviewer of Terrorism Legislation. Presented to Parliament by the Secretary of State for the Home Department, by Command of Her Majesty.* UK: Crown.

Carter, H. (03/08/2012) *Shafilea Ahmed: the murder that tore her family apart.* The Guardian. [Online]. Available from: http://www.guardian.co.uk/uk/2012/aug/03/shafilea-ahmed-murder-background?intcmp=239 (Accessed 02/03, 2013).

Change Institute. (2009) *The Pakistani Muslim Community in England. Understanding Muslim Ethnic Communities.* UK: Crown.

Coles, M.I. (2008) *Every Muslim Child Matters: Practical Guidance for Schools and Children's Services.* Trentham Books Limited.

Croft, S. (2012) *Securitizing Islam Identity and the Search for Security.* Cambridge: Cambridge University Press.

Dale A., Lindley, J. and Dex S. (2006) A life course perspective on ethnic differences in Women's economic activity in Britain, European Sociological Review, 22 (3), pp. 323–337.

Dale, A., Shaheen, N., Kalra, V. and Fieldhouse, E. (2002) Routes into education and employment for young Pakistani and Bangladeshi women in the UK. *Ethnic and Racial Studies*, 25 (6), pp. 942–968.

Dodd, V. (22/09/2015) 'School questioned Muslim pupil about Isis after discussion on eco-activism,' The Guardian, Available from: http://www.theguardian.com/education/2015/sep/22/school-questioned-muslim-pupil-about-isis-after-discussion-on-eco-activism (Accessed 11/13, 2015).

Fanon, F. (1967) *Black Skin White Masks*. England: Pluto Press.

Fekete, L. (2009) *A Suitable Enemy Racism, Migration and Islamophobia in Europe*. London: Pluto Press.

Gilroy, P. (1987) *"There Ain't No Black in the Union Jack"*: *The Cultural Politics of Race and Nation*. London: Hutchinson.

Githens-Mazer, J., Lambert, R., Baker, A.H., Cohen-Baker, S. and Pieri, Z. (2010) Muslim Communities Perspectives on Radicalisation in Leicester, UK.

Hall, S. (2000) Old and New Identities, Old and New Ethnicities. In *Theories of Race and Racism: A Reader*, eds. L. Back and J. Solomos, London: Routledge, pp. 144–153.

Hall, S. (1996) New Ethnicities. *Stuart Hall: Critical Dialogues in Cultural Studies*, eds. D. Morley and K. Chen, London: Routledge, pp. 442–451.

Her Majesty's Government (HM Government). (2015a) *Counter-Terrorism and Security Act 2015*. Available from: http://www.legislation.gov.uk/ukpga/2015/6/notes/contents (Accessed 03/28, 2015).

Her Majesty's Government (HM Government). (2015b) *Channel Duty Guidance. Protecting vulnerable people from being drawn into terrorism. Statutory guidance for Channel panel members and partners of local panels*. UK: Crown.

Her Majesty's Government (HM Government). (2011a) *Prevent Strategy*. UK: Crown.

Her Majesty's Government (HM Government). (2011b) *CONTEST The United Kingdom's Strategy for Countering Terrorism*. UK: Crown.

Her Majesty's Government (HM Government). (2006) *Terrorism Act 2006*. UK: Crown.

Her Majesty's Government (HM Government). (2000) *Terrorism Act 2000* (Available from:http://www.legislation.gov.uk/ukpga/2000/11/part/I#commentary-c1675655 (Accessed 02/03, 2012) UK: Crown.

Hooper, S. (23/07/2015) 'Stifling freedom of expression in UK schools,' Al Jazeera, Available from: http://www.aljazeera.com/indepth/features/2015/

07/stifling-freedomexpression-uk-schools-150721080612049.html (Accessed 11/15, 2015).

Hussain, S. (2008) *Muslims on the Map A National Survey of Social Trends in Britain.* London: Tauris Academic Studies.

Hussain, Y. and Bagguley, P. (2005) Citizenship, Ethnicity and Identity British Pakistanis after the 2001 'Riots'. *Sociology,* 39 (3), pp. 407–425.

Ijaz, A. and Abbas, T. (2010) The impact of inter-generational change on the attitudes of working-class South Asian Muslim parents on the education of their daughters. *Gender and Education,* 22 (3), pp. 313–326.

Jackson, R. (2015) The epistemological crisis of counterterrorism, *Critical Studies on Terrorism,* 8:1, pp. 33–54.

Jackson, R. (2007) Constructing enemies: 'Islamic terrorism' in political and academic discourse. *Government and Opposition,* 42 (3), pp. 394–426.

Jacobson, J. (2006) *Islam in Transition. Religion and Identity Amongst British Pakistani Youth.* UK: Taylor and Francis.

Jacobson, J. (1997) Religion and ethnicity: Dual and alternative sources of identity among young British Pakistanis. *Ethnic and Racial Studies,* 20 (2), pp. 238–256.

Khattab, N. (2009) Ethno-religious background as a determinant of educational and occupational attainment in Britain. *Sociology,* 43 (2), pp. 304–322.

Klausen, J. (2009) British counter-terrorism after 7/7: Adapting community policing to the fight against domestic terrorism. *Journal of Ethnic and Migration Studies,* 35 (3), pp. 403–420.

Kureshi, H. (2011) *Collected Essays.* London: Faber and Faber Ltd.

Macey, M. (2007) Islamic Political Radicalism in Britain: Muslim Men in Bradford. In *Islamic Political Radicalism A European Perspective,* ed. T. Abbas, Edinburgh: Edinburgh University Press, pp. 160–172.

Mason, R. and Sherwood, H. (18/01/2016a) *Cameron 'stigmatising Muslim women' with English language policy,* The Guardian. Available from http://www.theguardian.com/politics/2016/jan/18/david-cameron-stigmatising-muslim-women-learn-english-language-policy (Accessed, 02/20, 2016).

Mason, R. and Sherwood, H. (18/01/2016b) *Migrant spouses who fail English test may have to leave UK, says Cameron.* The Guardian. Available from http://www.theguardian.com/uk-news/2016/jan/18/pm-migrant-spouses-who-fail-english-test-may-have-to-leave-uk (Accessed, 02/20, 2016).

Meer, N. (2010) *Citizenship, Identity and the Politics of Multiculturalism: The Rise of Muslim Consciousness.* Basingstoke, England & New York: Palgrave Macmillan.

Meer, N. (2008) The politics of voluntary and involuntary identities: Are Muslims in Britain an ethnic, racial or religious minority? *Patterns of Prejudice,* 42 (1), pp. 61–81.

Meer, N. and Noorani, T. (2008) A sociological comparison of anti-Semitism and anti-Muslim sentiment in Britain. *The Sociological Review*, 56 (2), pp. 195–219.

Mellor, J. (2011) "I Really Couldn't Think of Being Married, Having a Family with Nothing Behind Me": Empowerment, Education and British Pakistani Women." In *Pakistan and Its Diaspora. Multidisciplinary Approaches*, eds. M. Bolognani and S.M. Lyon, UK: Palgrave Macmillan, pp. 217–238.

Moddod, T. (1990) British Asian and Muslims and the Rushdie affair. *The Political Quarterly*, 61 (2), pp. 143–160.

Modood, T. (2013) Multiculturalism, Ethnicity and Integration: Some Contemporary Challenges. In *Global Migration, Ethnicity and Britishness*, eds. T. Modood and J. Salt, Basingstoke: Palgrave Macmillan, pp. 40–62.

Modood, T. (2005) *Multicultural Politics Racism, Ethnicity, and Muslims in Britain*. Minneapolis: University of Minnesota Press.

Modood, T. and Salt, J. (2013) Migration, Minorities and the Nation. In *Global migration, ethnicity and Britishness*, eds. T. Modood and J. Salt, Basingstoke: Palgrave Macmillan, pp. 3–13.

Modood T. and Dobbernack J. (2011) A left communitarianism? What about multiculturalism?, *Soundings* 48, pp. 54–65.

Muslim Council of Britain (2015). *British Muslims in Numbers*. Available from: https://www.mcb.org.uk/wp-content/uploads/2015/02/MCBCensus Report_2015.pdf (Accessed 09/15, 2015).

Office for National Statistics (2012) *Religion in England and Wales* 2011. UK: Crown.

O'Toole, T., DeHanas, D.N., Modood, T., Meer, N. and Jones, S. (2013) *Taking Part Muslim Participation in Contemporary Governance*. Bristol: University of Bristol.

O'Toole, T., Meer, N., DeHanas, D.N., Jones, S.H. and Modood, T. (2015) Governing through Prevent? Regulation and Contested Practice in State–Muslim Engagement. *Sociology*, pp. 1–18.

Ouseley, H. (2001) *Community Pride not Prejudice. Making Diversity Work in Bradford*. Bradford Vision.

Panayi, P. (2010) *An Immigration History of Britain : Multicultural Racism Since 1800*. Harlow, England; New York: Pearson Longman.

Parekh, B. (2011) Defining National Identity in a Multicultural Society. In *People, Nation and State: The Meaning of Ethnicity and Nationalism*, eds. E. Mortimer and R. Fine, London: I.B. Taurus & Co. Ltd, pp. 66–74.

Parekh, B. (2010) What is Multiculturalism? In *The Ethnicity Reader Nationalism, Multiculturalism and Migration*, eds. M. Guibernau and J. Rex, Cambridge: Polity Press, pp. 238–243.

Payton, M. (18/01/2016) *David Cameron prompts backlash by announcing plans to teach Muslim women English*. Independent. Available from: http://www.independent.co.uk/news/uk/home-news/backlash-as-david-cameron-announced-plans-to-teach-muslim-women-english-a6818496.html (Accessed 03/01, 2016).

Pearson, A. (27/8/2014) *Rotherham: In the face of such evil, who is the racist now?* The Telegraph. Available from: http://www.telegraph.co.uk/news/uknews/crime/11059138/Rotherham-In-the-face-of-such-evil-who-is-the-racist-now.html (Accessed 10/03, 2015).

Piscatori, J. (1990) The Rushdie affair and the politics of ambiguity. *International Affairs (Royal Institute of International Affairs 1944–)*, pp. 767–789.

Qureshi, A. (2015) PREVENT: creating "radicals" to strengthen anti-Muslim narratives, *Critical Studies on Terrorism*, 8(1), pp. 181–191.

Ramadan, T. (2010) *What I Believe*. Oxford: Oxford University Press.

Rizvi, S. (2007) *A Muslim Girl's School in Britain. Socialization and Identity*. Doctorate of Philosophy. University of Oxford.

Saeed, T. and Johnson, D. (2016) Intelligence, global terrorism and higher education: Neutralising threats or alienating allies? *British Journal of Educational Studies*, 64(1), pp.37–51.

Saeed T. (forthcoming) Muslim Narratives of Schooling in Britain: From "Paki" to the "Would-Be Terrorist". In *Education, Neo-liberalism and Muslim Students: Schooling a 'Suspect Community'*, eds. M.M. Ghaill, and C. Haywood, UK: Palgrave Macmillan.

Sahoo, A.K. and Maharaj, B. (2007) Introduction: Globalization, Migration, Transnationalism and Diaspora: Some Critical Reflections. In *Sociology of Diaspora A Reader, Volume 1*, ed. Sahoo, A. K. and Maharaj, B., New Delhi: Rawat Publications, pp. 1–18.

Samad, Y. (1992) Book burning and race relations: Political mobilisation of Bradford Muslims. *Journal of Ethnic and Migration Studies*, 18 (4), pp. 507–519.

Sanghera, G. and Thapar-Björkert, S. (2007) 'Because I am Pakistani … and I am Muslim … I am Political'—Gendering Political Radicalism: Young Femininities in Bradford. In *Islamic Political Radicalism A European Perspective*, ed. T. Abbas, Edinburgh: Edinburgh University Press, pp. 173–191.

Sardar, Z. and Ahmad, W.I.U. (2012) Introduction. In *Muslims in Britain: Making Social and Political Space*, eds. W.I.U. Ahmad and Z. Sardar, USA: Routledge, pp. 1–16.

Shah, S. (1998) Flash-Backs-and-Forth: Re-searching the Roots. In *Educating Muslim Girls Shifting Discourses*, ed. K. Haw, Buckingham: Open University Press, pp. 43–62.

Shirazi, F. and Mishra, S. (2010) Young Muslim women on the face veil (niqab) A tool of resistance in Europe but rejected in the United States. *International Journal of Cultural Studies*, 13 (1), pp. 43–62.

Siraj, A. (2011) Meanings of modesty and the hijab amongst Muslim women in Glasgow, Scotland. *Gender, Place & Culture*, 18 (6), pp. 716–731.

Talib, M. (1997) The Tablighis in the making of Muslim identity. *Comparative Studies of South Asia, Africa and the Middle East*, 17 (1), pp. 32–51.

Taylor, C. (1994) The Politics of Recognition. In *Multiculturalism: Examining the Politics of Recognition*, ed. G. Amy, Princeton: Princeton University Press, pp. 25–74.

Thapar-Bjorkert, S. and Sanghera, G. (2010) Social capital, educational aspirations and young Pakistani Muslim men and women in Bradford, West Yorkshire. *The Sociological Review*, 58 (2), pp. 244–264.

Triandafyllidou, A., Modood, T. and Meer, N. (eds) (2012) *European Multiculturalisms: Cultural, Religious and Ethnic Challenges*. Edinburgh: Edinburgh University Press.

Tyrer, D. (2010) 'Flooding the Embankments': Race, Bio-Politics and Sovereignty. In *Thinking through Islamophobia: Global Perspectives*, eds. S. Sayyid and A. Vakil, London: Hurst & Co. (Publishers) Ltd, pp. 93–110.

Tyrer, D. and Ahmad, F. (2006) *Muslim Women and Higher Education: Identities, Experiences and Prospects. A Summary Report. Liverpool John Moores University and European Social Fund*. Oxford: Oxuniprint.

Virdee, S. (2014) *Racism, Class and the Racialized Outsider*. London: Palgrave Macmillan.

Werbner, P. (2007) Veiled interventions in pure space honour, shame and embodied struggles among Muslims in Britain and France. *Theory, Culture & Society*, 24 (2), pp. 161–186.

Werbner, P. (2005b) Honor, shame and the politics of sexual embodiment among South Asian Muslims in Britain and beyond: An analysis of debates in the public sphere. *International Social Science Review*, 6 (1), pp. 25–47.

Werbner, P. (2005c) The translocation of culture: 'Community cohesion' and the force of multiculturalism in history. *The Sociological Review*, 53 (4), pp. 745–768.

Williamson, M. and Khiabany, G. (2010) UK: The veil and the politics of racism. *Race & Class*, 52 (2), pp. 85–96.

Yaqoob, S. (2007) British Islamic Political Radicalism. In *Islamic Political Radicalism A European Perspective*, ed. T. Abbas, Edinburgh: Edinburgh University Press, pp. 279–294.

3

Securitizing the Muslim Female: Islamophobia and the Hidden Terrorist

I feel that many of them think that we are being forced to wear it or we've got something to hide that is why we are covering our faces. If they care that much then why don't they try and find out instead of having this stereotype, going out and try to educate themselves about why some of us are doing this, wearing the niqab and things like that […] I think it's just people that have a bad attitude towards Islam without being educated about Islam, without knowing what Islam is.
—Faiza, West Yorkshire2, 22, Undergraduate (Humanities), British

Women in general are more prone to being vulnerable. Women who wear the headscarf are already quite mentally strong because they know what they are going to come across. But the girls who don't wear it, like people think it is all good for them, but really they attract different type of people and will be approached by different people so it is up to them to be strong.
—Aisha, London4, 22, Undergraduate (German), British

Media and political discussion on Muslim women primarily focuses on the 'veiled figure'. The female is perceived as a victim of religion or culture by being forced into the veil; she is practising her agency and making a political statement by wearing the veil; she is a physical or ideological threat to Western liberal values as a result of the veil; while acceptance of the veil represents an open, accommodating and multicultural society. The level of acceptance also varies, where the burqa/niqab is perceived as less acceptable (extreme) to the basic hijab (between moderate and extreme), where the 'non-veiled' Muslim (integrated) is the most acceptable member of the Muslim community. What is acceptable Muslimness is determined by a socio-political discourse, which, as illustrated in Chap. 2, is situated within an ideological framework of 'Britishness'. The appearance of the Muslim woman makes her an easy marker of such identity politics; yet, as Faiza and Aisha's accounts reveal, she is seldom included in the debate about her identity. As a 'marker', though, she becomes an easy target of Islamophobia, personifying the primitiveness of a religion that is antithetical to modern British values (see Tyrer and Ahmad 2006; Allen 2010a; Githens-Mazer and Lambert 2010a; Meer and Modood 2010; Williamson and Khiabany 2010; Zebiri 2011; Faith Matters 2013a; Zempi and Chakraborti 2014).

While a great deal has been written about the veiled Muslim woman, both in academic scholarship, as well as in media and political accounts (see Dwyer 1999b; Franks 2000; Werbner 2007; Afshar 2008; Khiabany and Williamson 2008; Haw 2009, 2010; Joppke 2009b; Bilge 2010; Brown 2010, 2011; Meer et al. 2010; Shirazi and Mishra 2010; Siraj 2011; Bhimji 2012; Contractor 2012), this chapter focuses on the securitization of the veiled figure and its implications for both veiled and non-veiled Muslim women. In particular, the chapter highlights the cases of Samina Malik, Roshonara Choudhry, Shasta Khan and the more recent 'jihadi brides'. The chapter explores notions of acceptability, the resultant moderate/extremist binaries, and how young women negotiate these. The second part of the chapter examines Muslim women's opinions about such stereotypes, revealing how they are caught within the moderate/extremist binary, exposing how such socio-political narratives about Muslim women has an impact on their everyday lives.

Framing Muslim Women: The Socio-political Narrative

In his book *Covering Islam: How the Media and the Experts Determine How We See the Rest of the World*, Edward W. Said examined how media, whether broadcast or print, has always had an uneasy relationship with Muslims, drawing on an Orientalist imagination in representing Muslims. In a foreword for the revised edition of his book in 1996, Said explained how media representation of Islam in the news was plagued with 'ignorance' and 'hostility' (Said 1997: xlviii). Media narratives about Muslims in the West drew on simplistic accounts of the 'clash of civilizations', especially when Western countries were involved in conflict in the Middle East, such as the Gulf wars. The ideological clash was therefore projected as the primary cause of discontent between Muslims and the civilized West. In Britain, Muslims were portrayed as the 'new folk devil [...] scapegoated for being criminally inclined and socially problematic because of failure to "integrate"' in the aftermath of the 2001 Bradford riots. (Massey and Tatla 2012: 161; see also Werbner 2005a, 2012). Similar portrayals were evident after the Rushdie affair in 1988 and the Danish cartoon controversy in 2006 (Abbas 2011: 67–68, 70–72).

The Muslim female also became a figure of contention for liberal feminists, who reduced the veil to a symbolic representation of patriarchy that visibly oppressed women (Bullock 2002; Brown 2008; Khiabany and Williamson 2008). The alternative narrative of Islamic feminists and post-colonial feminists celebrated the veil as resistance or agency (Macleod 1991; Afshar et al. 2005; Mahmood 2005; Werbner 2005b, 2007; Afshar 2008; Bilge 2010). Added to this was the emergence of the authentic voice that primarily focused on Muslim liberal feminists who reinforced the veil as a symbol of oppression (see Mojab 2001; Bullock 2002; Manji 2007; Ali 2015). Far from exploring the diverse experiences and narratives of Muslim women, both veiled and non-veiled, such debates resulted in contesting hegemonic discourses that sought to promote an authentic overarching discourse about Muslim women and the veil (see also Abu-Lughod 2002; Haw 2010). These debates therefore reinforced artificial categories, such as the moderate and extremist

Muslim female as determined by physical appearance, with the niqab situated at the extreme end of the spectrum.

Muslim women also continued to be portrayed as victims of culture, especially with reports of honour killings, forced marriages and female genital mutilation being reported amongst different Muslim communities. This is particularly true of the South Asian communities, especially those of the Bangladeshi and Pakistani (Dwyer 2000, 1999b; Werbner 2005b; Dwyer and Shah 2009). As discussed in Chap. 2, while such crimes against young women were being committed in the name of culture or religion,[1] these acts were often projected as a cultural or religious problem, demonizing entire communities despite many members not ascribing to such practices. In July 2015, Prime Minister David Cameron highlighting these barbaric practices, blamed 'passive tolerance' as one of the factors that had enabled such beliefs to persist in Britain (Cameron 2015). The practices were placed against the 'power and liberating force' of British values that had failed to rescue British Muslim females from such primitive beliefs (ibid.). The rhetoric about religious and cultural practices of Muslims continued to be placed within an ideological spectrum of the existing 'clash' between 'civilisations'. It also revealed a macho 'saviour complex', drawing on an Orientalist imagery of the civilized male rescuing the oppressed female from the clutches of a primitive patriarchal culture and religion (Brown 2008). While this socio-political narrative about Muslim women in Britain had been located within the spectrum of the oppressed and the fanatic, the events of 7 July 2005 and the more recent emergence of Isis has now placed them directly within the security agenda.

British Muslim women emerged as a potential security threat after the discovery of Samina Malik, Shasta Khan and Roshonara Choudhry. Samina Malik was the first Muslim woman to be convicted under the Terrorism Act 2000 for 'possessing records likely to be useful in terrorism' (Bowcott 2007). Malik, who appeared to be an ordinary 23-year old British Muslim, working at an 'airside [...] branch of WH Smith' (ibid.), called herself the 'lyrical terrorist', and wrote poetry that glorified terrorism, such as '"How To Behead" and "The Living Martyrs"'

---

[1] The murder of Shafilea Ahmed in 2012 by her parents in the name of 'honour' is one example of a recently reported crime of honour (*The Huffington Post* 2012a).

(Truscott 2007). Despite the name 'lyrical terrorist', Malik claimed to be innocent, using the phrase because 'it was cool' (ibid.). While her 'sentence was suspended for 18 months', since she was not an 'active' terrorist, the case was nonetheless important in illustrating the danger that seemingly ordinary Muslim women posed to the general public (Bowcott 2007; Truscott 2007).

Shasta Khan, a hairdresser and a wife, was found guilty of helping her husband to plan an attack against the local Jewish community (BBC News 2012d). At her trial, she blamed her husband for intimidating her into supporting his cause. As with Malik, she did not claim to be a terrorist, but was radicalized after she met her husband (*The Telegraph* 2012). Both Malik and Khan met the criteria of the 'vulnerable' Muslim female, who was easily intimidated and was in need of being protected from extremist elements. However, the case of Roshonara Choudhry was different.

Choudhry was studying English and Communications at King's College London but left in her third year (Dodd 2010a). A few months later she 'stabbed a 55 year old MP for East Ham twice in the stomach ... "to get revenge for the people of Iraq"' (BBC News 2010b). In her police interview, she revealed how she had been radicalized through the Internet, and believed that she was fulfilling her duty as a Muslim. Discussing the ideology of Sheikh Abdullah Azzam that she discovered on YouTube, she was clear about her actions:

> He was saying that when a Muslim land is attacked it becomes obligatory on every man, woman and child and even slave to go out and fight and defend the land and the Muslims and if they can't handle like the forces they are facing, then it becomes obligatory on the people who live in [...] closest to that country and if those people refuse to fulfil their duty then it, then it becomes to the next closest people and the next closest until it goes all the way round the whole world and it's obligatory on everyone to defend that land. (Dodd 2010a)

Choudhry's case revealed how young Muslim women could be radicalized into becoming active terrorists. The three cases further represented three ordinary Muslim women, with Choudhry an educated student, the most committed to an extremist ideology. The Muslim female was no longer an oppressed, helpless figure; she was also a potential physical threat. The securitization of the Muslim female identity—and the resultant fear of the 'hidden terrorist' amidst the mundane—was now located within the notion of the vulnerable-fanatic, reinforced by the emergence of the jihadi bride.

More than 50 Muslim women—including young girls from Britain—and over 500 from Europe have joined Isis (Sanghani 2015). They have been labelled 'jihadi brides', leaving their families and loved ones to support terrorists fighting in Syria to establish an Islamic state. Media and tabloid outlets have promoted a narrative of the jihadi bride whose only ambition, as reflected in Tareena Shakil's narrative in the Introduction, is to marry Muslim jihadists, to procreate and willingly to be subjugated and veiled (Brown 2014; Halliday 2015).

However, the jihadi bride concept is both reductionist and flawed (Hoyle et al. 2015; Saltman and Smith 2015). According to the Institute of Strategic Dialogue's report, there are multiple reasons for young women to join terrorist groups such as Isis that range from the individual to the political. Individual reasons may include 'isolation' and alienation, while political may include 'empathy' with an internationally 'persecuted' Muslim community, and 'anger' and frustration 'over a perceived lack of international action in response to this persecution' (Saltman and Smith 2015: 9). The report also highlights pull factors, such as helping to establish a 'Caliphate state', the idea of 'belonging and sisterhood' with other Muslim women who have common beliefs, and a 'romanticisation' and idealization 'of the experience' (Brown 2014; Hoyle et al. 2015; Saltman and Smith 2015: 9). However, while teenagers may be deemed easy to manipulate, older women have also joined Isis— the assumption that they are being lured towards extremism through online manipulation is incomplete and simple. There is both a religious and political conviction that guides such behaviour, a similar conviction to that of Roshonara Choudhry. Choudhry's rationale for stabbing an MP was both religious and political, targeting a politician who actively supported the war in Iraq, where fellow Muslims were being persecuted, with the government actively taking part in the destruction. The isolation and alienation that is experienced in the West is further linked to political frustration, where international governments are seen to be implicit, if not active, in persecuting Muslim communities across the world. The Muslim female is not simply an oppressed, helpless victim any longer; rather, she is a real security threat paradoxically hidden in plain sight. However, the security threat posed by some Muslim women has resulted in a paranoia that implicates the entire Muslim community in Britain. A population of 2.7 million Muslims (Office for National Statistics 2012) has become a securitized community as a result of the actions of home-grown terrorists. Innocent Muslim women are further implicated in this securitization (see also Sanghani 2014). The next section explores how Muslim women are affected by the security narrative and how it impacts their everyday lives.

The Framed Muslim Female: Experiencing Securitization and Islamophobia

> You know the part of linking it. You know if you look at a Christian or other religions a lot of people have done similar kind of things. I think when it is a Muslim it becomes a headline which makes things worse. Yes there is this one person doing it but it is not about the religion. You should focus on the individual or group but not society or religion, it is not related to that. If you are a Christian or from any other religion they would not emphasize that much but it seems like in the media it is all Muslims who do these things.
> —Zahra, West Yorkshire2, 19, Undergraduate (Social Sciences), British

Dekker and Noll's research on Islamophobia in the Netherlands utilized 'intergroup contact theory'[2] to illustrate how 'negative attitudes' towards 'ethnic outgroups' are more 'the result of processing [...] emotional and informative messages that individuals receive from relevant others', which include 'family, school, church, *mass media*, peer group, and political leaders' (Dekker and Noll 2012: 113, discussing the works of

---

[2] The theory shows how interactions with 'outgroups' may reduce the level of 'negative [...] attitudes' towards those groups. Their study demonstrated how greater contact with Muslims who make up the outer group plays a positive role in reducing Islamophobia in society (Dekker and Noll 2012: 113, 119–123).

Laswell 1977, Jennings 2007, Jennings et al. 2009, and Boomgaarden and Vliegenthart 2007, Italics added by me; see also Githens-Mazer and Lambert 2010a). Representations of Muslims as terrorists and of Muslim women as a potential threat provide rationalization for Islamophobia, where the association between insecurity and the Muslim identity is strengthened. Participants in this study highlighted a strong link between media representations and their experiences of Islamophobia. While they acknowledged the existence of a problem posed by individuals who were committing acts of terrorism in the name of Islam, for most, these individuals did not represent Islam, while others completely dismissed the claim that they could be Muslims. However, with the power of media, and the actions of a few evoking the name of Islam in acts of terrorism, it was believed that Islamophobia was only a natural consequence:

> Whatever is happening is just kind of [umm] I don't think the media does it on purpose, but things are still happening and unfortunately in most cases Muslims somewhere down the line are involved. That doesn't mean that other races and other religions aren't involved but it is an easy target. Easy target that no one at the moment can confidently stand up and question and say you know what you are wrong because pretty much we are wrong being Muslims. There is some level of truth to the media, but then again it is a level it is not all true.
> —Kulsoom, North West1, 22, Undergraduate (Science), British

Media portrayal of Muslims, particularly young women as the vulnerable-fanatic, further locates their identities within the moderate-extremist spectrum. Such terms influence the way Muslim women are positioned within society, with young women negotiating their identity often against such overarching categories. With media and state actors using words such as 'moderate', 'extremist' or 'radical', young Muslims in their everyday experiences are limited by such vague terms. As Mehnaz notes:

> I believe that these terms do exist. There are some Muslims who are more extreme than others. But what is a moderate? Would you call someone who does not stand up for their religious rights moderate, or someone who does as non-moderate? Who decides? The media? [...] You can be extreme in many cases [...] these terms are to narrow people down. You have got so

many people you can't narrow it down. I don't think they are the correct terms. They may explain ideas but who decides what they mean. Does extremist mean someone who will go bomb or someone who is going to stand up for their rights? [...] A person who goes bombs people and calls themselves jihadis. I don't see them as jihadis but I think of them as stupid idiots who have been brainwashed [...] I do not believe in stuff like this
—Mehnaz, West Yorkshire2, 22, Undergraduate (Law), British

Mehnaz's narrative about the definition of an 'extremist' is one that was echoed in David Cameron's speech in July 2015, in which he highlighted both violent and non-violent Islamic extremism as part of the problem. In tackling non-violent extremism, policies are aimed at preventing such extremists from accessing any public platform, including the Internet[3] (Travis 2014). Yet, by placing what is akin to a gag order on people who are deemed non-violent extremists, the conversation may be silenced, but it will not disappear. The problem with such policies, with the extremist-moderate, vulnerable-fanatic stereotype is that, instead of promoting debate, it aims at silencing discussion. The narratives in this research of women who may be deemed extreme because of their appearance reveal that they are law-abiding, peaceful individuals who have been swept away in a socio-political discourse about their identities. Hafsa's struggle in asserting her religion clearly establishes how such terms do not address the problem of extremism but, rather, create a superficial discourse about the acceptable moderate Islam:

> when they use terms like radicalization in a context that is definitely definitely negative, associated with suicide bombers, they automatically put in the general public including the Muslim population's head that radicalization of your religion is really bad. By that they stop you from going into the extreme of your religion, or really looking too much into it, and they make you realize, keh [that] if you are a moderate Muslim, the one who chills and hangs out, has a beard occasionally, you are okay because you are moderate, but the moment you start going too much into your religion be that daari [beard], hijab, whatever praying a little more, fasting more, then you

---

[3] Monitoring of such suspicious individuals may include accessing personal correspondence on 'instant messaging apps'. Failure on the part of app companies to share data with security agencies may result in the company being banned (see Curtis 2015).

are in the danger zone. You are in the zone that you can become one of those fundamentalists, you can become an extremist, so it's one of those very subconscious subtle ways of putting in the people and the masses head that this is not right. So they have confused the two concepts by making you focus on the black sheep [...] So extremism for me is just a term that they have coined so that people tend to be happy with the moderate Muslim state.

—Hafsa, North East1, 22, Graduate (Law), Overseas[4]

Muslims, then, who are in 'the danger zone' by becoming too religious, have to prove their innocence, lest they are thought to be extremists. How does one prove one's innocence if one appears to be an extremist? For David Cameron, denouncing groups such as Isis is not enough, as the existence of anti-Semitism amongst some Muslims (but also other ideologues), sectarianism or conspiracy theories (where what entails a conspiracy theory is not quite clear) also need to be tackled (Cameron 2015). The framework of the extremist/moderate highlights Mehdi Hasan's observation about how Muslims constantly need to prove they are 'moderate' enough, while people are deliberately trying to 'out' the secret 'extremists' within them (Hasan 2012). The moderate-extremist stereotype not only interrupts the place of Muslims in British society, but also creates complications within a religiously diverse Muslim community. Self-proclaimed moderate Muslims, for instance, avoid the more extreme looking elements, out of fear of being found guilty by association. Zahra has encountered this in her interaction with the 'moderate' Muslim:

Zahra:	Yeah I have come across some of them. You know they want to be 'moderate' so they get confused and they'd think that you know what if somebody is practising, they would think they are extremist. At the same time, they get scared that we are moderate so we don't get stereotyped
[...]	
Interviewer:	These are Muslims saying that?
Zahra:	Yes, these are Muslims. I think they have taken that concept that moderate Muslims are okay. They don't take things to

---

[4] See also Brown and Saeed (2015: 1955–1956).

	the extreme. They want to be called moderate so they tend to stay away from people like me.
Interviewer:	How does it make you feel?
Zahra:	It makes me feel a bit useless. You do feel like you don't fit in or something. But you know we are human (she laughs)

—Zahra, West Yorkshire2, 19, Undergraduate (Social Sciences), British

If the state's prerogative with the security agenda is to counter the extremism often linked to isolation and alienation, then terms like 'extremist' and 'moderate' are, in essence, failing this agenda. Terminology, and the resultant atmosphere of insecurity that it breeds about different Muslims, is an impediment that should be corrected in the existing security agenda. These terms have meanings and direct implications for young women such as Zahra, who are placed on the extreme end of the extremist-moderate spectrum by virtue of being overtly religious. Her narrative, as with other veiled women, points to a misunderstanding and fear that exists both outside and within the Muslim community—one that leads to further isolation. An overarching narrative that makes some Muslims acceptable by virtue of their physical appearance while others are considered a physical and ideological threat creates greater discord and alienation. This discord is one of the reasons given by young women who have fled to join groups such as Isis, looking for a 'sisterhood' where they belong (Hoyle et al. 2015; Saltman and Smith 2015). Yet, this sisterhood does exist in British society; a sisterhood that should be promoted in media and political narratives, but one that is often undermined by the moderate/extremist rhetoric. Faiza, who wears the niqab, highlights this:

> I don't believe in any such thing liberal, fundamental Islam, moderate. I think Islam is in each person. And I don't believe that women who wear hijab or don't wear it, even the head scarf or niqab as long as they are kind, good mannered, don't have anger, not ignorant, even those people are true Muslims they don't have to wear a niqab or anything. Islam is in each person.
> —Faiza, West Yorkshire2, 22, Undergraduate (Humanities), British

While bearded men are also securitized within such stereotypes, women tend to be located within the vulnerable-fanatic nexus; in need of being rescued. Unlike the experiences of Muslim men, who are portrayed as a physical threat (Gottschalk and Greenberg 2008), the experiences of veiled Muslim women often evoke feelings of being patronized, and considered inferior:

> They think us being religious is being tied to chains. And they feel like since we can't do anything about it they want to come and free us from religion, which is completely the opposite if you think about it. Ask a religious person they would say we are happy where we are, more happy than the place where you are, to be quite honest [...] they don't even know what religion is and because of the wrong representation of religion because of hundreds of factors going on in this world they think you are going away from your freedom, when you become more religious.
> —Areesha, West Yorkshire2, 20, Undergraduate (Social Sciences), Overseas

Muslim women therefore continue to be placed within a continuum of extremes, fluctuating between the victim who needs to be saved and a physical and existential threat that needs to be defeated. Further added to this mesh of ascribed identities is the notion of 'normality', located within a 'socio-ideological' consciousness that defines normality against the abnormal Muslim in a niqab/burqa, hijab or a *shalwar kameez*.[5] Young Muslim women who stand out because of their physical appearance are further accused of rebelling against the norm, while simultaneously becoming a security threat:

> And then there is the idea that these people wearing the burqas or hijab are rebelling against British society. Even if it is true, what is wrong with that? You see people dressing like punks, all in black or goth, or piercing all over their body, or whatever they chose to do. It is their way of self-expression. If they want to rebel against society why shouldn't they? That is probably the right of a free society. [...] If I chose to wear it or not, it is my choice. As long as I am not hurting you, why can't I choose to dress the way I please.
> —Lyyla, North West1, Alumna, Activist, British

Securitization of the Muslim female identity and the subsequent experiences of Islamophobia reinforce notions of what it means to be 'normal' in a Western context, where Muslim women are guilty of a socio-religious

---

[5] A *shalwar kameez* consists of trousers and a tunic (Vakulenko 2007: 721).

abnormality determined by their outward appearance (Ryan 2011). Preconceived notions and opinions about the Muslim identity have become an everyday feature for Muslim women, where second- or third-generation Muslims continue to be treated as outsiders; their religion perceived as a constant threat within the British social psyche.

The Niqabi 'Ninja'

While the overtly practising Muslim woman is securitized as a vulnerable yet potentially dangerous threat, the niqab is perceived to be the most problematic. In 2006, for instance, the 'niqab' became a point of contention in media and political discourse after Jack Straw's remarks about 'the niqab' as a 'visible statement of separation and of difference' (Abbas 2011: 67–68; 70–72). The sentiment was echoed in tabloid and media narratives, such as *The Sun*, *The Daily Mirror*, *The Daily Mail*, where the female Muslim became an embodiment of the struggle between nationhood and identity (Khiabany and Williamson 2008; Meer et al. 2010). The niqabi female is further caught between the stereotypical oppressed Muslim and the potential hidden terrorist. A FOSIS representative shares the difficulties experienced by young niqabi women in educational institutions:

> A few years back Imperial College is an example where they tried to impose a niqab ban. I think they did but it was overturned because we took the case to the NUS and made a big deal about that. Definitely this happens. There are other issues with the niqab—there was another case as well where it was a college student who wasn't allowed to enrol into college if she wore the niqab. They gave all sorts of excuses, that oh because of security reasons you can't put it on, problems with identification. So she said okay for my ID card I can take a picture without the niqab for you. She was prepared to do that. She said if in class people have trouble understanding me then I won't wear it in class. So she was prepared to make those concessions just to be accepted and enrolled. But they overruled it saying no you can't wear the niqab. They just did not want someone on campus wearing the niqab. That is happening.
>
> —FOSIS Representative (2011)[6]

---

[6] See also Brown and Saeed (2015: 1958–1959).

While the act of gaining admission and studying at a higher educational institution should be encouraged, the 'niqabi' woman is further isolated because of the stereotype of suspicion that informs her reality, both within and outside her university. Ironically, the security agenda through the creation of the suspicious Muslim figure behind the niqab has further removed agency from young women, many of whom choose to take on the niqab (Brown and Saeed 2015: 1958–1959). The narrative of Hafiza, who wears the niqab, testifies to the difficulty young niqabi women have in accessing educational opportunities. Hafiza has opted to stay away from the public domain. She dropped out of her old university because she felt uncomfortable wearing the niqab and decided to join the Open University instead. In her experience, women who wear the niqab are perceived to be threatening, despite being law-abiding, peaceful citizens,

> I am not going to go against society. It is a symbol of my religion [...] why are we made to look as women who cause problems. Niqabi women are an asset to the community. We don't smoke, drink or gamble.
> —Hafiza, London, 25, Alumna, British

Other women who have worn the niqab have also found it more difficult, and more unacceptable, than the hijab. Nadia, who normally wears the hijab and jilbab has, on occasion, taken on the niqab in public, and found that it attracted more anger and resentment,

> [L]ike myself I don't wear the niqab but I have worn it a couple of times [...] That was the only time I have had someone just openly come up to me in (West Yorkshire) and just in my face [...] he just started yelling stuff and he was just like oh you want us to be scared of you, I am not scared of you, not scared of you and I was like have a nice day. He couldn't see me smiling [...] he was English, quite an old man must have been in his 50s. But these people are confused and they want to take it out on someone. Once it was Jews, and then Pakis and now it is Muslims.
> —Nadia, West Yorkshire2, 20, Undergraduate (Law), British

Nadia's explanation for this experience draws on the need for the general public to find someone they can physically hold responsible for the events of 7 July. The niqabi woman, hidden behind the veil provides the perfect scapegoat, falling victim to a security narrative that 'securitizes' her very existence. She is also often subject to slurs such as 'ninja':

> Ninja is that you know cartoon strips, that some kind of monster that has its face covered in those cartoon strip, a cloth around their eyes tied behind their back, like the niqab [...] I just ignore them. I feel sorry for them. I just think you don't even know who I am, what I'm doing, why I'm wearing this. You just feel the need to you know name call.
> —Faiza, West Yorkshire2, 22, Undergraduate (Humanities), British

For Faiza, who also wears the niqab, such experiences are a common occurrence. She believes that 'as a minority', despite being a second-generation British Muslim, she has to 'put up' with such discrimination. While it is alienating, Faiza's strategy is to ignore it, by rationalizing this bigotry as a natural consequence of terrorism committed in the name of Islam. The rationalization and acceptance of Islamophobia is the most dangerous element of the securitization discourse, one that can encourage a feeling of alienation. Faiza shared her experiences of Islamophobia in the university, revealing how it made her feel vulnerable:

> there was also an incident where I had an exam. Obviously I had the niqab on, and the man, he should have told me that come to the side and lift your niqab up for ID check, but he actually told me there, he just goes lift your niqab up and at that time I got loads of emails from all my fellow students telling me to complain but I really didn't want to cause a fuss about it. I don't know I just didn't want to fuss about it [...] I just thought that as a minority I was the only person wearing the niqab in that whole exam room and there were about 200 people in the exam room and only one me wearing the niqab and I thought I don't know I might as well instead of drawing attention to myself I just as well do as he says and lift my niqab up and get it over and done with [...]
>
> But then again another exam I had this female and she spoke to me in a really patronizing way, like I'm sorry but we really have to you know how they sometimes speak to you in a really slow way like you don't understand English and that annoyed me more than that man who told me in front of everyone to lift my niqab up. Because I don't know I had a feeling that she

assumed I didn't know what she was talking about and she patronized me so I felt worse and was more annoyed about that than the previous incident.
—Faiza, West Yorkshire2, 22, Undergraduate (Humanities), British

To counter alienation and Islamophobia, Muslim women, especially those who wear the niqab, should not be made to feel like outsiders, abnormal, or a menace to society for dressing a certain way. They are British Muslims who, as law-abiding citizens, contribute to society. Attempts should be made in media and political discussions to include them within the discourse on acceptability. The security agenda, with its emphasis on the 'acceptable Muslim', on 'moderates' and 'extremists', promotes a superficial understanding of radicalization, where physical appearance determines whether a British Muslim is 'civilized' enough. Similar narratives inundate media accounts of jihadi brides, clad in black niqabs, carrying guns. Such meta-narratives have repercussions for Muslim women in their everyday lives, from the streets, to educational institutions and the workplace. However, while the niqabi 'ninja' is singled out, the hijabi Muslim female, while less dangerous, is also caught in the securitization discourse.

The Hijabi Muslim: From the Lesbian to Bin Laden's Wife

I was walking on the street. Two students follow me. One says to the other guy 'but she [...]' as if to stop the other guy from stopping me. I heard him move to the left so I crossed the street, but as I was doing that he spat at me. It did not reach me. Other people call me a lesbian since I wear the hijab. If such people are in a group I can hear the others trying to stop them as if they think I might react, or there might be a reaction from the Muslim community.
—Mehreen, South East1, 28, Graduate (Science), Overseas

Women who wear the hijab are also representative of an Islamic ideology that is increasingly perceived as hostile to British values. Mehreen's narrative reveals the intersection between oppression and insecurity, where lesbian is associated more with sexual oppression, rather than sexual choice, while the Muslim reaction is linked with a fear of violence. Other women who wear the hijab have also reported such name-calling, but to use the word 'lesbian' as an insult reveals an undercurrent of a hetero-normative discourse on oppression, where the Muslim woman, by being sexually inactive, is believed to be oppressed and incapable of action. Such insults move beyond the oppression narrative of liberal feminists, where the 'lesbian' attack invokes different notions of normality, and acceptability, including heterosexuality, against the abnormally veiled Muslim female. This heterosexual normality is juxtaposed with a hyper-macho and securitized male, where the Muslim community's reaction is perceived to be one of male violence, drawing on Orientalist tropes of violence, abnormality and sexualization. Slurs such as 'Osama bin Laden's wife' which have also been used against Muslim women who wear the hijab (or the niqab), again, invoke the violent male Muslim, linked to the Muslim female, where the securitizing socio-political narrative places her as both a direct and indirect threat. For the hijabi Muslim, then:

> you are visually Muslim and all the issues around terrorism which all Muslims face but also bigger issues around how Islam oppresses women so they have to put up with literally interrogation to prove that they are not oppressed.
> —FOSIS Representative (2011)

Mehreen also experienced discrimination within the university when applying for a research assistant job but did not report it, a problem she believes many young Muslim women who wear any of the religious symbols face—both within the university as well as outside, when seeking employment. Sabahat, a schoolteacher who started wearing the hijab recently, revealed how the attitude of fellow teachers and parents changed towards her. She shared similar feelings of being ignored, or considered inferior, both within and outside her workplace. Whether travelling on a bus or grocery shopping, she stood out as a Muslim in her community. Sabahat also revealed how there is an instant feeling of guilt that is internalized by Muslims, even when they are innocent:

> I sat on the city bus and because I had quite a few stops before I got off, I sat on a seat and there was this really big sports bag or something near my legs. There were three seats [...] that was the only seat available. Everybody was staring at me and every time someone would get off they would look at me almost is she getting off is she getting off, and it is funny because I was actually praying in my heart that oh please let me be okay [...] what if there is something in that. I was thinking that and you could tell they were thinking that as well and when I did get off you could tell there was a sigh of relief, but when I didn't pick the bag up they absolutely stared at me. You feel like, you feel guilty you are doing something wrong. They are making you look suspicious. So the fact that I was wearing the hijab I didn't want to go to the driver and tell him there is a bag here because I felt like because I am wearing the hijab it would seem suspicious.
> —Sabahat, West Yorkshire2, 25, Alumna, Teacher, British

For Sabahat, being a Muslim female who wears the hijab not only frames her as a potential threat, but also creates a sense of paranoia within Muslims. Her reaction to an unmarked, suspicious bag was similar to any other non-Muslim citizen in the bus, yet her expression of this apprehension and unease was limited by virtue of being a hijabi female, thereby becoming a prime suspect. Other participants have also reported a form of internalizing paranoia that illustrates how the securitization discourse enters the social psyche, with Islamophobia operating within a socio-psychological framework. Muslims themselves are overtly conscious of their identity as 'suspects', carrying the added burden of proving their innocence, of denouncing acts of violence committed by strangers in the name of their religion.

> It's like Muslim women have to keep justifying all their actions, keep justifying that they are British, all these stereotypes that we don't walk 10 steps behind our husbands, we are not married by the age of 19, we don't have kids. I know people I was directing this course, who kind of have this stereotype of me. They are like oh you socialize. I think with them it's this whole the headscarf, a bit confused. I am like no you need to move beyond that. It is an issue you have with yourself not me. I can get over people who have crazy hair or what. You know I am just kind of okay with tattoos or whatever, I can get over that, I can see beyond that. Some students they have never obviously integrated with other communities but it's difficult.
> —Tehmina West Midlands1, 19, Undergraduate (Social Sciences), British

This added pressure of constantly defending one's right to practise Islam, of denouncing terrorism, defending Islam as a peaceful religion, has become a part of being Muslim in Britain, as well as in other Western countries. The feeling of guilt associated with the actions of terrorists is the result of a post 7/7 securitized psyche that effects British Muslims, and one that has created a permanent state of suspicion and paranoia about the Muslim community.

The Moderate Muslim Woman: One of 'Us'

> I have had English people come up to me say they feel scared when a woman comes on a subway with a hijab or burqa. They tell me that they are scared. I think those kind of women get more because of religion, way they are just because of how much they embrace it. Unlike me. I don't want to use the word Westernized because that would mean I am on their side, when it is not about sides, or like wanting to be white. It is just weird. It is almost like a comment referred to like, you are one of us.
> —Zubaida, London1, 30, Graduate (Science), British

The moderate-extremist spectrum also implicates the non-veiled Muslim female, who is perceived as the most acceptable and integrated of the Muslim community. Her clothing is a testament to her Westernized lifestyle, becoming a model of British Muslimness. By framing Muslim women within such a spectrum of acceptability, the non-veiled Muslim female encounters a different set of reactions, where the nature of her moderate identity is placed against that of the extremist. Aisha, like other non-veiled Muslims highlights this struggle:

> They'll say oh why don't you drink and it will turn into a big thing, why don't you wear a headscarf, or why don't you have sex before marriage. People need an excuse to start. A lot of young British Muslims nowadays especially in university are getting integrated [...] We are brought up in a way that you know people don't like it that we can still do both sides, be

Westernized and still have our culture intact [...] I think it is just as hard if you are not wearing a headscarf [...] when you are not wearing one then it really begins, then they really try to psychoanalyze you and it is just as hard.
—Aisha, London4, 22, Undergraduate (German), British

Her account draws on both the notion of sexual freedom and the resultant control that is associated with Islam and its treatment of Muslim women. As a Muslim woman who looks like 'one of us', Aisha, like Zubaida, has to defend her 'Muslimness' where she is neither too Westernized nor too Muslim to be completely acceptable. Aisha's narrative, like those of other non-veiled practising Muslim women, highlights a diversity of religiosity that is located at different points within the moderate-extremist spectrum. As 'one of us', Aisha enters the moderate Muslim discourse in so far as she willingly assimilates to a Westernized lifestyle. There are therefore limitations to how acceptable moderate Muslims such as Aisha are, within the defined spectrum. Tabussum highlights how all Muslims, irrespective of their degrees of religiosity, are considered suspect to an extent:

Then 7/7 happened [...] it has made people very suspicious of Muslims. Maybe for people like you and I, who don't wear hijabs, you wouldn't really necessarily know we are Muslims, unless you knew a lot about Arabic names, and people would be like yeah yeah they're cool, but then maybe when they find out that we are Muslims I think they will be suspicious of us. I think that's the effect it has had on people. Just this thing of distrust, and I think with all the right wing information out there about Islam both from the West and from the East it's made people really misunderstand the whole religion.
—Tabussum, South East1, Racism and Equality Advisor

Muslims, whether veiled or non-veiled, are part of the security discourse that results in experiences of Islamophobia that essentialize religious symbols as markers of differentiation, where the lack of symbols nonetheless confine individuals to external categories. Looking a certain way or having certain names are 'naturally' associated with a wider 'securitized' group of Muslims, echoing a sense of otherization projected towards Muslims. The level of insecurity about the moderate Muslim and the amount of permissible acceptability also creates a greater fear of the extremist Muslim, especially when those who appear moderate still indulge in religious practices, that may appear to be extreme:

> You know when people look at me and they see I wear jeans I look quite modern and stuff but I pray. They look at me and they say they can't believe that I pray, you know those kind of anti-Islamic comments. It kind of makes them scared because they look at me and think if people like her are religious then imagine how fanatical the others who wear headscarves are […] The media is making everybody more stupid or feeding them whatever they want […] Moderate is kind of, almost like degrading in a sense. If someone said to me I am a moderate Muslim, I would be offended. I would be like you don't know what is in my heart. I'd be like what just because I am not wearing a headscarf. As a Muslim person if someone calls me moderate it is saying to me that you are not practising your faith properly. Either way you are kind of damned, whether you are an extremist or a moderate, you don't want to be either really.
> —Aisha, London4, 22, Undergraduate (German), British[7]

However, the only terminology that defines Muslims in the socio-political discourse of Islam in Britain is that of the extremist or the moderate. Muslims are positioned at different points within the spectrum of acceptability, which not only limits their expression of being Muslim, but also simplifies a diverse Muslim community.

Security, Muslim Women and the Social Psyche

Muslims, after the tragedy of 7/7 and the emergence of terrorist groups such as Al Qaeda and Isis, have been drawn into a security discourse where they are constantly implicated as prime suspects. If they are overtly religious, they are a threat; if they are moderate, they may not be moderate enough, or still vulnerable to radicalization. Women such as Malik, Khan and Choudhry, as well as the 50 to 60 women—a minority, out of the majority population of 2.7 million Muslims who have joined Isis—have placed Muslim women within the security discourse. They are

---

[7] See also Brown and Saeed (2015: 1955–1956).

located within a spectrum of the moderate-extremist, where the level of acceptability is determined by the socio-political discourse, where even the non-veiled Muslim female is placed against the extremist hijabi and niqabi woman.

The narratives examined in this chapter reveal how securitization intersects with Islamophobia against the Muslim female, creating a constant state of paranoia and fear in the social psyche. As a result, law-abiding Muslim women are made to feel guilty about the terrorist activities of individuals who have no connection to them, and are also a threat for them. Their experiences of Islamophobia are rationalized as a natural consequence of the actions of terrorists. Muslim women who wear the hijab and the niqab are deemed too extreme, often encountering verbal abuse that sheds more light on the abuser than the victim. With slurs such as 'ninja' and 'Bin Laden's wife', the woman behind the veil becomes a scapegoat, perceived to be a monster, or a submissive spouse of a terrorist. With terms such as 'lesbian' used as an insult, the reference is not only to the sexually inactive Muslim female who does not interact with men and is part of a strong sisterhood, but also highlights a heteronormative discourse, whereby the Muslim female is considered abnormal. The non-veiled Muslim female is also questioned about both her Muslimness and her Britishness, where acceptability depends on her ability to assimilate. Hence, in tackling the Muslim female extremist threat, Muslim women in Britain have become securitized as an oxymoronic threat that is hidden in plain sight. They are, indeed, vulnerable but, as the narratives reveal, this vulnerability is less about extremism, and more about Islamophobia and discrimination. Such vulnerability contributes to an atmosphere of isolation and alienation, where Muslim women may question their place in British society, seeking out a more 'romanticised' 'sisterhood'. With cases of jihadi brides and the rise of Isis, the Muslim female will continue to be drawn into a securitized discourse, reinforcing a social paranoia about Muslims that is increasingly becoming the norm in Britain.

Bibliography

Abbas, T. (2011) Islamophobia in the United Kingdom: Historical and Contemporary Political and Media Discourses in the Framing of a 21st-Century Anti-Muslim Racism. In *Islamophobia The Challenge of Pluralism in the 21st Century*, eds. J. L. Esposito and I. Kalin, Oxford: Oxford University Press, pp. 63–76.

Abu-Lughod, L. (2002) Do Muslim women really need saving? Anthropological reflections on cultural relativism and Its others. *American Anthropologist*, 104 (3), pp. 783–790.

Afshar, H. (2008) Can I see your hair? Choice, agency and attitudes: The dilemma of faith and feminism for Muslim women who cover. *Ethnic and Racial Studies*, 31 (2), pp. 411–427.

Afshar, H., Aitken, R. and Franks, M. (2005) Feminisms, Islamophobia and identities. *Political Studies*, 53 (2), pp. 262–283.

Ali, A.H. (2015) *Heretic: Why Islam Needs a Reformation Now*. USA: HarperCollins.

Allen, C. (2010a) *Islamophobia*. England: Ashgate Publishing Limited.

BBC News. (30/03/2012d) *Lecturer Rod Thornton to leave Nottingham University after terror row*. BBC News. [Online]. Available from: http://www.bbc.co.uk/news/uk-england-nottinghamshire-17563715 (Accessed 03/15, 2013).

BBC News. (04/02/2010b) *Campus Islamic extremists under police scrutiny*. BBC News. [Online]. Available from: http://news.bbc.co.uk/1/hi/education/8496066.stm (Accessed 03/15, 2013).

Bhimji, F. (2012) *British Asian Muslim Women, Multiple Spatialities and Cosmopolitanism*. UK: Palgrave Macmillan. (second generation).

Bilge, S. (2010) Beyond subordination vs. resistance: An intersectional approach to the agency of veiled Muslim women. *Journal of Intercultural Studies*, 31 (1), pp. 9–28.

Bowcott, W. (11/09/2007) *Woman called 'lyrical terrorist' celebrated act of beheading*. The Guardian. [Online]. Available from: http://www.theguardian.com/uk/2007/nov/09/terrorism.ukcrime (Accessed 02/19, 2013).

Brown, E.K. and Saeed, T. (2015) Radicalization and counter-radicalization at British universities: Muslim encounters and alternatives. *Ethnic and Racial Studies*, 38 (11), pp. 1952–1968.

Brown, K. (06/10/2014) *Analysis: Why are Western women joining Islamic State?* BBC News. [Online]. Available from: http://www.bbc.com/news/uk-29507410 (Accessed 07/03, 2015).

Brown, K.E. (2011) *Gender matters, soundings policy matters for Muslims in Britain.* Muslim Council of Britain. [Online]. Available from: http://soundings.mcb.org.uk/?p=44 (Accessed 08/03, 2012).

Brown, K. (2008) The promise and perils of women's participation in UK Mosques: The impact of securitisation agendas on identity, gender and community. *The British Journal of Politics & International Relations*, 10 (3), pp. 472–491.

Brown, K.E. (2010) Contesting the securitization of British Muslims: Citizenship and resistance. *Interventions*, 12 (2), pp. 171–182.

Bullock, K. (2002) *Rethinking Muslim women and the veil: Challenging historical & modern stereotypes.* The International Institute of Islamic Thought (IIIT).

Cameron, D. (2015) *Extremism: PM speech. Her Majesty's Government.* [Online]. Available from: https://www.gov.uk/government/speeches/extremism-pm-speech (Accessed 28/07, 2015).

Contractor, S. (2012) *Muslim Women in Britain: De-mystifying the Muslimah.* Routledge.

Curtis, S. (13/07/2015) *Will WhatsApp really be banned in the UK?* The Telegraph. [Online]. Available from: http://www.telegraph.co.uk/technology/social-media/11736230/Will-WhatsApp-really-be-banned-in-the-UK.html (Accessed 07/20, 2015).

Dekker, H. and Noll, J. (2012) Islamophobia and Its Explanation. In *Islamophobia in the West Measuring and Explaining Individual Attitudes*, ed. M. Helbling, London: Routledge, pp. 112–123.

Dodd, V. (03/11/2010a) *Roshonara Choudhry: Police interview extracts.* The Guardian. [Online]. Available from: http://www.theguardian.com/uk/2010/nov/03/roshonara-choudhry-police-interview (Accessed 07/10, 2015).

Dwyer, C. and Shah, B. (2009) Rethinking the Identities of Young British Pakistani Muslim Women: Educational Experiences and Aspirations. In *Muslims in Britain Race, Place and Identities*, eds. P. Hopkins and R. Gale, Edinburgh: Edinburgh University Press, pp. 55–73.

Dwyer, C. (2000) Negotiating diasporic identities: Young British South Asian Muslim women. *Women's Studies International Forum* Elsevier, pp. 475.

Dwyer, C. (1999b) Veiled Meanings: Young British Muslim women and the negotiation of differences. *Gender, Place & Culture*, 6 (1), pp. 5–26.

Faith, M. (2013a) *Tell MAMA measuring anti muslim attacks.* Faith Matters. [Online]. Available from: http://tellmamauk.org/ (Accessed 03/22, 2013).

Franks, M. (2000) Crossing the borders of whiteness? White Muslim women who wear the hijab in Britain today. *Ethnic and Racial Studies*, 23 (5), pp. 917–929.

Githens-Mazer, J. and Lambert, R. (2010a) *Islamophobia and Anti-Muslim Hate Crime: A London Case Study*. University of Exeter, European Muslim Research Centre.

Gottschalk, P. and Greenberg, G. (2008) *Islamophobia Making Muslims the Enemy.* USA: Rowman & Littlefield Publishers, Inc.

Halliday, J. (05/02/2015) *Female jihadis publish guide to life under Islamic State.* The Guardian. [Online]. Available from: http://www.theguardian.com/world/2015/feb/05/jihadist-girl-marry-liberation-failed-islamic-state (Accessed 07/09, 2015).

Hasan, M. (08/07/2012) *We mustn't allow Muslims in public life to be silenced.* The Guardian. [Online]. Available from: http://www.guardian.co.uk/commentisfree/2012/jul/08/muslims-public-life-abuse (Accessed 10/09, 2012).

Haw, K. (2010) Being, becoming and belonging: Young Muslim women in contemporary Britain. *Journal of Intercultural Studies*, 31 (4), pp. 345–361.

Haw, K. (2009) From hijab to jilbab and the 'myth' of British identity: Being Muslim in contemporary Britain a half-generation on. *Race Ethnicity and Education*, 12 (3), pp. 363–378.

Hoyle, C., Bradford, A. and Frenett, R. (2015) *Becoming Mulan? Female Western Migrants to ISIS.* Institute for Strategic Dialogue.

Joppke, C. (2009b) *Veil: Mirror of Identity.* Cambridge: Polity.

Khiabany, G. and Williamson, M. (2008) Veiled bodies—Naked racism: Culture, politics and race in the Sun. *Race & class*, 50 (2), pp. 69–88.

Macleod, A.E. (1991) *Accommodating Protest. Working Women, the New Veiling and Change in Cairo.* New York: Columbia University Press.

Mahmood, S. (2005) *Politics of Piety. The Islamic Revival and the Feminist Subject.* NJ: Princeton University Press.

Manji, I. (2007) *The Trouble with Islam: A Muslim's Call for Reform in Her Faith.* New York: St Martin's Press.

Massey, J. and Tatla, R.S. (2012) Moral Panic and Media Representation: The Bradford Riot. In *Global Islamophobia: Muslims and Moral Panic in the West*, eds. S. Poynting and G. Morgan, England: Ashgate Publishing Ltd, pp. 161–180.

Meer, N. and Modood, T. (2010) The Racialisation of Muslims. In *Thinking through Islamophobia: Global Perspectives*, eds. S. Sayyid and A. Vakil, London: Hurst and Co. (Publishers) Ltd., pp. 69–84.

Meer, N., Dwyer, C. and Modood, T. (2010) Embodying Nationhood? Conceptions of British national identity, citizenship, and Gender in the 'Veil Affair'. *The Sociological Review*, 58 (1), pp. 84–111.

Mojab, S. (2001) Theorizing the politics of 'Islamic Feminism' *Feminist Review*, 69 (1), pp. 124–146.
Office for National Statistics. (2012) *Religion in England and Wales 2011.* UK: Crown.
Ryan, L. (2011) Muslim women negotiating collective stigmatization: 'We're just normal people', *Sociology*, 45 (6), pp. 1046–1060.
Said, E.W. (1997) *Covering Islam: How the Media and the Experts Determine How We See the Rest of the World.* London: Vintage Books.
Saltman, E.M. and Smith, M. (2015) *'Till Martyrdom Do Us Part' Gender and the ISIS Phenomenon.* Institute for Strategic Dialogue.
Sanghani, R. (28/05/2015) *AK47s, heart emoji and feminism: How jihadi brides are luring British girls to join Isil.* The Telegraph. [Online]. Available from: http://www.telegraph.co.uk/women/womens-politics/11635643/How-Isil-jihadi-brides-lure-British-girls-AK47s-emoji-and-feminism.html (Accessed 07/20, 2015).
Sanghani, R. (01/10/2014) *British Muslim girls: 'We're sick to death of these 'jihadi brides' going to Syria—It's disgusting'.* The Telegraph. [Online]. Available from: http://www.telegraph.co.uk/women/womens-life/11133324/British-Muslim-girls-Were-sick-to-death-of-these-jihadi-brides-going-to-Syria-its-disgusting.html (Accessed 07/10, 2015).
Shirazi, F. and Mishra, S. (2010) Young Muslim women on the face veil (niqab) A tool of resistance in Europe but rejected in the United States. *International Journal of Cultural Studies*, 13 (1), pp. 43–62.
Siraj, A. (2011) Meanings of modesty and the hijab amongst Muslim women in Glasgow, Scotland. *Gender, Place & Culture*, 18 (6), pp. 716–731.
Travis, A. (30/09/2014) *What are Theresa May's new 'extremism disruption orders'?* The Guardian. [Online]. Available from: http://www.theguardian.com/politics/2014/sep/30/theresa-may-extremism-disruption-orders (Accessed 07/10, 2015).
Truscott, C. (06/12/2007) *'Lyrical terrorist' sentenced over extremist poetry.* The Guardian. [Online]. Available from: http://www.guardian.co.uk/uk/2007/dec/06/terrorism.books (Accessed 05/06, 2010).
Tyrer, D. and Ahmad, F. (2006) *Muslim Women and Higher Education: Identities, Experiences and Prospects. A Summary Report. Liverpool John Moores University and European Social Fund.* Oxford: Oxuniprint.
Vakulenko, A. (2007) Islamic Dress in Human Rights Jurisprudence: A critique of current trends. *Human Rights Law Review*, 7 (4), pp. 717–739.

Werbner, P. (2012) Folk devils and racist imaginaries in a global prism: Islamophobia and anti-Semitism in the twenty-first century. *Ethnic and Racial Studies*, (ahead-of-print), pp. 1–18.

Werbner, P. (2007) Veiled interventions in pure space honour, shame and embodied struggles among Muslims in Britain and France. *Theory, Culture & Society*, 24 (2), pp. 161–186.

Werbner, P. (2005a) Islamophobia: Incitement to religious hatred–Legislating for a new fear? *Anthropology Today*, 21 (1), pp. 5–9.

Werbner, P. (2005b) Honor, shame and the politics of sexual embodiment among South Asian Muslims in Britain and beyond: An analysis of debates in the public sphere. *International Social Science Review*, 6 (1), pp. 25–47.

Williamson, M. and Khiabany, G. (2010) UK: The veil and the politics of racism. *Race & Class*, 52 (2), pp. 85–96.

Zebiri, K. (2011) Orientalist Themes in Contemporary British Islamophobia. In *Islamophobia: The Challenge of Pluralism in the 21st Century: The Challenge of Pluralism in the 21st Century*, eds. J.L. Esposito and I. Kalin, USA: Oxford University Press, pp. 173–190.

Zempi, I. and Chakraborti, N. (2014) *Islamophobia, Victimisation and the Veil*. London: Palgrave Macmillan.

4

Securitizing the Educated Muslim: Islamophobia, Radicalization and the Muslim Female Student

In securitizing Muslim women, as discussed in Chap. 3, degrees of religiosity play a crucial role in placing them within the spectrum of normality/abnormality, of moderate/extremist. However, drawn into the securitizing discourse are also *educated* Muslim women and men, who are perceived to be a greater threat. This is illustrated not only in the conviction of Roshonara Choudhry, but also through the emergence of Umar Farouk Abdulmutallab, a graduate student from a university in London who later attempted to blow up a plane bound for the USA, and Jihadi John, another educated Muslim who joined Isis and brutally executed fellow British citizens. The 'securitized' Muslim student is presumed to be an intelligent yet vulnerable young individual, susceptible to radical ideologies of extremist groups. While Muslim male students are more likely to fall within the potential extremist category, Muslim female students continue to oscillate between the vulnerable and fanatic. As a result of this fear of the educated Muslim, educational institutions have become part of the government's security apparatus. The government's Counter Terrorism and Security Act 2015, which imposed a 'statutory' responsibility on educational institutions including universities to pass on information about 'vulnerable' students 'at risk' of radicalization,

© The Author(s) 2016
T. Saeed, *Islamophobia and Securitization*, Palgrave Politics of Identity and Citizenship Series, DOI 10.1007/978-3-319-32680-1_4

predominantly focuses on Muslim students (HM Government 2015a; Saeed and Johnson 2016). Any radical behaviour within an educational context by Muslim students places them in the category of at risk and thereby vulnerable to extremism.

By framing universities within a security discourse, Muslim students' freedom of expression and freedom to challenge the status quo is compromised. With a statutory duty imposed on universities, the 'better safe than sorry' approach (Thornton 2011) is often adopted by universities, which are becoming overly cautious in their dealings with Muslim students. Students who are politically active or are members of Islamic student societies (ISocs) are particularly considered to be at risk, as the narratives in this chapter illustrate. The chapter examines the notion of radicalization in relation to Muslims, its location within the university and its implications for Muslim students. It further explores the experiences of ISoc sisters, exposing how ISocs and their members have to defend their right to exist within a university context that constantly holds them suspect.

Explaining Radicalization

The term 'radicalization' in a post-Al Qaeda/Isis context is encumbered by a complex mesh of politics, religion and culture. Defining radicalization is a difficult task, since different definitions have been presented, almost all linking radicalization with some form of extremism in the context of Muslims.

For Patel (2007: 42), radicalization entails 'seeking fundamental change in the present political order'. Burgat (2008) discusses different meanings of radicalization from 'violent' 'struggle' to 'sectarian radicalisation', which creates division between communities, denying the very 'existence' of another group; such 'sectarian radicalisation fuels racist postures', resulting in violence against a community during 'times of peace' (2008: 90). Johnson (2006) describes it as a process that reorients individuals towards a particular path. The idea of radicalization as a process is also discussed in the works of Stemmann, who describes 'the radicalization process' as beginning 'with the emergence of anti-integration tendencies and the desire to disengage from the host society. It continues with hostility towards the host society, rejection of the principles and institutions of liberal democracy, and the growing acquisition of violent attitudes, all of which make individuals a potential target for recruiters' (2006: 8). The 'anti-integration' tendencies are not just the result of the minority's inability to belong to a society, but also the host community's inability to accommodate 'difference' within its dominant 'discourse' on citizenship and belonging (Wieviorka 2004; Barnes 2006; Strabac and Listhaug 2008).

Radicalization, as these definitions suggest, is an attempt to bring about a change: this could take the form of a 'violent struggle', or an internal struggle; it could be present at one moment in some individuals and groups, but completely absent in others. For Rehman (2007), radicalization has roots in individual experiences of 'ostracization, neglect, and alienation from the mainstream', which he considers particularly problematic for second- or third-generation Muslims. Generational differences amongst parents and children lead to greater isolation, making young people more vulnerable to radical ideologies (Rehman 2007: 847). Roy also calls it a 'youth movement', led by young Muslims who have no roots in the homeland of their fathers. In Roy's words (2007: 55), 'they are a lost generation' not a 'militant vanguard of the Muslim community'. Vertigans (2007) positions radicalization within local, national and international influences. While alienation and discrimination are local or national factors, atrocities committed against the innocent in places such as Palestine, Chechnya and Kashmir become catalysts, giving young individuals a purpose. Hence, 'for many recruits, the sense of belonging to a group, sharing values, explanations and companionship, is part of the attraction' (Vertigans 2007: 454). O'Duffy also explores the nexus between 'local grievances', such as structural unemployment, inequality and government 'foreign' policies towards Muslim countries (O'Duffy 2008). The role of 'alienation', feeling disconnected from the community, as part of the process of radicalization has also been signalled as one of the many reasons why young people turn to extremism, with radicalization reflecting and being 'a product of increased fragmentation and self-reflexivity, where people look for meaning in their lives' (Spalek 2007: 193; see also Duffy 2009). While these discussions focus on the radical individual, Wiktorowicz (2004) extends the debate to radical groups.

Drawing on 'social movement theory', he demonstrates how groups such as the Al Muhajiroun[1] are organized in such a way as to 'attract' individuals looking for meaning and a place to 'belong' (Wiktorowicz 2004: 16). Discrimination and a sense of dislocation play an important role, but these factors alone are insufficient for the path from radicalization to extremism. Wiktorowicz and Kaltenthaler (2006) further use 'rational choice theory' to illustrate the 'incentives' for potential members to join such groups, which include 'spiritual' incentives, though the nature of these incentives might vary for different individuals (2006: 318–319, see also Wiktorowicz 2005a).

These interpretations and explanations for radicalization suggest one clear fact; the one-size-fits-all approach to radicalization—and, more importantly, how it relates to terrorism—is problematic. In such a context, then, evoking 'radicalization' in relation to Muslims and extremism creates greater confusion, where even peaceful political behaviour by Muslims is placed within the assumed 'process of radicalization', leading to terrorism. Githens-Mazer and Lambert (2010b) highlight how 'conventional wisdom' often dictates an understanding of radicalization for 'policy makers and the media' (Githens-Mazer and Lambert 2010b: 889–890). For Kundnani (2012a: 21), exploring 'what causes' one person to 'engage in violence' and not another 'in the same political context [...] is beyond analysis'. Githens-Mazer (2012) further illustrates how present day understanding of the concept either as 'a process' or as 'causation' may be too simplistic. This has resulted in 'a conceptual back-formation', moving away from 'the 18th and 19th centuries radicalization' that fundamentally challenged 'those shibboleths held by religious and political elites' as to 'how one of us becomes one of them—how an "ordinary" person enters on the path to becoming a terrorist who wants to kill me and you' (Githens-Mazer 2012: 560; see also Githens-Mazer 2010b). Hence, the manner by which radicalization is explained in media and policy circles simplifies it in a desperate attempt to understand modern

---

[1] An Islamist group started by Omar Bakri Mohammad, a member of another Islamist group banned by the British government:Hizb-ut-Tahrir. Al Muhajiroun was considered radical because of its 'support for the use of violence [...] the use of military coups to establish Islamic states wherever there are Muslims, including Britain', while condoning' the use of violence against Western militaries operating in Muslim countries' (Wiktorowicz and Kaltenthaler 2006: 302).

day terrorism, where individuals, despite their varied background and life experiences, are clumped together under the category of a radical extremist, where an interpretation of Islam makes Islam itself suspect. Such 'claims' to 'the causality of certain process or factors' are logically unsound, as similar 'processes' can be observed in 'cases beyond the sample' of Islamic extremism (Sedgwick 2010; Githens-Mazer 2012: 564; Kundnani 2015).

Given this problematic nature of radicalization and security, it is not surprising to find policies of counter radicalization, such as Prevent, encountering greater challenges and obstacles, especially where the Muslim community as a whole is rendered 'suspect'. With the British state attempting to counter radicalization in universities, such a narrative, instead of supporting Muslim students against extremist ideology, encourages a framework of otherization, where Muslims have constantly to prove their legitimacy as British and Muslim students. Thus, as long as the meaning of radical and the radicalization process is located within a framework of security around the Muslim subject, there is a greater likelihood of a misdiagnosis of the problem of Islamic extremism and terrorism. Policies that aim to disrupt a process that continues to baffle academics and policy makers have, in fact, contributed to further isolation and disengagement amongst the Muslim community.

The Radical Muslim Student

> it has become a taboo word to be called a radical. Before it was something to be proud of, radicals are our best activists in history, radicals were people who changed thoughts, changed society through their radicalism [...] I think it has been really hijacked by certain individuals. I think when such a depiction is there the term itself is highly problematic. Student activism is radical but the way we use student activism is not even related to radicalism which is seen as behind closed doors their thoughts changing.
> —FOSIS Representative (2011)[2]

---

[2] See also Brown and Saeed (2015: 1957).

> Radical are people who have used the name of Islam and they have committed certain acts under that name, or they have voiced their opinions about certain acts under the name of Islam. They are not from Islam, or within Islam because Islam is not dirty or filthy like they make it. It is not like that. Islam is something beautiful that is meant to make you feel at peace not make you feel filthy.
> —Kiran, London1, 22, Graduate (Science), British

As highlighted by the FOSIS representative and Kiran, the stereotype of the radical and dangerous Muslim student who may be on the path to terrorism found credence in the aftermath of 9/11 and 7/7. Glees and Pope's (2005) report *When Students Turn to Terror. Terrorist and Extremist Activity on British Campuses* highlighted how young Muslims involved in these terrorist attacks had met on university campuses in Britain (Glees and Pope 2005; Hamid 2007). Further investigation into groups classified as extremists, such as the Hizb-ut-Tahrir, showed how higher educational institutions were targeted as recruiting grounds (Centre for Social Cohesion 2010a). In response to such findings, the UK government further implicated universities and Muslims in its securitization process. Under Prevent 2011, university 'staff' and 'administration' were 'advised' to be vigilant about any 'signs of radicalization' for the sheer purpose of ensuring the 'welfare' and wellbeing of their students (HM Government 2011a: 76; see also Secretary of State for the Home Department 2012).

While, in 2012, the Home Affairs Committee (2012: 13) acknowledged that 'there may be a much less direct link' 'between university education and terrorist activity', 'than was thought in the past', a 'statutory duty' was nonetheless imposed on universities under the Counter Terrorism and Security Act 2015 to 'prevent' radicalization of students. As the Prevent duty highlights, '[s]ome students may arrive at RHEBs[3] already committed to terrorism; others may become radicalized whilst attending a RHEB due to activity on campus; others may be radicalized whilst they are at a RHEB but because of activities which mainly take place off campus' (HM Government 2015c: 3). The student—in particular, the Muslim student—becomes a suspect the moment they enter

---

[3] Relevant higher education bodies.

the university; either they are already radical, or are vulnerable to radicalization. The university body therefore has a duty to identify the student radical in its midst and to ensure that a 'safe' atmosphere exists where no student is radicalized. In order to protect students from radicalization, universities work with 'Prevent coordinators', building on an already existing relationship with the police and the Prevent team to stop students from turning radical (Association of Chief Police Officers 2012).

Furthermore, under the 'Prevent duty' university personnel have the following responsibilities: conducting a 'risk assessment' to ensure that students are safe from 'not just violent extremism but also non-violent extremism'—i.e. radicalizing ideologies; monitoring student speaker events to ensure radical speakers are not given a platform; outlining clear policies for 'the use of prayer rooms and other faith-related facilities'; outlining the role and scope of the Students' Union and student societies in addressing radicalization; ensuring that the Internet is filtered 'as a means of restricting access to harmful content'; training staff and university personnel to look out for 'radicalised students' who may become 'focal' points for 'radicalisation through personal contact with fellow students and through their social media activity'.; and these duties will be monitored by a 'monitoring' body appointed by the 'Secretary of State' (HM Government 2015c: 4–6). Instead of utilizing the space for dialogue and discussion that universities possess by virtue of being educational institutions of higher learning, in response to the dangerous Muslim radical the Prevent duty has turned these institutions into mediums of surveillance (Saeed and Johnson 2016). While this piece of legislation was amended to ensure that 'freedom of speech' is also upheld in universities (HM Government 2015a; McGarry and Mythen 2015), the measures put in place to root out radicalization stifles free speech within the university, especially for Muslim students, reinforcing a 'fear of Muslim political agency' (Birt 2010: 117), where students who are politically active, albeit for Muslim campaigns, are viewed with suspicion.

The case of Mohammed Umar Farooq illustrates this paranoia. Farooq was suspected of terrorism and questioned by an official after he was caught in the university library reading a book on terrorism that was part of his postgraduate degree course. While Staffordshire University apologized for the incident, it also highlighted the fact that the 'prevent duty' was 'very broad' and 'was "underpinned by guidance [...] that contains insufficient detail to provide clear practical direction in an environment such as the university's"' (Ramesh and Halliday 2015). Other incidents have also been reported in schools in which Muslim students are accused of being 'potential terrorists' for expressing political views, or using political terms within the legitimate context of a classroom discussion (Dodd 2015; Saeed forthcoming). While these cases emerged after the imposition of a statutory duty to protect students 'at risk', Rizwaan Sabir's ordeal predates this legislation.

Sabir was a Master's student who downloaded the Al Qa'ida training manual from the US Department of Justice website, 'a manual [...] which could be bought at WH Smith, Waterstones and Amazon as well as the university's own library' (Townsend 2012). He sent it to a 'friend' for advice on his research, 'a friend' who 'was well known on campus as a mentor for Muslim students' (Thornton 2011: 423). When a member of staff discovered the document on Sabir's computer, he was reported to the authorities and arrested along with his friend (Jones 2011). 'Sabir and his friend were held and questioned for 6 days because of their possession of the Al Qaeda Training Manual' (Thornton 2011: 423), and were eventually released without charge. In this case, the two actors who could have helped Sabir and his friend became a source of the problem: the 'university authorities' who claimed that the student had no right to access such a document, despite his supervisor's insistence that the document 'was relevant to his research' (Jones 2011; Thornton 2011), and the police authorities who were later discovered to have 'fabricated key elements of the case against' him (Townsend 2012).

While the police authorities later monetarily compensated Sabir and issued an apology, the level of bias against Sabir, and against Farooq, or Muslim students who have constantly to defend their right to be regular students, demonstrates how dominant stereotypes about the Muslim student radical influences the perceptions of local actors. As Thornton observed, 'the university' implemented '[t]he "better-safe-than-sorry" approach by calling the "police straightaway" instead of carrying "out some basic checks"' (Thornton 2011: 423–424). This 'safe college' image in the case of Sabir compromised his rights as a researcher, which has further implications for Muslim researchers in universities. It further compromises the function of a university which, according to Said, provides a 'Utopian space' for research on minorities in plural societies (1994: xxix). This space is politically neutral, where individuals can challenge dominant narratives without the fear of being persecuted for their distinct views. However, the danger of transforming the university into a *Big Brother* for the state, 'where social and political issues are actually either imposed or resolved would be to remove the university's function and turn it into an adjunct to whatever political party is in power' (Said 1994: xxix).

The radical student was not always a source of such paranoia. Far from it, the Saidian Utopia was an expression of such student radicalism. Historically, student movements in Britain have varied, given the changing social and economic environments, from the 'town and gown' clash of 1354 at the University of Oxford[4] (Halsey and Marks 1968) to the 1960s, where student activism was related to 'internal university or college issues [...] [rather] than national or international issues' (Blackstone and Hadley 1971: 3). Rootes (1980), in a discussion on student radical movements explains how 'student movements are creatures of the societies in which they occur', highlighting in some form 'all the excellences and deformities of their circumstances' (Rootes 1980: 473). Present day student activism can similarly vary from internal demands to more national or international concerns, such as anti-war protests, anti-austerity protests, or animal rights. Muslim students are also active around issues of access to 'prayer rooms' or *halal*[5] food, and more international issues around the Israeli-Palestinian conflict, Kashmir, the invasion of Iraq and Afghanistan, and so on (Ahmad 2001; Tyrer 2003; Tyrer and Ahmad 2006).

By simplifying the radical and violent extremist connection amongst Muslim students, not only is there a danger of implicating Muslim student radicals who are politically active but do not harbour any violent

---

[4] Clash between the residents of Oxford and the University. Some accounts argue that the clash was the result of Oxford students who constantly 'flouted' the laws, 'destroyed property' and 'harmed' the citizens, resulting in an eventual clash, also known as the 'St Scholastica's Day Riot' (Boren 2001: 12).

[5] 'Literally "released" from prohibition. The Hebrew equivalent, *kashar*, implies something that is fit, or suitable.' (Halliday 2002: 13).

tendencies, but it also results in an Islamophobic perception of Muslim students that would breed resentment and promote isolation. As H. A Hellyer, a research fellow at the University of Warwick and deputy convener of a Home Office working group on tackling extremism and radicalization observed in 2010, '[u]niversities are generally not held accountable for the actions of their graduates; not for IRA sympathisers who graduated from British universities, nor extremists from any background—the British National Party chairman is a University of Cambridge graduate' Newman 2010. Despite his warning that universities are not 'security establishments' (Newman 2010) and that treating them as such would compromise intellectual and academic freedom, the Counter Terrorism and Security Act 2015 has nonetheless made them part of the state's security machinery.

The preceding examples of Muslim students who have been victims of the radical student 'witch hunt' (Allen 2014) predominantly concern Muslim male students. Muslim women, on the other hand, as discussed in Chap. 3, are placed within the vulnerable-fanatic spectrum; one which is also true of the female student. The Muslim male radical may be considered a direct physical threat, but the Muslim female radical, while dangerous, is nonetheless considered vulnerable as well, a victim of fanaticism, who can be rescued from the clutches of a primitive religo-cultural belief system. Muslim females are also more susceptible to experiences of Islamophobia within the everyday context of the university. However, even Muslim female students who are not politically active but are, nonetheless, part of suspicious student societies, such as the Islamic student society (ISoc), are considered vulnerable and 'at risk'. This fear was reinforced by Umar Farouk Abdulmutallab, the 'President' of the UCL ISoc in 2006–07, who attempted to blow up a plane bound to the USA in 2009 (BBC News 2011d; Universities UK 2011). His association with the ISoc reignited the debate on Islamic societies and their ability to radicalize young students.

Organizations such as the Federation of Student Islamic Societies (FOSIS), which represents all ISocs across England and Wales, pride themselves on being progressively radical. This kind of radicalism is about 'empowering Muslim students towards a culture of civic and political participation with remarkable results […] seen in every level of campaigning from feminist and social issues, to international conflict, human rights, ethical investment and accessible education'. The height of the success of such radicalism is evident in the election of 'the first Muslim vice-president of the National Union of Students (NUS)' (Hanjra 2010). While, in theory, the kind of radicalism that Hanjra is proposing should be considered legitimate, part of the Utopian university that Said emphasized, the existing reality of British universities with an unclear 'statutory duty' of vigilance towards Muslim students, renders such behaviour risky and highly suspect. FOSIS, in opposition to the Counter Terrorism and Security Act 2015, released a statement highlighting the failure of existing counter terrorism legislation that had created an atmosphere where 'Muslim students' felt 'under siege', with such a 'Prevent duty' likely to 'disproportionately target Muslim students, leading only to further stigmatization and alienation, perhaps most ironically doing little to prevent the appeal of extremist narratives' (FOSIS 2015).

However, FOSIS has continuously come under attack by both state and non-state actors for not doing enough to combat extremism amongst young Muslims (HM Government 2011c: 11; Sutton 2012). The Centre for Social Cohesion had previously highlighted the extreme nature of such student societies, some of which were infiltrated by members of Hizb-ut-Tahrir. Song (2012) highlights how ISocs are unfairly singled out as potential student sites of radicalization, where generalizations about 'extremism' amongst Islamic societies overlooks 'all the other aspects of ISOC membership within universities, and all the students who join ISOCs for entirely innocuous, and indeed, laudable, reasons' (2012: 158). In examining this problem further, the next section focuses on the experiences of members of the 'sister wing' of ISocs, and their negotiation with the stigma of radicalization.

Sisters of the ISoc: Guilty Until Proven Innocent

The ISoc sisters who participated in this research varied from defining themselves as political to completely apolitical. Yet, by virtue of being associated with their university's ISoc, and by being practising Muslim women who stood out, they felt they were often unfairly attacked for being radical. The main role of an ISoc is not political activism but welfare; however, quite a few ISoc sisters highlighted the importance of political activism in ensuring the welfare and safety of its Muslim students, a view that was shared by some but not all ISoc members. FOSIS, has tried to encourage greater political participation of ISocs in student politics:

> Islamic societies try to avoid politics in general. So for me who deals with political participation is to convince Islamic societies to be more politically involved on campus, get to know your rights. Running in elections, just speaking to your officials so they know who you are. Know the system which is in your favour. So then such things will not happen. It is about empowerment. So you know what is right and wrong and they know which individuals to talk to if something happens.
> —FOSIS Representative (2011)

The level of student campaigning for ISocs is predominantly limited to fund-raising during times of natural disaster or devastation. Lyyla, an alumna of a West Yorkshire university, describes ISocs as providing a 'safe environment' for students who are 'away from home' where, far from radicalization, 'no one pushes their' boundaries. However, in providing such a safe environment, for Lyyla ISocs also reinforce patriarchal structures that prevent Muslim women from realizing their full potential:

> The men are more vocal and they hold positions in these societies but they are bloody useless. They got like head brother and head sister but everything goes through the head brother. Why? What makes him special? And why do they always need a head brother? Why can't a woman be head of an ISoc [...] and that offends me because these women are so much more smarter than the brothers but because they are men they have to have a male leading it and women buy into that, they don't question it. When I speak to ISoc sisters, they are on ball politically and want to do stuff but they will say oh I have to ask the ISoc brother. Why? [...] every problem that we have in the Muslim community, sexism towards women and women's lack of self-confidence is projected toward the ISoc [...] I know Muslim women who are amazing organizers [...] but who speaks in these events—the brother.
> —Lyyla, North West1, Alumna, Activist, British

Lyyla herself is a practising Muslim who wears the hijab, but she is also a strong socialist and anti-war campaigner. In her own experience with Muslim men as well as non-Muslim socialist comrades, she has confronted ignorance and Islamophobia, with remarks that question her ability to be both a Muslim woman and an activist. As a practising Muslim woman, either she is considered stereotypically oppressed, and therefore not politically active, or the act of her wearing the hijab is judged by her socialist colleagues as a political choice, but not religious. Ironically, even campaigns that challenge the status quo struggle with giving Muslim women the space to define their own identities, without superficially bracketing them within an *either/or* category. Furthermore, while Lyyla's critique of the ISoc highlights the limitations of religious student societies (not just Islamic societies), it also reveals the importance of such structures in providing a 'safe' and familiar space that is a source of comfort for Muslim students away from home (see also Sondy 2013). While these boundaries need to be challenged—and are being challenged by some, though not all ISocs—the challenge needs to come from the ISoc sisters themselves.

However, the limits placed on ISoc sisters are not just the result of the patriarchal structure of the ISoc, but also the universities themselves. Nadia, the head sister of an ISoc in West Yorkshire, is a case in point. Nadia is politically active, and also defines herself as a socialist; yet, the extent to which she can be political is limited to the space provided by her university:

> I think the problem with us is that if we just did you know sat around and did the spiritual stuff then they would be okay with that. It is as soon as you start talking about politics and as soon as you start saying we want to change things on campus that they don't like that activism side of it and if I was an abstract activist or socialist activist or general activist that'd be different, but when it comes under the banner of the Islamic society pushing for something even if it is something like for example establishing a vegetarian canteen purely on the basis that they are not following at the moment halal and kosher regulations […] but then because it is the Islamic society that is doing it, it comes under a different banner […]. Or even if I as an individual because I am the head sister […] it is different because we are active. Because there are other Muslim societies […] like the Middle

East society, they do have solid stuff but they would never for example campaign for a prayer room and things like that. That is not the purpose of their society. The purpose of an Islamic society is that it brings together all branches of Islam, all people, all Muslims, whatever they follow and it campaigns for their rights and it makes sure that they have a place and for the students in general we are a welfare society and I think that is the issue they have with us.
—Nadia, West Yorkshire2, 20, Undergraduate (Law), British

For the ISoc at Nadia's university both male and female members who were active in student politics were considered problematic. However, West Yorkshire2 had the additional problem of being linked with Muslim alumni that were later accused and convicted of terrorism. Even though the men in question were not university students or members of ISocs at the time of their arrest, their previous association with the university and its ISoc was enough to make the society suspect. The ISoc's tainted reputation resulted in current members struggling to prove their innocence not just to society outside, but also often to their own Muslim and non-Muslim fellow students. The ISoc is further accused of having Hizb-ut-Tahrir sympathizers, a fact that Nadia and the ISoc members have repeatedly denied. Despite these rumours, the welfare staff of the university interviewed did not mention any such problems with the ISoc but, rather, highlighted the university's constant engagement with Muslim students through the Islamic society.

Yet, Nadia believes that her ISoc is deliberately targeted by the middle management. Their society has confronted issues of booking rooms on campus for their ISoc events, or inviting speakers, a problem that none of the other societies faced. She felt it was 'Islamophobic to a degree', where 'the middle management' had this image of the ISoc and Muslim students as being extreme, even though none of them had ever made the effort of meeting ISoc members:

> I also hate this idea of moderate and extremist Islam. Because Islam is Islam and if somebody is moderating it they are just diluting it and then it is just slam or lam or whatever. You know I was having this discussion with the welfare officer and she was saying that I think radicalization is good and she

kind of stopped herself and then said no I mean politicization. And I was like are you saying that because of the context of the term and she was like yeah I guess because I don't like radical ideology and then we had to take the whole discussion back. These terms are quite the snappy media terms that make people go oo radicalization.
—Nadia, West Yorkshire2, 20, Undergraduate (Law), British

The ISoc sisters are tainted with the reputation of being radical. Zahra, an active member of ISoc, has constantly to defend herself not only to other non-Muslim students, but also the self-proclaimed 'moderate' Muslims.

People when you tell them you are Muslim and from the Islamic society they think you are trying to convert them. If you invite them to events or talks, they know you are Muslim they will just think you are trying to make them Muslim even though you are just inviting them to a talk. And you are just giving them knowledge about Islam, they don't have to become Muslim to attend a talk, but for them they think you are trying to make them Muslim.
—Zahra, West Yorkshire2, 19, Undergraduate (Social Sciences), British

While the West Yorkshire2 ISoc stands out because of its history, members of other ISocs also feel they are constantly under surveillance. Romeena, who works both as a university welfare advisor for her university in South East England and with the Islamic student society, highlights how similar actions on the part of the university—whether it is the administration, middle management or, at times, the faculty—restricts students from actively engaging in student events, especially student politics.

It does suppress students. In the Islamic society if we were to invite somebody to talk about Palestine we have to think a hundred times before doing that […] This is a well known speaker, been on the BBC but we have to be cautious […] that kind of suppression is not always beneficial.
—Romeena, South East2, Alumna, University Welfare and Islamic Society Executive

With the 'Prevent duty', this kind of control over student activities—in particular, Muslim and ISoc activities—will increase. Far from engaging with Muslim students on controversial topics that inundate media and political rhetoric, this control will, instead, 'suppress' it further, thereby limiting the potential of a university to debate such issues intellectually. While the Prevent duty highlights the need to ensure that students are protected from radicalizing and extremist points of view, by curbing the ability to debate and discuss, any extremist point of view is not going to be challenged, thereby defeating the entire premise of a 'counter' terrorism agenda— instead, creating conditions that further silence Muslim students.

By making the ISocs, and thereby the ISoc sisters, more suspicious, the existing policies towards ISocs have increased discrimination and Islamophobia, especially for those who wear the hijab or niqab, often exacerbated in instances where the sisters are campaigning—albeit raising funds, or publicizing an ISoc event. Fatima wears the hijab and jilbab, and actively supports her ISoc, has experienced this occasionally. The following are two examples—one within the university; the other outside, where she felt the encounter was a result of her being a member of the ISoc and campaigning for an ISoc cause:

Fatima: Come across quite a few people who are Islamophobic type of people when we had events, had charity events, explore Islam week. You could hear people saying negative things like oh look stalls to recruit terrorists and stuff like that.
Interviewer: Did they come up to you and say that?
Fatima: They never said it upfront. I think they would be scared of saying that to your face but you can hear them sniggering and talking, you have to push that aside. You can't confront them. If you confront them we are practically reinforcing their view of us that we are violent or we are bad so we just ignore it. But if someone actually comes across to us we try to explain the true nature of Islam to them […]

We had a charity event with the Islamic society. We went to [a town next to our university] with boxes. We don't ever go there because it is too far […] we had boxes to collect money and there was this professor who had two pounds or something and he was about to put it in there and he put it on the box and he asked what is it for. And I told him we are from ISoc and we are trying to raise money for needy children. He looked at the Islamic Relief sign, and the sign is like a mosque. He looks at that and he says what's that. I told him the charity that we are doing it for is Islamic Relief. He takes the pound, puts it in his pocket and walks off.

Interviewer: This was a professor?
Fatima: Yes it was a professor. Old. [...] white. We didn't know who he was and then later we found out that he was a professor. I didn't take it any further because it happened within a second. I wouldn't even remember the person's face.
—Fatima, West Yorkshire2, 21, Undergraduate (Law), British Pakistani

The image that ISocs radicalize students or 'recruit terrorists'—one that is reinforced by the media, as well as political actors who accuse ISocs and FOSIS for not doing enough to fight radicalization—is one that impacts the sisters as much as the brothers. As the FOSIS representative notes, the difference is based on their location within the extremist-fanatic spectrum, in comparison with Muslim male students:

> I think Muslim women face a lot more challenges on campuses just because of ongoing debates and because they are more Muslim looking. After stabbing happened at City they would tell the women don't hang around campus just go home. Always to travel in groups as there was fear that they might be targeted since they look more Muslim. The other challenges, the cases I've heard with regards to anti-terror legislation, it is more male in terms of being stopped and detained. I have heard very few cases of that happening to women but on campuses I think women face more challenges whether people think you are, if you wear a hijab they instantly assume you are unapproachable.
> —FOSIS Representative (2011)

Muslim female students have suffered Islamophobic abuse on university campuses as highlighted in Chap. 3 (see also Tyrer and Ahmad 2006; Office for Public Management and Hussain 2009). As representatives or members of ISocs, there is an added dimension of suspicion and the potential for radicalization that makes the Muslim female student—but, in particular, an ISoc sister—more vulnerable to Islamophobia.

While the interview with FOSIS took place in 2011, recent incidents of British Muslim girls fleeing to join Isis, as discussed in Chap. 3, has further moved the Muslim female student towards the radical (read: fanatic) end of the spectrum. The accusations and stigmatization that both Fatima and Romeena highlight have been continuous features in the everyday existence of Islamic society members since 7/7. Such accusations minimize the important welfare role of ISocs in catering to the religious needs of Muslim students and providing support to Muslims who may not take part in general student events' as a result, these students may feel left out or alienated within the university. While non-Muslim students are also welcomed to ISoc events, the society mainly attracts Muslim students, especially those who often feel isolated because of their religion. As Sanam observes:

> for example in terms of drinking or partying or casual sex or things like that I think most Muslims are quite specific about those things […] I feel like too many times, I know that the administration doesn't organize the fun events for students, but too many times it is easy for the university environment to build up this idea of fun revolving around those things which then side-lines a lot of young Muslims … for people who don't want that kind of lifestyle what do they do. Then you have ISOC organizing separate events …
> —Sanam, South East1, 26, Graduate (Social Sciences), Overseas

Sanam's narrative highlights the problems that many Muslim students confront in a predominantly non-Muslim university context. Their inability to participate in the 'fun events' in universities often makes them stand out within the student body. The ISoc provides a space for Muslim students who cannot find such a sense of belonging in the widespread activities of the university, where the university itself is limited in its ability to cater to the specific requirements of its Muslim student population. Mehreen, who belongs to the same university as Sanam, initially restricted her socializing to the Islamic society as she felt that non-ISoc events did not offer much in terms of her religious and cultural needs. She often could not eat food properly at dinners or departmental BBQs, which served mostly non-*halal* meals; she could not engage in the drinking culture; and she stood out because of her appearance. However, while the ISoc provided a place to belong, both Sanam and Mehreen, as with some of the other ISoc members (though not all), also highlighted their continued efforts to join other student societies despite the differences, thereby mingling with both Muslim and non-Muslim students. The ISoc, however, provided a place for them to meet young people who held similar views, where they did not feel like an outsider.

Participants from other universities also highlighted this important welfare role of ISocs. Nargis, who belongs to South West1, discussed the problems she encountered when she first arrived in the UK, unfamiliar with living in a non-Muslim country. Her colleagues at work were friendly but her interaction with them was restricted because of their different lifestyles:

> The colleagues I work with are mostly who I interact with [...] One is from Mexico and one is from Thailand they are the only two girls in my research group but I really cannot interact with them. Hundreds of issues that they talk, they are quite irrelevant to me. Boyfriends and loads of other things that they talk about I would be like okay, going to the pub—I never go to the pub, talking about sex—I'd be like okay. They live with their boyfriends and I'm like okay. So really can't make good friends. The only friends I talk to are on Skype, the old ones. I am just like okay with people and lots of work.
> —Nargis, South West1, 25, Graduate (Sciences), Overseas

Alluding to Mehreen's and Sanam's narrative, Nargis constantly felt she could not communicate with her colleagues and was unable to participate in their lifestyle. The ISoc, however, provided her with a sense of community. She felt 'comfortable' talking to members of the ISoc, who would organize events where she could equally participate.

> I really felt very nice and I do not really find time to go to lots of ISoc events. It really feels nice because you can talk to people from different departments [...] You can talk to them loads, because of the common thing of being Muslim. We went to some iftar parties [...] we made lots of friends [...] exchanged numbers. I feel very comfortable talking to them.
> —Nargis, South West1, 25, Graduate (Sciences), Overseas

Aliya, a British Muslim with a Pakistani heritage, had less trouble making friends, but her closest friend was a Muslim, as it was easier for her to be friends with someone from a similar background. While she herself was not as actively involved in the ISoc as her friend, she nonetheless felt the ISoc was important in getting Muslim students together, particularly in a university where they are in a minority. Her mother also encouraged her to find her university ISoc and stay on the 'straight and narrow' path, mixing with the right people. Ironically, it is precisely this space provided to Muslim students to come together that makes ISocs especially suspect, perceived as an ideal recruiting point for Islamic extremist organizations. With academics such as Glees and Pope (2005) highlighting the radicalizing role of Islamic societies in the lives of the 7/7 terrorists; with think-tanks, such as the Centre for Social Cohesion (2010a), that had also issued constant warnings about the vulnerability of Muslim students; and also government and media constantly focusing on universities and their ISocs as potential recruiting targets, Islamic societies in the wider narrative are tainted with a reputation for being radical. Tehmina, who is an active member of her Students' Union but has also been involved in the National Union of Students, particularly within a welfare capacity, highlights the problem that various ISocs across the country encountered after the tragedy of 7 July 2005.

> I think it did affect the way Muslim students were seen on campuses. There was a discussion on whether to get rid of Islamic societies in some universities that were happening [...] There was a fear that they all would be radical. People started to question more Islamic societies and Pakistani societies. But the whole debate about with me was not every Muslim is a terrorist and not every terrorist is a Muslim [...] I kept having to justify myself as a Muslim after that [...] Constantly justify which I don't do any more. It did affect us.
> —Tehmina, West Midlands1, 19, Undergraduate (Social Sciences), British

Tehmina also pointed to the limitations placed on the advocacy role of these student societies as a result of such accusations. ISocs have continued to provide an avenue for young Muslims both to access and to demand services such as prayer room facilities, *halal* food on campus and the like. With their reputation under suspicion, the role of Muslim campaigners can often be misunderstood; they are in danger of being labelled radical for campaigning about Muslim student rights in universities or for supporting international causes such as Palestine, or inviting speakers to raise awareness about Islam can often limit their activities on campuses. The line between ISoc activism and extremism as perceived by state and media actors has become highly permeable within the security lens. This is further complicated with incidents of ISocs being approached by security agencies, as reported to FOSIS, where young Muslims are unsure about 'how to respond' since they cannot 'say no' but also 'don't want that association'. Such an association also impacts the way other students perceive ISocs. Zebunnisa is involved with her ISoc's charity events and has friends who are members, but her narrative captures the suspicion to which other ISoc members have alluded:

> Zebunnisa: To be honest, I enjoy student politics *bauhat ziyada* [a lot], but there are certain things I won't get involved with. Like with the Islamic society I will not be part of their committee [...] because of the incidents that have happened, UCL *walla* [one] and in other places. To be very honest I am new here and I don't want that because of that and the fact that I don't have a family here, someone tries to make use of the fact that I am alone here and someone tries to brainwash me because well I won't be brainwashed for starters. I can help them volunteering, charity week.
> Interviewer: Do such things happen?
> Zebunnisa: They don't happen here but these people have been living here for long, and they might be my friends but I don't know them well enough [...] I just don't want to give someone that chance.
> —Zebunnisa, North West1, 21, Undergraduate (Law), Overseas

The suspicion that Zebunnisa expresses of ISoc members—some of whom are her friends—who have not committed a crime, but are untrustworthy simply because of their affiliation with an ISoc, demonstrates the divisive nature of framing ISocs as a radicalizing force. Zebunissa is not alone, as Fatima's narrative highlights, in observing that other students are also constantly suspicious of ISoc activities. While fellow students keep their distance from such student societies, parents have also started discouraging their children from joining such societies, especially after the Abdulmutallab incident.

> My mom told me don't get involved in the Islamic society [...]they get after these people only, *pehla koi masla hota hai tu inkei peechei aatei hain, yeh woh* [whenever there is a problem, the first ones they come after are these people, this and that]. This is generally a concern that does exist. I don't really know what the grounds for it are perhaps the whole UCL incident did exacerbate it a bit.
> —Hafsa, North East1, 22, Graduate (Law), Overseas

Unlike before, when parents such as Aliya's had encouraged their children to join the Islamic society with the hope that they would not stray far from their religious and cultural values, Hafsa's parents and others like them now actively discourage them from joining the society, fearful for their children's safety. Parents also became more cautious about their children's religiosity. Nadia, for instance, narrates her experience with Muslim female students who complained about their parents being worried if they started praying too much, thinking they were turning into extremists. Nadia's own father became worried when she started praying more, afraid that 'MI5 would arrest' her (Saeed and Johnson 2016: 43). The fear is not restricted to male students; it also affects females whose parents have become more protective of their children and are concerned about the kind of activities they are involved in within the university. With the government also encouraging Muslim mothers to watch over their children to ensure they are not being radicalized, Muslim students are constantly being framed within this insecure narrative. Lyyla highlights the absurdity of expecting parents constantly to monitor their teenagers:

> which parent knows what their teenage child is doing. There is something wrong with you or something wrong with your teenage child if the parent knows. That is the whole point of teenager, rebelling [...] if you got teenage

children, you don't know what they are doing on a Saturday night [...] You hope they are not doing drugs or whatever, but they are teenagers.
—Lyyla, North West1, Alumna, Activist, British

By encouraging parents to look out for signs of radicalization amongst their children, parents are also drawn into the security framework. Children joining organizations such as ISocs, or praying too much, reinforce the paranoia that such actions amount to radicalized and potentially terrorist tendencies. This fear is further exacerbated when organizations such as FOSIS are criticized by government officials, the media and think-tanks such as the Quilliam Foundation and the Centre for Social Cohesion. Yet, FOSIS and the ISocs continue to challenge this negative image in their individual capacity by engaging with other student societies, and have achieved a limited level of success. While this level of activism is discussed in detail in Chap. 6, the challenges and successes of FOSIS are summarized by Ahmed who, as a representative of his university's Students' Union, witnessed a high level of engagement between FOSIS and other student groups and societies at the national level.

The best way to test how Muslim students are progressing in mainstream student politics is sort of to look at the national picture and so FOSIS is a prime example, and I think as long as they are attacked for being an extremist group on campus, even though they represent all Muslim students, I think that is going to be very very negative for tackling extremism, if we are to agree that that is a problem. And I think the problems reduce over the past few years. I was a delegate ... elected to represent my university at the National student conference. I saw first-hand how the different organizations ran their campaigns and got involved in the national picture so the union of Jewish students, FOSIS, Socialist Workers' Party, Labour students ... There the picture is that FOSIS are very very involved and integrated in the national picture. You have members in the executive, they have had members on the actual leadership centre, vice-president of the NUS. When you see that happening you realize that there is potential to organize Muslim students in the mainstream of student politics.
—Ahmed, London3, Student Union Anti Racism Officer

While ISocs are challenging the negative stereotype attached to them, they have also constantly to defend their right to invite speakers and hold events. The 2015 Prevent strategy is attempting to regulate the kind of speakers that are invited to universities—an action that was also taken by the Centre for Social Cohesion (2010a), when they drafted their own list of speakers whom they deemed extremist and circulated it amongst universities. The problem with such lists and policies is that, often, these are drafted without consulting Muslim students or societies. As a consequence of this, Muslim groups, instead of engaging with think-tanks and security agencies, are equally suspicious of them (see also Saeed and Johnson 2016). The participants further suspected organizations such as Quilliam (see Dodd 2010b) and the Centre for Social Cohesion for promoting their own limited agendas that had nothing to do with Islam or Muslims. The problematic relationship is best captured by the FOSIS representative:

> When we look at examples of Centre for Social Cohesion or Quilliam their reports […] they don't even have any credentials as researchers. They don't have the academic degree to go with their research. They are just people with an agenda, that is what they are, they would look at news in a way that suits their way of thinking and their agenda.
> —FOSIS Representative (2011)

Such lack of engagement with student societies results in resentment and further isolation, and young Muslim students and their ISocs feel targeted. Romeena also witnessed this problem in her university in the South East of England, highlighting how the problem with inviting speakers was more the result of a lack of communication between university and the ISocs, who were often excluded from the decision making process. In one speaker event organized by the ISoc, the university decided to place 'security guards' to check students without informing the student society, which she described as 'an alienating experience' (see also Saeed and Johnson 2016). The problem she highlights is one of a lack of communication and a level of suspicion that prevents universities from trusting their own Muslim students. Romeena shares another example that illustrates this lack of discussion and communication:

People do things and there is no sense of accountability. Why did the chaplain turn up to *Jumma*[6] every week. She was a woman to a *jumma* that was all men [...] a bit uncomfortable for the men [...] They need to have dialogue about how to better manage [...] but people jump into action and no accountability.
—Romeena, South East2, Alumna, University Welfare and Islamic Society Executive

Such a level of distrust further reinforces suspicion of university authorities. Despite facing these problems from parents, fellow students, university administration, the government and the media, ISocs are still willing to engage with different actors provided there is a level of mutual engagement, rather than dictation. Ahmed's ISoc, for instance, cooperated with its university; this was because the university administration, rather than simply preventing them from inviting speakers, were willing to have a conversation with the ISoc, and explained their reasons for being critical of the chosen speakers. Furthermore, organizations such as FOSIS do not shy away from the problem of extremist speakers or radicalism, having organized conferences with academics, policy and security personnel aimed at jointly formulating ways of combatting extremism on campuses (Saeed and Johnson 2016). However, they are quick to point out that often the response from university authorities is exaggerated, thereby creating an atmosphere of distrust and suspicion. As Romeena highlights:

We at universities should not be living in a big brother society. That is what causes the isolation of students [...] people who feel they are being spied on [...] what happens is that you just end up secluding them further, because you make them your targets, you are honing in on them ... students are aware of it.
—Romeena, South East2, Alumna, University Welfare and Islamic Society Executive

This suspicion is particularly problematic when students believe their ISoc is under surveillance. Both Hafsa and Nadia, in their narratives,

---
[6] The Friday afternoon prayer congregation.

reiterate the belief that they were being spied on. For Hafsa, there were 'spies' in her ISoc who were informing the university administration about potential speakers and events before they were made public knowledge. Nadia believed she was being monitored by MI5—a fear that was reiterated by her father. It is worth noting that this fear of being spied on, or being under surveillance, existed before the introduction of the 'Prevent duty'. Such a fear is further exacerbated by the Counter Terrorism and Security Act 2015, with both ISoc sisters and brothers feeling 'under siege', further alienated and stigmatized by their own universities (FOSIS 2015).

ISocs, Sisters and the Radical Student

Universities are supposed to be places of higher learning where students should be encouraged to be radical; should be able to experiment, debate, and challenge the status quo through such radical behaviour. They provide a 'safe' space for students to challenge their limits, not be confined by them. However, as this chapter has demonstrated, a 'radical student'—especially in relation to Muslims—is one to be feared and controlled; one who is assumed to be on the path to terrorism. Even though there is no substantial evidence to suggest that such a path or process exists (Githens-Mazer 2010a; Kundnani 2015), the university is turning into a 'safe space' where students are not only protected from violence, but also from radical thought, thereby defeating the purpose of a higher educational institute of learning.

Framing Muslim students within a counter terrorism framework in universities reduces them to nothing more than would-be terrorists. This assumption that a process of radicalization can be interrupted within a university setting, thereby imposing a 'prevent duty' on university personnel to monitor its predominantly Muslim students, where the exact nature of these 'signs' of radicalization continues to baffle both policy makers and academics, has propagated an atmosphere of distrust amongst the student body. If the threat of extremism is not just physical violence, but also a conservative and extremist mindset, then limiting free speech—which the security framework in universities has inadvertently done—does not counter any threat; rather, it deliberately ignores it. There is no denying the fact that young educated Muslims have travelled to countries such as Syria to join Isis; that educated Muslims such as Roshonara Chaudhry or Jihadi John, in fact, became terrorists—but the majority of the remaining educated young Muslims are peaceful and law-abiding citizens.

Furthermore, Muslim students who are members of ISocs particularly stand out. There is a stigma attached to ISocs across British universities in the aftermath of 7 July, but especially after the discovery of the Abdulmutallab connection. While ISocs provide a place for Muslim students to come together, such a space also creates an ideal opportunity for extremist groups to target students. However, by curtailing and controlling the activities of ISocs, universities further isolate them, rather than challenging any form of extremism. Organizations such as FOSIS are willing to work with security personnel and universities in ensuring that Muslim students are provided a 'safe' environment; however, they are seldom given the opportunity to engage and are expected simply to follow orders.

The narratives of ISoc sisters reveal how they are equally implicated in a discourse about insecurity and vulnerability, where their affiliation with the ISoc also reduces them to the category of a 'potential terrorist'. For the ISoc sisters, their student society serves a welfare function, providing a space on campus where they can practise their religious beliefs, a place to belong in a university context in which they mostly feel out of place. Not all ISoc sisters are politically active—in fact, many claim to be apolitical; the ISoc, far from radicalizing them, has been accused of reinforcing a patriarchal status quo (Lyyla). Yet, the sisters who are trying to be more proactive often face resistance from the university itself, or from parents, or from fellow students, all of whom suspect them of being too radical. The narratives also reveal how ISoc sisters are more vulnerable to Islamophobic attacks, as both their physical appearance and their ISoc affiliation makes them highly suspect. With the fear of being under surveillance for holding political views, or simply belonging to an Islamic student society, ISoc members, both male and female, have constantly to tread with caution, afraid that their actions might be misconstrued, thereby making them 'vulnerable' and 'at risk' to radicalization.

Bibliography

Ahmad, F. (2001) Modern traditions? British Muslim women and academic achievement. *Gender and Education*, 13 (2), pp. 137–152.

Allen, C. (2014) 'Operation Trojan Horse: examining the 'Islamic takeover' of Birmingham schools,' *The Conversation*. http://theconversation.com/operation-trojan-horse-examining-the-islamic-takeover-of-birmingham-schools-25764 (Accessed 11/10, 2015).

Association of Chief Police Officers. (2012) *Prevent, Police and Universities Guidance for Police Officers and Police Staff to Help Higher Education Institutions Contribute to the Prevention of Terrorism*. UK: Office of National Coordinator Prevent.

Barnes, H. (2006) *Born in the UK: Young Muslims in Britain*. London: The Foreign Policy Centre.

BBC News. (12/05/2011d) *Protestors call for reinstatement of Dr Rod Thornton*. BBC News. [Online]. Available from: http://www.bbc.co.uk/news/uk-england-nottinghamshire-13380860 (Accessed 03/15, 2013).

Birt, Y. (2010) Governing Muslims After 9/11. In *Thinking Through Islamophobia Global Perspectives*, eds. S. Sayyid and A. Vakil, London: Hurst & Co. (Publishers) Ltd, pp. 117–128.

Blackstone, T. and Hadley, R. (1971) Student Protest in a British University: Some Comparisons with American Research. *Comparative Education Review*, pp. 1–19.

Boren, M.E. (2001) *Student Resistance: A History of the Unruly Subject*. London: Routledge.

Brown, E.K. and Saeed, T. (2015) Radicalization and counter-radicalization at British universities: Muslim encounters and alternatives. *Ethnic and Racial Studies*, 38 (11), pp. 1952–1968.

Burgat, F. (2008) *Islamism in the Shadow of Al Qaeda, translated by P. Hutchinson*. USA: University of Texas Press.

Duffy, D. (2009) Alienated radicals and detached deviants: what do the lessons of the 1970 Falls Curfew and the alienation–radicalisation hypothesis mean for current British approaches to counter-terrorism? *Policy Studies*, 30 (2), pp. 127–142.

Dodd, V. (22/09/2015) 'School questioned Muslim pupil about Isis after discussion on eco-activism,' The Guardian, Available from: http://www.theguardian.com/education/2015/sep/22/school-questioned-muslim-pupil-about-isis-after-discussion-on-eco-activism (Accessed 11/13, 2015).

Dodd, V. (04/08/2010b) *List sent to terror chief aligns peaceful Muslim groups with terrorist ideology.* The Guardian. [Online]. Available from: http://www.guardian.co.uk/uk/2010/aug/04/quilliam-foundation-list-alleged-extremism (Accessed 08/07, 2012).

Federation of Student Islamic Societies (FOSIS). (17/01/2015) Press Releases FOSIS Expresses Concern over Consequences of Counter-Terrorism & Security Bill on UK Campuses. Available from: http://media.fosis.org.uk/press-releases/1606-fosisexpresses-concern-over-consequences-of-counter-terror-bill-on-uk-campuses (Accessed 05 March, 2015).

Githens-Mazer, J. (2012) The rhetoric and reality: Radicalization and political discourse. *International Political Science Review*, 33 (5), pp. 556–567.

Githens-Mazer, J. (2010a) *Rethinking the causal concept of Islamic radicalisation. Political Concepts: Committee on Concepts and Methods Working Paper Series* Montreal: International Political Science Association.

Githens-Mazer, J. (2010b) Mobilization, Recruitment, Violence and the Street: Radical Violent *takfiri* Islamism in Early Twenty-First-Century Britain. In *The New Extremism in 21st Century Britain*, eds. R. Eatwell and M.J. Goodwin, UK: Routledge, pp. 47–66.

Githens-Mazer, J. and Lambert, R. (2010b) Why conventional wisdom on radicalization fails: The persistence of a failed discourse. *International Affairs*, 86 (4), pp. 889–901.

Glees, A. and Pope, C. (2005) *When Students Turn to Terror. Terrorist and Extremist Activity on British Campuses.* London: The Social Affairs Unit.

Halliday, F. (2002) *Two Hours that Shook the World September 11, 2001: Causes and Consequences.* London: Saqi Books.

Halsey, A.H. and Marks, S. (1968) British student politics. *Daedalus*, 97 (1), pp. 116–136.

Hamid, S. (2007) Islamic Political Radicalism in Britain: The Case of Hizb-ut-Tahrir. In *Islamic Political Radicalism. A European Perspective*, ed. T. Abbas, Edinburgh: Edinburgh University Press Ltd, pp. 145–159.

Hanjra, F. (22/04/2010) *Student Islamic societies are radical, not extremist.* The Guardian. [Online]. Available from: http://www.guardian.co.uk/commentisfree/2010/apr/22/student-islamic-societies-radical (Accessed 04/27, 2010).

Her Majesty's Government (HM Government). (2015a) *Counter-Terrorism and Security Act 2015.* Available from: http://www.legislation.gov.uk/ukpga/2015/6/notes/contents (Accessed 03/28, 2015).

Her Majesty's Government (HM Government). (2015c) *Prevent Duty Guidance: for Higher Education Institutions in England and Wales.* UK: Crown.

Her Majesty's Government (HM Government). (2011a) *Prevent Strategy.* UK: Crown.

Her Majesty's Government (HM Government). (2011c) *Report to the Home Secretary of Independent Oversight of Prevent Review and Strategy by Lord Carlile of Berriew Q.C.* UK: Crown.

Home Affairs Committee. (2012) *Roots of Violent Radicalisation. Nineteenth Report of Session 2010–12, Volume 1.* London: The Stationery Office Limited.

Johnson, D. (2006) *Education and Radicalisation.* St Antony's College, University of Oxford.

Jones, S. (14/09/2011) *Student in al-Qaida raid paid £20,000 by police.* The Guardian. [Online]. Available from: http://www.guardian.co.uk/uk/2011/sep/14/police-pay-student-damages-al-qaida (Accessed 03/05, 2012).

Kundnani, A. (2012a) 'Radicalisation: the journey of a concept,' *Race & Class*, 54 (2), 3–25.

Kundnani, A. (2015) *A Decade Lost. Rethinking Radicalisation and Extremism.* UK: Claystone.

McGarry, R. and Mythen, G. (03/03/2015) *Beware the security creep into British universities, The Conversation.* Available at: http://the conversation.com/beware-thesecurity-creep-into-british-universities-37867 (Accessed 03/10, 2015).

Newman, M. (07/01/2010) *Universities should not be 'security establishments', say experts on terror.* Times Higher Education. [Online]. Available from: http://www.timeshighereducation.co.uk/news/universities-should-not-be-security-establishments-say-experts-on-terror/409863.article (Accessed 02/09, 2011).

O'Duffy, B. (2008) Radical atmosphere: explaining Jihadist radicalization in the UK. *Political Science and Politics*, 41 (1), pp. 37–42.

Office for Public Management and Hussain, S. (2009) *The Experiences of Muslim Students in Further and Higher Education in London.* London: Greater London Authority.

Patel, I.A. (2007) The Scales for Defining Islamic Political Radicalism. In *Islamic Political Radicalism. A European Perspective*, ed. T. Abbas, Edinburgh: Edinburgh University Press Ltd, pp. 42–53.

Ramesh, R. and Halliday, J. (24/09/2015) *Student accused of being a terrorist for reading book on terrorism*, The Guardian. Available from: http://www.theguardian.com/education/2015/sep/24/student-accused-being-terrorist-reading-book-terrorism (Accessed 03/02, 2016).

Rehman, J. (2007) Islam, "war on terror" and the future of Muslim minorities in the United Kingdom: Dilemmas of multiculturalism. *Human Rights Quarterly*, 29 (4), pp. 831–878.

Rootes, C.A. (1980) Student radicalism: Politics of moral protest and legitimation problems of the modern capitalist state. *Theory and Society*, 9 (3), pp. 473–502.
Roy, O. (2007) Islamic Terrorist Radicalisation in Europe. In *European Islam Challenges for Public Policy and Society*, eds. S. Amghar, A. Boubekeur and M. Emerson, Brussels: Centre for European Policy Studies, pp. 52–60.
Saeed, T. and Johnson, D. (2016) Intelligence, global terrorism and higher education: Neutralising threats or alienating allies? *British Journal of Educational Studies*, 64(1), pp.37–51.
Saeed T. (forthcoming) Muslim Narratives of Schooling in Britain: From "Paki" to the "Would-Be Terrorist". In *Education, Neo-liberalism and Muslim Students: Schooling a 'Suspect Community'*, eds. M.M. Ghaill, and C. Haywood, UK: Palgrave Macmillan.
Said, E. (1994) *Culture and Imperialism*. London: Vintage Books.
Secretary of State for the Home Department. (2012) *The Government Response to the Nineteenth Report from the Home Affairs Committee Session 2010–12 HC 1446 Roots of Violent Radicalisation*. UK: The Stationery Office Limited.
Sedgwick, M. (2010) The concept of radicalization as a source of confusion. *Terrorism and Political Violence*, 22 (4), pp. 479–494.
Sondy, A. De (2013) British Pakistani Masculinities: Longing and Belonging. In *Men, Masculinities and Religious Change in Twentieth-Century Britain*, eds. L. Delap and S. Morgan, UK: Palgrave Macmillan. pp. 252–278.
Song, M. (2012) Part of the British mainstream? British Muslim students and Islamic student associations. *Journal of Youth Studies*, 15 (2), pp. 143–160.
Spalek, B. (2007) Disconnections and Exclusion: Pathways to Radicalisation? In *Islamic Political Radicalism. A European Perspective*, ed. T. Abbas, Edinburgh: Edinburgh University Press Ltd, pp. 192–206.
Stemmann, J.J.E. (2006) Middle East Salafism's influence and the radicalization of Muslim communities in Europe. *MERIA*, 10 (3), pp. 1–14.
Strabac, Z. and Listhaug, O. (2008) Anti-Muslim prejudice in Europe: A multilevel analysis of survey data from 30 countries. *Social Science Research*, 37 (1), pp. 268–286.
Sutton, R. (13/12/2012) *FOSIS must do more to demonstrate its rejection of extremist narratives*. HuffPost Students. [Online]. Available from: http://www.huffingtonpost.co.uk/rupert-sutton/post_4207_b_2291779.html (Accessed 15/12, 2012).
The Centre for Social Cohesion. (2010a) *Radicalism on UK Campuses a Comprehensive List of Extremist Speakers at UK UNIVERSITIES*. London: The Centre for Social Cohesion.

Thornton, R. (2011) Counterterrorism and the neo-liberal university: Providing a check and balance? *Critical Studies on Terrorism*, 4 (3), pp. 421–429.

Townsend, M. (14/07/2012) Police 'made up' evidence again Muslim student. The Guardian. [Online]. Available from: http://www.guardian.co.uk/uk/2012/jul/14/police-evidence-muslim-student-rizwaan-sabir (Accessed 02/16, 2013).

Tyrer, D. (2003) *Institutionalized Islamophobia in British Universities. Degree of Doctor of Philosophy.* Institute of Social Research, University of Salford.

Tyrer, D. and Ahmad, F. (2006) *Muslim Women and Higher Education: Identities, Experiences and Prospects. A Summary Report. Liverpool John Moores University and European Social Fund.* Oxford: Oxuniprint.

Universities UK. (2011) *Freedom of Speech on Campus: Rights and Responsibilities in UK Universities.* London: Universities UK.

Vertigans, S. (2007) Routes into 'Islamic' terrorism: Dead ends and spaghetti junctions. *Policing*, 1 (4), pp. 447–459.

Wieviorka, M. (2004) The making of differences. *International Sociology*, 19 (3), pp. 281–297.

Wiktorowicz, Q. (2004) Joining the Cause of Al-Muhajiroun and Radical Islam. *The Roots of Islamic Radicalism conference*, Yale University.

Wiktorowicz, Q. (2005a) *Radical Islam Rising: Muslim Extremism in the West.* USA: Rowman & Littlefield.

Wiktorowicz, Q. and Kaltenthaler, K. (2006) The rationality of radical Islam. *Political Science Quarterly*, 121 (2), pp. 295–319.

5

Securitizing the Ethno-Religious Identity(s): Exploring Islamophobia as Pakophobia

> Once again, we are Pakistanis, so we have that situation of having different types of stereotypes and negative perceptions associated with us because Pakistan is not popular [...] I think as a Pakistani Muslim it is quite difficult to sometimes see whether it is a religious resentment or is it a cultural resentment. You never know where the other person might be coming from or might potentially go because both are not seen as the best possible scenarios.
> —Salma, North West1, 28, Graduate (Business), Overseas

Securitization of the Muslim identity has an impact not only on British Muslims, but also non-British Muslims who are either temporary residents, immigrants or refugees fleeing war-torn countries such as Syria, or others in search of education and employment opportunities in Britain. Amongst these non-British Muslims are also Muslim students who, as Chap. 4 highlights, are as much implicated in the security narrative of a university by virtue of being Muslim as other British Muslim students. However, in certain cases. added to the Muslim issue is a problematic ethnic identity, which may result in a form of hyper-securitization. Salma's narrative highlights this problem for the Muslim Pakistani identity where 'both are not seen as the best possible scenarios'.

This chapter examines the hyper-securitization of the Muslim Pakistani identity, especially during the period 2009–2011, at a time when the Af-Pak problem was at its peak. Pakistani students in the North West of England were accused of terrorism, and eventually deported, with Pakistan's notoriety reaching new heights on the discovery and death of Osama bin Laden in Pakistan. Different from the British Muslims with a Pakistani heritage, the Pakistani Muslim females in this study had travelled from Pakistan for the purpose of education, where the problems they faced were linked to their religion and nationality. For many of the Pakistani Muslim women, this hyper-securitization takes the form of a Pakophobia, where being both Muslim and Pakistani creates a greater sense of vulnerability and insecurity.

The discussion in this chapter highlights how the Muslim Pakistani is constantly aware of her 'outsider' status, but unlike the British Muslim, she is a non-citizen with a passport of a country that was labelled the hub of terrorism. These narratives provide insights into the complex ways in which Muslim communities—and Muslim women, in particular—experience the state's securitization agenda, with differences in experience not only based on physical appearance, but also ethnic and racial signifiers.

Pakophobia: Muslims and Their Other Identities

Following on from Croft's (2012) discussion of securitization in the Introduction, the double bind—i.e. the ethnic-religious connection in cases where both identities are caught in a wider socio-political narrative of insecurity—results in a form of hyper-securitization. The extent to which particular groups of Muslims are more vulnerable than others is determined by the political context. Today, post-Isis, any Muslim with a link to Syria or the Levant lends themself to a hyper-securitized discourse. In 2009 to 2011, the Muslim-Pakistani connection was perceived to be hyper-securitized, as both identities were considered particularly conspicuous, given Pakistan's role in the then 'war on terror'. While Muslim Pakistanis continue to be part of the narrative of counter terrorism, where their identity is still suspect, the political security lens has refocused towards the Middle East. Despite this shift, stricter immigration laws in the UK have implicated students from high risk countries, including Pakistan—amounting to what some critics have called 'racial discrimination' (Havergal 2015).

Frances Stoner Saunders, in her discussion of immigration, calls the 'visa—from the French *visé* "having been seen"' as 'another key document of the verified self'. It exposes the hypocrisy of Western liberalism, what she calls the liberalism of possession, defended by ever thickening borders, sharply rising enforcement budgets, new and more invasive surveillance technologies, and other mechanisms of exclusion of which stricter visa regimes are one powerful example (Saunders 2016). This 'verification' of the self is similar to the bureaucratic management of minority identities as discussed in Chap. 2, where the 'liberal ethic of mutual recognition—however unequally and unevenly distributed […] is now read largely from the perspective of "exclusionary" misrecognition', where the identity of a high risk nationality/ethnicity is managed through a system of surveillance that begins from the moment the 'alien' applies for the 'visa'—the permit to enter the civilized world (Bhabha 1998: 131). The entry of the Pakistani citizen therefore begins from this point of securitized (mis)recognition, where the 'verifiable self' is located in an 'inferior' position against the verifying self. It is within this context that British visas and work permits for Pakistani citizens have become more difficult to obtain, where '[s]ome universities' have been directly 'told by the Home Office to stop recruiting from certain regions, mainly in Pakistan' (Havergal 2015).

This section offers insights on the issue of such hyper-securitization which participants in this study called 'Pakophobia', a fear of the Muslim Pakistani. Pakophobia is understood as a type of Islamophobia, which is interspersed with both the ethnic (Pakistani) and religious aspects of the individual's identity. It is not a phenomenon that is different from Islamophobia but, rather, is situated within the same category, where the specific ethnic characteristic of a Pakistani may often be the defining feature of the discrimination experienced, rather than the religious aspect alone.

Young Pakistanis entering the UK are aware of their suspect status. The narrative of Dalia, an undergraduate student, highlights this heightened sense of awareness, where she shares the problems her male friend faced in getting a student visa for Britain, who in the end decided to give up when his visa was rejected. While having similar credentials as Dalia, she believed he was discriminated against for being a Pakistani male. As a Pakistani female, she believed she had an advantage—ironically, as a consequence of the stereotype of Pakistani women being victims of patriarchy and culture, which is further reinforced by the British Pakistani community. As Pakistanis enter this larger socio-political discourse associated with the British Pakistani community, further situated within an international discourse on Pakistan and terrorism, their identities are hyper-securitized in the British socio-political imagination. Abida calls this Pakophobia:

> Interviewer: You mentioned Islamophobia and then Pakophobia. What do you think is the link between the two?
> Abida: Most Pakistanis are thought to be Muslims.
> Interviewer: Being Pakistani, does that make one more vulnerable towards Islamophobia or is it a completely different kind of discrimination.
> Abida: It is exactly the same thing [...] I've seen people react differently towards people belonging to as I said other countries who are Muslims.
> —Abida, West Yorkshire1, 21, Undergraduate (Law), Overseas

Abida highlights the experiences of other non-British Muslim females from the United Arab Emirates or Lebanon who were more 'Westernized' and did not experience the same kind of discrimination that she and her Pakistani friends had experienced:

> I know Pakistani and Bengali people are targeted more, more than Saudi Arabian people, more than Indian people. Pakistani and Bengali people are targeted more and accused more of being Islamic extremists, I don't know why but I hear they are.
> —Faiza, West Yorkshire3, 22, Undergraduate (Humanities), British Pakistani

The vulnerability of the Pakistani Muslim is further reinforced by the country's high risk status in the bureaucratic machinery of immigration and alien control. The experiences of Pakistani Muslims further reinforce this position of insecurity where, as students, they enter a British university context governed by draconian policies such as the Counter Terrorism and Security Act 2015.

> especially since 7/7 […] debates started on madrassas in Pakistan and how these militants were trained in Pakistan and sent abroad to do all these activities. After that they started looking at Pakistan in a very suspicious way.
> —Rukshanda, London2, 28, Graduate (Science), Overseas

Coming from a high risk country to a context where educational institutions have become part of the state's security apparatus (Allen 2014; Saeed and Johnson 2016), many of the women in this research expressed their constant struggle in proving that they were educated and trustworthy, fighting not only against Islamophobia, but also Pakophobia. They were often subject to racial slurs that highlighted this troubled outsider status:

> Abida: I have had people call me T.W.A. Didn't understand what that meant at all. It means Third World Assassin. I have started owning that persona now.
> Interviewer: What do you mean?
> Abida: It means that if you think I am a third world assassin which I am not, you better run and hide because if I find you I am going to smack the a-wax out of you. So yeah, if being a part of Pakistan means being called that then let it be I don't really care.
> —Abida, West Yorkshire1, 21, Undergraduate (Law), Overseas

The term 'third world assassin' alludes to a security threat which, for Abida, was linked to her being Pakistani, from a country that in media and political rhetoric continued to be defined as the 'world's most dangerous country' (Moreau 2007, 2010). Encountering racial slurs such as T.W.A. or 'Paki', was a common theme expressed by other young Pakistanis, as well. In his discussion on racial insults in Brazil, Guimaraes describes racial insults as 'tools of humiliation'. Often, 'the social and racial position of the insulted is already historically established by means of a long process of prior humiliation and subordination, the very term that designates them as a racial group (*preto* or *negro*) has already become, in itself, a pejorative term' (Guimaraes 2003: 136). Hence, as Bernard-Donals' observes, 'regardless of the "interested" or "naïve" uses of language and its history, subjects cannot go *outside* of that history: it is always already there' (Bernard-Donals 1994: 164).

The term 'Paki' is one such insult, which is historically situated in the narrative of the South Asian community in Britain. As Singh describes it, the term 'Paki' 'exists in a system of associative relationships with signs which negatively label other ethnic groups' (2004: 23; see also Kureshi 2011: 6–7). 'Paki-bashing' became more prominent in 1969 or 1970 which, according to Pearson, signalled the 'emergence of a "moral panic" when the official and semi-official view of "public opinion", the mass media, the courts, and the police found a new word to describe acts of "unprovoked assault" on people who are said to be racially inferior' (Pearson 1976: 49–50). However, with the Muslim identifier gaining prominence, the term Paki gradually became associated not just with being South Asian, but also Muslim.

> I think it used to be just anti-Asian [...] but now you hear Paki being used and the next word they would use is Osama bin Laden's wife or Al Qa'ida. So they are making that link themselves.
> —Nadia, West Yorkshire2, 20, Undergraduate (Law), British

'Paki' therefore evolved to include Islamophobic connotations, directed at South Asians, Pakistanis but also Muslims. The term had been heard by both Pakistanis and British Muslims though their association and the awareness of 'Paki' was different. The British Muslims were more aware of the history of the term, and its implications as a form of racist abuse, some making a personal connection:

> I hate that word Paki. What I understand from it is when our forefathers came to Britain to work because the British people, the English people didn't want to work in factories and do that kind of jobs. So [...] when my grandfather came that term was used in a derogatory way, it was demeaning. When a Pakistani uses the word Paki I have negative feelings about that.
> —Tamana, West Yorkshire2, 19, Undergraduate (Social Sciences), British

The term continues to be 'used in a derogatory way' by non-South Asians, but it is also a word that has been taken up by young British South Asians, in the attempt to invert its meaning. While used jokingly for each other, the racist implications are nonetheless obvious when a non-South Asian uses the term directed towards a Muslim or a South Asian. Many of the British Muslim women were critical of this inversion, believing that the word was demeaning to South Asians submerged in a history of bigotry and xenophobia. Nadia shares her struggle with the term:

> I remember when my grandma came here they were literally expecting the roads to be paved with gold. They realized it wasn't at all what it was cut out to be […] and I always get angry with people here, the term 'Paki' is used to refer to each other but I know that my aunty got beaten up by someone calling her that name. [In West Yorkshire] you know when there were a lot of problems, when my family first came here, my mother's family in the 60s, you know when Enoch Powell and everything was at large and I know they wanted to get rid of the term not just for the word, because of what it carries. And I know there is a lot of ignorance in my generation that they don't understand what their parents did, they don't understand why they wanted them to have the freedom.
> —Nadia, West Yorkshire2, 20, Undergraduate (Law), British

For many of the British Muslims with a Pakistani heritage, the history of the term 'Paki' is linked with racist experiences of family members. Many of the Pakistanis, however, were unfamiliar with the nature of this racist term until they had arrived in Britain. Hafsa, for instance, knew there was a problem with the term but did not realize the magnitude of its racist connotations, having used it in drafts of her dissertation. For her, the term meant purity, since that was the definition she associated with Pakistani. It was her advisor who cautioned against the use of the term in her final paper, reminding her that the word had a different meaning in Britain. Hafsa, though, continued to encounter the term in her small town in the North East:

> They would be driving the car, they were drunk. They would throw something, they would shout at you and go like "you bloody Paki" something

like that, something Paki related, Muslim related. But I think [...] the connection was made really easily, in the sense that if you are Pakistani you must be Muslim. They never say you bloody Indian. I can look Indian, some people think that I look Indian. But they just assume that okay she is wearing the hijab and that she looks like she is from the South East Asian place. She has to be a Paki, so Paki would have to come up.
—Hafsa, North East1, 22, Graduate (Law), Overseas

The racial slur 'Paki' therefore fluctuates between a racist association with South Asians and Pakistanis and an Islamophobic connotation for the Muslim outsider. For Faiza, who wears the niqab, her experience of discrimination was more the result of ignorance about Islam than her brown skin. Yet, the permeability of the boundary between anti-Pakistani and Islamophobic abuse is evident in this changing nature of the term 'Paki':

If you are white as white can be, and you wear the hijab you are still called Paki. [...] Now it's anyone who covers themselves, wears the hijab can be called Paki.
—Faiza, West Yorkshire2, 22, Undergraduate (Humanities), British Pakistani

Whether directed at a South Asian looking individual or a 'white' Muslim, 'Paki' is a pejorative term, meant to essentialize and otherize the individual. For the Pakistani students, such terms took the form of a racism against their Pakistani-Muslim identity, thereby being not only Islamophobic in nature, but also Pakophobic. The perception that such insults were directed towards the Pakistani-Muslim identity is important, irrespective of whether that was the intention of the racist, as such perceptions are often internalized by young Pakistanis, who accordingly restrict their behaviour to avoid standing out. The term is used for both men and women; however, for men such incidents have resulted in physical violence. Hafsa narrates an incident of her Pakistani friend:

Hafsa: He's my friend, he left from my friend's room actually, very late at night. They were working on some assignment, due the next morning [...] he was crossing the library he got

	beaten up by like four boys. Punched, slapped, hit, he bled a little.
Interviewer:	When was this?
Hafsa:	This was last year and we really made him try to press charges because they had the car plate number since another friend was coming along the way and he took picture of the car plate number. The only reason he said it was a racial thing because I look Pakistani that's it. He didn't have a beard, nothing he was just pure Pakistani looking. It was a very Pakistani directed thing. It was just for that reason and no other reason. He didn't say anything, he just stood there and didn't hit them, which was a very smart thing to do because they were obviously four boys, and they were pretty big, butch and drunk. So yeah they just hit and left. The police got involved, all security around college was increased because of that. They really encouraged him to press charges but he was just like I don't want to get involved in all of this because I don't know where this will go and I don't want to come on record and oh victim of racist stuff, it's my last year here, get the hell out of here, let's not bother. He is in Pakistan now.

—Hafsa, North East1, 22, Graduate (Law), Overseas

Whether the racists in the case of Hafsa's friend thought he was Pakistani, Muslim or South Asian we will never know, but the perception of the friend that he was abused because of his Pakistani identity is more important as this 'feeling' has an impact on the insider/outsider status. This status, then, determines the behaviour of the Pakistani in question, who has to constantly negotiate and play the role of an 'acceptable outsider'. The 'outsider' perception is different for a temporary resident who is not entitled to the privileges of a British citizen in multicultural Britain (see also Parekh 2010: 241), but is always considered a visitor. Even if this visitor manages to find a more permanent state of residence in Britain, they will still fall under the category of a first-generation immigrant, moving towards the 'insider-outsider' status of the British Muslim. Therefore, the 'let's not bother' response of Hafsa's friend, who is aware of his 'outsider' status, is more common in cases of non-British Muslims, especially those planning on returning to their home countries and not wanting to draw attention to themselves. The level of acceptability that is granted to any temporary Muslim resident is further dependent on the socio-political climate, one that is heavily influenced by media discourse about Muslims and their other identities. While the Muslim Pakistani is a highly suspect category, a Muslim from Dubai or Bahrain may be less suspect because of the acceptability of their nationality/ethnicity.

Furthermore, the gendered perception of Pakistanis in the British media and political discourse is also highly Orientalist, similar to the stereotype of Muslim men and women. In the case of Pakistanis, the oppressive religio-cultural meld sharpens that Orientalist lens even further, with the male Pakistani reduced to the perpetrator, and the female his victim. The nature of Pakophobia that women encounter is, once again, dependent on their physical appearance. Here, the cultural dress *shalwar/kameez* in connection with the Muslim hijab invokes a different perception of insecurity for the Pakistani female, as Mehreen observes:

> I get teased about my dress in the streets. I wore a shirt for my exam because I thought my *shalwar kameez* might give a negative impression so I wore a shirt then [...] I think the scarf is unacceptable to them. I have an Indian colleague, she wears *shalwar kameez* nothing happens to her.
> —Mehreen, South East1, 28, Graduate (Science), Overseas

While Mehreen's hijab was considered more problematic, she nonetheless decided to change her *shalwar kameez*, taking on a more acceptable Western dress. The hijab, as a practising Muslim, could not be compromised but the *shalwar kameez* that indicated her South Asian and Pakistani connection needed to be changed for her to become more acceptable. In Mehreen's narrative, the Indian colleague had not combined the Muslim hijab with the South Asian *shalwar kameez*, a combination that predominantly stands out in the case of either Pakistani or Bangladeshi Muslims, though the sari more often is associated with the Indian identity.[1] Such a combination then further makes Pakistani Muslims stand out; many

---

[1] These associations of clothing and identity are superficial—especially in the context of South Asian communities, where the *shalwar kameez* or saris are worn across different countries in South Asia. Yet, the simplistic association nonetheless essentializes the 'brown' skinned communities into

of them are more likely to experience Islamophobia or Pakophobia. The negotiation between the religious and ethnic identities was also highlighted in Abida's experience of setting up a Pakistani student society in her university, which most students either avoided or discouraged.

> That matter is one big problem. It is called a Pakistani society. People have suggested renaming it the South Asian society. Some kind of name which does not involve Pakistan, they say that it's not a good idea to have a society like this. I don't know the reasoning, probably because I don't understand it or I don't want to understand it. But they say oh don't name it the Pakistani society, we are not too keen about it, it's not a good country [...] I think I don't see it that much in overseas Pakistanis, I see it more in British Pakistanis [...] who again hate it because maybe they haven't been there [...] they think that Pakistan is extreme, fundamentally run.
> —Abida, West Yorkshire1, 21, Undergraduate (Law), Overseas

Abida's university had an Islamic society; the same members were willing to join a South Asian society, but not one going by the name of Pakistan. Her university, while small, is located in an area which has another larger university whose British Pakistani alumni were implicated in terrorist activity. The terrorists' visits to Pakistan for training inundated media accounts for months, where the Pakistan connection became further problematic. In such a context, then, an overseas female Pakistani has greater difficulty negotiating a place for her ethnic/national identity as Muslims with a Pakistani heritage are all too familiar with their hyper-securitized place. For the British Muslims, as discussed in Chap. 2, being Muslim could not be compromised, yet the hyper-securitization that resulted from the Muslim-Pakistani connection could be remedied. While Abida highlights her problem within the university, other Pakistanis visiting the UK also confronted these issues in public spaces, with some discouraged from disclosing the national connection:

> When I came here my phupho [aunt] [...] in London [...] said if someone asks you about your nationality, don't tell them you're Pakistani. This was

---

the more or less acceptable categories, especially when 'ethnic' clothing is matched with 'religious' garb in the form of a hijab.

kind of really strong. She said [...] you will face racism issues so don't typify yourself as a Pakistani [...] And then she explained it to me that after all the things that Pakistanis did people have had problems with being this and they tried to conceal their identity. Loads of people in London that I've met they say that being a Pakistani makes life more difficult, makes you less trustworthy.
   —Maryam, South West1, 28, Graduate (Social Sciences), Overseas

Maryam's visit to the UK was not in the immediate aftermath of 7/7 but in 2009, when media reports and political discourse continued to highlight Pakistan's role in terrorism and militancy. Even those participants who did not wear the *shalwar/kameez* but 'looked Western' had to defend their Pakistani identity to people who constantly accused Pakistan of supporting terrorism. This further led to an internalization of paranoia regarding being a Muslim Pakistani. Overseas students, for instance, monitored their own behaviour, embarrassed at the behaviour of other Pakistanis, or of events in their own country. Abida shares experiences of Pakistani female students in her classroom:

Abida: Most of the Pakistani girls don't talk during lectures [...] They are too scared of being noticed as a Pakistani. I remember we were doing constitution, there was a terrorism act, and of course everyone knows what terrorism means, especially Pakistanis. So I remember on the day of the lecture our slides are given about a week before [...] There was no Pakistanis and no Asian British present during that lecture, I was so ashamed of it. I don't know the reason why because our professor in the beginning mentioned the first organization to invent terrorism was the IRA, the Irish. So it's the fact that they think we are terrorists is what makes them ashamed of the you know [...]
Interviewer: Are you saying that Pakistani and British Pakistanis themselves think they are terrorists?
Abida: They themselves think they are part of that group. In TV, on the news when they say that these many people were arrested, some of them were from Pakistan, even if they don't say it, they sound like Pakistani names. Mohammad

> Hussain[2] is not going to be an Arab guy, it sounds Pakistani, so we have got this self-loathing quality that we have adopted, which is not a good quality which makes us think we are inferior, because we think now that our own people are blowing up planes and are blowing themselves up. We see that in our own country and we know that there are Pakistanis who are blowing up hundreds of people in political rallies, just because someone has a different view.
> —Abida, West Yorkshire1, 21, Undergraduate (Law), Overseas

Being a Pakistani Muslim in Britain, whether male or female, lends itself to a form of subliminal conditioning in which certain biases against the Muslim Pakistani community are internalized by the community itself. This internalization is reflected in Abida's narrative about her class fellows and echoes Sabahat's guilt by association in Chap. 3; where she felt both guilty and afraid on seeing an abandoned bag on a bus, fearful of both its contents but also that she would be accused of being its owner since she looked Muslim. Hence, appearing Muslim or Pakistani can be a problem in a context where both identities are securitized. Added to this sense of insecurity is a troubling theme that emerges between the overseas Pakistani and the British Pakistani—in particular, women who hold British Pakistanis responsible for the stereotypes that define their Pakistani experience in Britain.

> Also my *shalwar kameez* when I wear it. I am sorry to say that Pakistani/Bangladeshi/Indian, especially Pakistani community, are labour class, not educated people. They think you are uneducated but I try to overcome this, and people are often happy that I make an effort.
> —Mehreen, South East1, 28, Graduate (Science), Overseas

Mehreen, despite being an educated doctoral student, is placed within the category of the backward, uneducated Pakistani woman, an association for which the Pakistani community in Britain is blamed. Her narrative wreaks of elitism, where the women from the British Pakistani community are condemned as 'labour class' or uneducated, echoing

---

[2] Changes to a deep Pakistani accent when she pronounces this name.

Prime Minister David Cameron's suggestion that Muslim women cannot speak English and, hence, are not productive and integrated members of British society (Mason and Sherwood 2016a, 2016b). Areesha echoed similar sentiments:

> I always have this argument with my friend. I tell her I feel like I am talking to someone from the village over here. These people have lived all their lives in Britain but they act like they haven't left their village, haven't seen the world. That is how I feel when I talk to them. What do they think of Pakistan? We only have donkey carts, don't have cars. It is absolutely ridiculous [...] these people haven't been to Pakistan for 10 or 12 years. I don't understand these guys.
> —Areesha, West Yorkshire2, 20, Undergraduate (Social Sciences), Overseas

Mehreen and Areesha are not alone in holding such elitist views about the British Pakistani community. Terms such as 'BBCD' (British Born Confused Desis) were also used by other Pakistanis in their description of the British Pakistani community. While the Muslim Pakistani women tended to blame the BBCDs, in particular their inability to adapt thereby increasing the outsider status of Pakistani citizens who were visiting as students, the British Pakistanis were also critical of the Pakistani students. The Pakistani women were often described as being too Westernized, of flaunting and misusing the independence given to them by their families, with Pakistan perceived as either dangerous or corrupt.

> Like the other day the girl was saying, oh I am too scared to go to Pakistan. I said why? Oh it is so dangerous [...] There are bombs going on, this going on that going on. I said excuse me I just came from Pakistan my family is there, and nobody is at risk. These are British Pakistanis.
> —Areesha, West Yorkshire2, 20, Undergraduate (Social Sciences), Overseas

The level of disconnect between overseas Pakistanis and British Pakistanis differed across locations, but was most prominent in small towns. However, in West Yorkshire, where there is a large South Asian and, in particular, Pakistani community, these sentiments were also quite prevalent. The British Pakistani women were perceived to have led sheltered lives, never having left the protection of their immediate families. Those interviewed either associated Pakistan with the land of their parents or grandparents that was predominantly rustic, or with the more recent problems of terrorism and political corruption. Even the British media had an easier time identifying the Pakistani aspect of a terrorist's identity or his link to Pakistan than the Saudi aspect of a person such as Osama bin Laden who, as far as media narrative was concerned, was more 'Arab' than 'Saudi'.

> I think especially now with the whole war on terror. Oh no Pakistan is helping the US, oh no you are helping the Taliban. If you are Muslim you are either Arab or Pakistani. That is what it seems like right now.
> —Shumaila, South West1, 20, Undergrad (Medicine), British

Such associations, while troubling for overseas Muslim Pakistanis, were also perceived to be a result of a political discourse where Pakistan was painted as a fragile and dangerous state. This assessment of the sociopolitical situation was particularly evident in the narratives of young Pakistani women who were politically active. For them, the discourse on Pakistan in British media and politics was connected to a grander agenda of counter terrorism:

> I think Pakistanis tend to suffer more because the point of Islamophobia is that you justify an unjustified war and that war is being fought in Pakistan. You know I used to take a bus and they used to play this news on the radio, a crappy tabloid. And three to four times every week there would be some lame news about some Ali or Usman Pakistanis who was being tried in some court on some terrorist suspicion, his trial date is moved forward or back. And the reason why they do this is because they want to keep that fear alive that these people are a real threat and every single one of them is plotting against you all the time […] normally it is the Pakistanis and it makes sense because the War is being fought in Afghanistan and Pakistan right now so you have to create a real fear amongst the British public that if we are using millions and billions of your tax pounds it's justified because these people are monsters and we have to combat this threat.
> —Amna, North West1, 28, Graduate (Social Sciences), Overseas

Amna's response, in particular, drew on the political elements of a war which, at that point, was 'being fought' in the Af-Pak region. The borders of this war have now shifted to the Middle East—in particular, Syria and the Levant—yet the place of Pakistan in the socio-political discourse continues to be located within a wider discourse of terrorism. This is particularly evident in the difficulty faced by Pakistani students in getting student visas for universities in Britain (Havergal 2015). However, the extent to which such sentiments about Pakistan were normalized was highlighted in Hafsa's narrative. She sat for a law exam, and was offended by a case study in their paper:

> Case study around Rushdie [...] anyway people are arrested on terrorism act ... this is all about how media covers the guilt of the people [...] they called them 'terrorists' [...] And the reason why I had issue with it is because they use the word Pakistan [...] statements like 'fanatics' 'hate preachers'[...] The issue that I had, yeah [...] you can talk about all these things [...] but you cannot name a particular place or region [...] but the point is that I went and checked back and in every single paper up till that year every single question that was a problem question instead of having a country named, it used to have country A country B, something like this. But in this year, in this paper, after this event, they decided very happily to write Pakistan. I complained that you know we are all sensitive about this issue [...] [the teacher] could have used this entire situation that is completely fair but why did she call it Pakistan [...] you cannot say that. This can be a reality but in a paper you can't do that. You can't prejudice Pakistani students who take them seriously. You don't know that we might even have, you know my friend has had an uncle killed by terrorists in Pakistan and she was giving that paper. So you can imagine how upset she was when she came out of the paper. It affected me more, because I hadn't slept for the past four days [...] so this was like the last straw kind of thing. I completely literally felt like I was going to fail the paper [...] And then I like passed, I got a low grade [...] I don't know how and I have a feeling that they on purpose passed me because they didn't want me to take this up as a proper proper issue.
>
> —Hafsa, North East1, 22, Graduate (Law), Overseas

The normalization of a narrative of insecurity about Pakistan is reflected in the lack of thought that went into planning an exam taken by both Pakistani and non-Pakistani students. The case study further included 'words like dangerous fanatics' who were 'coming from completely different traditions' and 'spoiling the country's ancient traditions', which she believed was akin to the rhetoric employed by the British National Party (BNP) that was active at that time. Hafsa's narrative further proves Sayeeda Warsi's claim that 'Islamophobia' has 'passed the dinner-table test' (Anthony 2011), though one could argue that, in 2016, it has moved well beyond the dinner table, becoming an acceptable part of the British social psyche. Added to this acceptance is the problem of non-reporting, with Pakistani and Muslim students ignoring such incidents of Islamophobia or Pakophobia out of fear of attracting unwanted attention to themselves. The extent to which such a fear interferes in the everyday lives of young Pakistanis is reflected in the case of the Justice for North West 10 (J4NW10) campaign, which was ongoing when Hafsa's teacher decided to use the Pakistani terrorist as a case study in her exam paper.

Justice for North West 10: Securitizing Pakistanis

In April 2009, 12 students, 11 of whom were Pakistani, were arrested on suspicion of terrorism. They were condemned by media and politicians, only later to be exonerated by the judicial system on grounds of insufficient evidence. Despite their innocence proven in a court of law, 'deportation orders' were issued against the students who remained in custody; 10 students appealed against the deportation, and the J4NW10 campaign was initiated for the release of these detainees. However, 8 students eventually voluntarily went back to Pakistan while two remained in prison appealing against the deportation.[3] In May 2010, these two students, Abid Naseer and Ahmed Faraz Khan, eventually were allowed to stay 'when a judge ruled that' while the 'two Pakistani students posed a serious threat to national security' they 'could not be deported because of

---

[3] For more information, see https://sites.google.com/site/j4nw10/Home.

the risk they would be tortured or killed in their own country' (Cobian and Norton-Taylor 2010). Hafsa's case study in the exam further alluded to the North West 10 with statements such as 'terrorists' taking 'advantage of the human rights act', 'not deported' but 'living on free housing benefits', which for Hafsa and her Pakistani Muslim friends was clearly about this case. Hafsa also believed that, even though they were acquitted, the Pakistani students in the North West 10 case were treated as though they were terrorists simply because they came from Pakistan:

> Interviewer: Do you think what happened to Manchester 10 from Pakistan would have happened with any other nationality.
> Hafsa: It wouldn't have happened with Indians. It was a combination. Definitely not Indian Hindus, potentially Indian Muslims but probably not because they don't perceive India as violent [...] I think with Arabs they have that Saudi Arabia thing looming on their head [...] at this point in time they know Pakistan does not have much power why not. If it was a weaker Arab country, yeah why not them even.
> [...]
> It all has to do with power. It is all about the power.
> —Hafsa, North East1, 22, Graduate (Law), Overseas

The power that Hafsa highlights is the same power that reduces Pakistan and its citizens to a high risk country, where they enter Britain as a hyper-securitized subject to be placed under surveillance. Despite the innocence of the Pakistani students involved, the J4NW10 campaign was primarily initiated and supported by lawyers and leftist parties. The response of the Pakistani and Muslim student body studying in universities in England was cautious, if not completely absent. Amna, who was active in this campaign, describes the difficulty she had in getting students involved:

> The problem is that this issue is so controversial that the last thing a Pakistani student wants to do is get involved in this. I did have some *gora*[4] friends over there, who were willing to get involved but Pakistani students

---

[4] Gora meaning 'White'.

were staying away from this. Even my own brother, I didn't tell him anything because if I told him that I was involved in this campaign, and you know he would have this fear that 'I working here and you involved in such activities and they will think that I am also a terrorist you know' [...] so I didn't tell them anything. There is a fear that anyone who is Muslim who gets involved in such activities will be labelled a terrorist and be picked up.
—Amna, North West1, 28, Graduate (Social Sciences), Overseas

The fear of being picked up, for being mistaken for a terrorist—one that was evident in Muslim students' responses to ISocs in Chap. 4—is also a factor that determines the behaviour of Pakistanis in Britain. There are acceptable and unacceptable political causes, the J4NW10 despite being about Pakistani students who were acquitted was considered an unacceptable campaign. Amna even approached her university's ISoc but they chose to stay away from this campaign. Yet, even though the same Muslim students supported the Palestinian cause, either directly or indirectly, they were apprehensive about this campaign. The FOSIS representative highlights the reluctance of Islamic societies and Muslim students to become involved in such campaigns.

With this, I think it is a new phenomenon and people don't know how to deal with it, and because it effects directly your position here, I think the fear of physical harm is a lot closer. It is much easier to support something far away than something that is so close.
—FOSIS Representative (2011)

The danger of association, whether physical harm from a would-be terrorist, or being picked up by security agencies, results in a sense of self-censorship; students, while passively supporting different campaigns, will not actively get involved. Campaigning for a cause such as J4NW10 is further problematic because of the negative hype that was generated by the media. Students were also unsure about the facts of the case. However, in their discussion of this campaign, students also mentioned the problematic nature of political campaigning for Pakistan. Tamana notices this problem:

> I think Pakistan is [...] so corrupt. What is the point of you doing something you know what I mean? Whereas Gaza is more to do with children dying and more to do with you know [...] I think Muslim students watch Al Jazeera. I think Gaza is mentioned more there but Pakistan is not mentioned there.
> —Tamana, West Yorkshire2, 19, Undergraduate (Social Sciences), British

The corruption that plagues Pakistan, together with the internal problems of the country, was enough to term any political campaigning for Pakistan almost illegitimate against the more legitimate support for Palestine where children are dying. Campaigns against drone attacks, which also include children dying, were still considered too controversial, given Pakistan's dismal record of democracy. Even Pakistani students, however, were staying away from the J4NW10 campaign out of fear of 'getting into trouble':

> There are things which are complicated and I could be in a lot of trouble with my parents for doing that because they are worried about me. It is not because they don't want me to, it's because they are worried about me. You know they keep saying that when we had a protest the only thing we kept being worried about was that we might say something which might be the next big thing on Pakistani media and you know we might be pointed fingers at for it. So there are things where you just have to play it safe. I don't know if it sounds logical or right but there are some things which may not be a certain way which could actually get you into a lot of trouble which you were actually not intending or looking for.
> —Tasneem, North West1, 21, Undergraduate (Social Sciences), Overseas

The fear that Tasneem points to is different from that of Amna's brother, yet both are afraid of being singled out by security agencies of their respective countries. The fact that, in the case of J4NW10, the students accused were acquitted by a British court of law was irrelevant, since there was always this Orwellian fear of 'things [...] may not be a certain way which could actually get you into a lot of trouble'. However, for overseas Pakistanis, the added fear was also their insecure status in Britain as students on a British visa.

> Even if people want to take part in such a thing they would refrain from doing it given it will affect their immigration or visas [...] I would think I don't want to screw up my own visa by getting involved in something like this [...] even if people want to get involved the last thing they would want is to get deported in the middle of your study.
> —Nazia, London3, 28, Graduate (Social Sciences), Overseas

Amna, who was involved in the campaign, also highlighted similar issues with her friends who were afraid their visas might be revoked, or those on government scholarships might lose their funding. Yet, the problem was not so much about political causes as it was about Pakistan and, in particular, the J4NW10 that involved Pakistanis who were suspected of terrorism. The Pakistani-terrorist link was the reason Pakistanis were afraid of becoming involved, even though these same students were involved in other causes, such as Palestine.

> I actually saw that those same people who were very active for Palestine and Gaza were not active for Pakistan which really bothered me. I thought they would be apolitical by nature, but a lot of the Pakistanis did not help me at all with the deportation campaign [...] for two reasons. First of all, everyone is sympathetic for Gaza, Pakistan has a very bad image [...] and secondly everyone was supporting Gaza so you don't feel singled out. It's Lebanese, Egyptian, Gora, heterosexuals, homosexuals, old, young, children [...] The same people told me that we are not taking any part in any protest for Pakistan because that is a political issue. Gaza for them is a Muslim issue [...] This is all the Pakistanis.
> —Amna, North West1, 28, Graduate (Social Sciences), Overseas

Reiterating the preceding discussion on Palestine, Amna's narrative illustrates how Palestine, for many, was viewed as a more Muslim concern, where human rights of fellow Muslims were being violated. It was also a campaign that did not involve a 'fear of getting into trouble' because it was a more widely 'accepted' cause. It was not viewed as something political in nature, where the act of protesting did not translate into political action but, rather, a demonstration of solidarity with Muslims whose rights were violated. While Palestine fell in the domain of a more Muslim issue, Pakistan, despite being a majority Muslim country, was viewed with suspicion. Zebunnisa, who was a member of her university's

Pakistani society's executive committee, observes this phenomenon amongst Pakistani Muslim students in her university:

> when you get involved with Pakistani issues, there is a lot of corruption involved, other third party issues involved which turns off people [...] Palestine there is no such issue. They unite on only one thing we are Muslims, we want our freedom. There is no corruption, no such problem. If you know Palestinians they are very passionate and united people. I think that is why people and Pakistanis it is overall they agree with the agenda of Palestinian people than Pakistan. It stems from the fact that with Pakistani issues it is not just religion [...] but other things. Unity in Palestinians is what inspires Pakistanis to be a part of that, because we don't have that, and that is what we look up to with the Palestinians.
> —Zebunnisa, North West1, 21, Undergraduate (Law), Overseas

The students who were staying away from the Pakistan campaign were Pakistanis themselves, yet the unity and legitimacy associated with the Palestinian cause made it more appealing, even to Pakistanis, at a time when their fellow Pakistani students were being deported after being acquitted in a court of law. The representative of the national student association for Pakistani students, an organization comprising of British/Pakistani students and alumni, also noticed how its own student association was quick to respond to the Gaza crisis, but was reluctant to become involved with politically sensitive issues pertaining to Pakistan. However, while students were clear in distancing themselves from Pakistan politically, the case of Dr Aafia Siddiqui, a Pakistani neuroscientist who was convicted of terrorism after being extradited to the USA (Al Jazeera 2008; Walsh 2009), was perceived differently, especially by the British Pakistanis. Her name came up in the accounts of three different British Pakistanis, who perceived her as a 'Muslim' woman who was being persecuted for her Muslimness. Kiran, for instance, was willing to get involved in campaigns for Dr Siddiqui, perceived as a humanitarian cause:

> Interviewer: Why Aafia Siddiqui?
> Kiran: Because I think I am inclined towards humanitarian causes. I can sympathize with her as many people do. Any area where human rights are being affected I think it is important.
> —Kiran, London1, 22, Graduate (Science), British

Zahra, a student in West Yorkshire2, shared similar sentiments. Her ISoc was actively involved in the case of Aafia Siddiqui which, despite her Pakistani nationality, was perceived as an issue of human rights in relation to Islam, not Pakistan.

> Because of what happened to her. She is Muslim and on that basis […] if you imagine yourself in that situation. Really how she is being brutalized. She didn't even do anything. I find it strange that people can characterize, you don't need evidence. It is like you are Muslim and you don't need any evidence for it.
> —Zahra, West Yorkshire2, 19, Undergraduate (Social Sciences), British

Hafiza, another British Pakistani, also expressed her support for Siddiqui who was, again, considered a victim of Islamophobia. Ironically, the case of the J4NW10, where there was clear evidence on the basis of which the Pakistani students were acquitted, was still considered to be an unclear cause, where one would never know what really happened, or could get into trouble. The case of Aafia Siddiqui, where a court of law—albeit an American court—had found her guilty, was not considered problematic; she was believed to be innocent. Even though the Pakistanis in the J4NW10 campaign were Muslims, the Muslim affinity was missing for them; however, in the case of Aafia Siddiqui that affinity, the need to defend the rights of a fellow Muslim being persecuted, was strongly felt by Muslim women. The extent to which their involvement was the result of a fellow Muslim woman being persecuted instead of a Muslim man was unclear; however, given their support for Palestine, the gender of the 'victim' may in fact have been irrelevant. While no Pakistani in this study expressed any affinity to this cause, it was still evident that young Pakistanis were also more willing to get involved in campaigns for Muslim causes, as opposed to campaigns related to Pakistan.

The extent to which this is true for other Muslim nationalities is a question that needs further investigation. Between 2009 and 2011, when the Arab Spring—i.e. revolutions in the Middle East—started gaining momentum, the participants interviewed during this time were well aware of these revolutions and openly supported them. Even those who did not attend a protest still verbalized their support. The universities that were visited for the purpose of these interviews had banners supporting these revolutions. Yet, with Pakistan the narrative shifted, as Faiza points out:

> I think no one is willing to get their hands dirty in politics, in a country where politicians are powerful. In Palestine the politicians aren't powerful. Pakistan might be a developing country but still their politicians are 'powerful'. I don't think nobody wants to mess around with people like that.
> —Faiza, West Yorkshire2, 22, Undergraduate (Humanities), British

The narratives of these young women suggest an active interest in international affairs, particularly those relating to human rights and Muslims. However, there is a sense of dissociation with politics and Pakistan, as evident in the nature of caution adopted by Pakistani students about campaigning for Pakistan. Such a sense of caution raises important questions about the perceived freedom to protest without 'getting into trouble', where apathy becomes an insufficient reason, particularly where support for Muslim causes such as Palestine exists. As Pakistani students are more willing to engage in Muslim causes—as opposed to Pakistani campaigns, where the Pakistani identity is seen as more high risk than the Muslim identity—an understanding of Islamophobia and the way it is internalized needs to consider the relevance of certain politicized ethnic identities and nationalities. The reason for such lack of involvement could be twofold. Either the Pakistani identity is not sufficiently significant to warrant a response from students, or there is an actual fear that such involvement might lead to the experience of *Pakophobia* through the dreaded association of being a *Pakistani*. The answer to this query can be found in Malika's response to the problem of student campaigning for Pakistan, which is to convert the issue into one effecting Muslims, rather than 'just Pakistanis':

> I would say that in a situation like that if it wasn't just Pakistani students but Muslim students of other racial descent, if they got together as well and they protested. It would probably, like these people the government, probably wouldn't have as much power to you know falsely accuse the students and just deport them back to their home countries. Because if it's like only

Pakistani students they would be like oh they are all to be tied with the same rope. But if it were Muslim students of other descents, they would also care about the image that they are portraying of themselves by like deporting students just because they are Muslims, just deporting them back because they are acting up [...] but if they were only Pakistani students then it would be more dodgy.
—Malika, North West1, 22, Undergraduate (Social Science), Overseas

The more 'dodgy' nature of campaigning for Pakistan—which, in the context of 2016, could translate into campaigning for Syria—highlights how certain nationalities and ethnicities are more troubling within the Muslim category. For universities, the Counter Terrorism and Security Act 2015 will reinforce this sense of insecurity; young overseas Muslims who were already afraid of being 'picked up' would especially avoid political causes related to problematic countries such as Pakistan or Syria. Hence, not only is the Muslim connection a problem for young Muslims, as witnessed in the case of ISocs in Chap. 4, but also the ethnic-religious link lends itself to a hyper-securitized discourse about Muslims and their other identities.

Pakophobia, Islamophobia and the Pakistani Citizen in Britain

Experiences of discrimination and securitization are located within national and international events, with media and political actors shaping the place of 'vulnerable' identities in the socio-political imagination. The Muslim community presents itself as a potentially dangerous group, with young people perceived as being more prone to violence, despite the small percentage of Muslims who have turned to terrorism. However, the Muslim community is not a homogenous entity. With differences in sect, culture, race and ethnicity, different groups of Muslims may face different types of vulnerability, while located within a larger suspect category. This chapter highlighted one such group—the Muslim Pakistanis, who experience a form of hyper-securitization because of their association with two identities: 'both' of which 'are not seen as the best possible scenarios'

(Salma, North West1, 28, Business Graduate, Overseas). Pakistan's role in the 'war on terror', the Af-Pak problem, not to mention the Pakistani identity of certain radicals or extremists, has placed the Pakistani Muslim within a hyper-securitized group.

The chapter further focused on the experiences of Muslim Pakistani women in the UK who stand out because of their physical appearance, alluding to both their skin colour and their cultural dress—i.e. the *shalwar kameez*. However, the narratives highlighted how young people have internalized the insecurity around their Muslim Pakistani identity, where the Pakistani identity can be compromised but the Muslim identity is non-negotiable. Such compromises are evident not only in Mehreen's narrative of replacing her *shalwar kameez* with a Western dress to appear more 'acceptable' while retaining the hijab, but also in Abida's struggle to establish a Pakistani student society in a university where the ISoc is fully functional and thriving. The narratives also highlight the tense relationship that exists between Pakistani citizens and British citizens with a Pakistani heritage, with Pakistani women blaming British Muslim women's inability to adapt as the reason for the discrimination they face, when they are associated with the British Pakistanis. British Pakistanis, however, are critical of the Pakistani lifestyle; but they are also disconnected from Pakistan, which has become an imagined land of their forefathers, or a hotbed of terrorism and political corruption.

Such stereotypes and insecurities therefore translate into the kind of campaigns and causes that young people join, with the J4NW10 campaign falling under the category of 'dodgy' because of its links to Pakistan, while Palestine is perceived as a Muslim cause legitimate enough to be supported. The kind of Pakophobia, then, that comes through in the narratives is one where not only do Pakistanis feel targeted because of their Muslim Pakistani identity, but also where this insecurity is internalized, which leads to avoiding political causes linked to Pakistan, or the non-reporting of incidents of Pakophobic violence. The Pakistani Muslim problem, however, will persist until Muslims themselves do not actively challenge it. Such a challenge will involve a proactive role of not just British Muslims, but also Pakistanis visiting as students who either tolerate Pakophobic encounters, or simply avoid causes and campaigns that are directly linked to their rights as Pakistanis in Britain.

If the Muslims and Pakistanis over there are so paralyzed by fear you can't expect the leftist unions on their own to fight our wars for us. Only the people who are directly affected, which is the Pakistani students themselves, until or unless they don't take a very active stand, like a consistent active front role you know, until they don't start doing this, then it will happen […] This is most relevant to the Pakistani students and the problem is that they are most scared of this. Because all they want to do is to come to England, get their education out of the way and go back to Pakistan.

—Amna, Overseas, West Yorkshire1, 28, Graduate (Social Sciences), Overseas

The Muslim-Pakistani connection explored in this chapter further highlights the danger that other communities may face, when their ethnic or racial identities also become securitized. With the danger of Isis, the Muslim-Syrian link may create a greater level of vulnerability for Muslim communities, whether from Syria, or from those with links to the region. Hence, the phenomenon of Pakophobia as a form of Islamophobia should be taken as a lesson of caution so that other hyper-securitized communities are prevented from experiencing the same kind of vulnerabilities that not only challenge their place in Britain, but also makes one question the notion of 'British values' that could permit such discrimination against its Muslim communities.

Bibliography

Al Jazeera. (06/08/2008) *Pakistani doctor faces US trial.* AlJazeera. [Online]. Available from: http://www.aljazeera.com/news/americas/2008/08/20088574059161528.html (Accessed 11/10, 2012).

Allen, C. (2014) 'Operation Trojan Horse: examining the 'Islamic takeover' of Birmingham schools,' *The Conversation.* http://theconversation.com/operation-trojan-horse-examining-the-islamic-takeover-of-birmingham-schools-25764 (Accessed 11/10, 2015).

Anthony, A. (23/01/2011) *Sayeeda Warsi: A matter of pride and prejudice.* The Guardian. [Online]. Available from: http://www.guardian.co.uk/theobserver/2011/jan/23/observer-profile-baroness-warsi-islamophobia (Accessed 08/12, 2011).

Bernard-Donals, M.F. (1994) *Mikhail Bakhtin Between Phenomenology and Marxism*. Cambridge: Cambridge University Press.

Bhabha, H.K. (1998) Anxiety in the Midst of Difference. APLA Distinguished Lecture 1996, *PoLAR*, 21(1), pp. 123–137.

Cobian, I. and Norton-Taylor, R. (18/05/2010) *Two Pakistani students pose 'serious threat' but can stay in UK*. The Guardian. [Online]. Available from: http://www.guardian.co.uk/uk/2010/may/18/pakistani-students-terror-suspects-deportation (Accessed 06/05, 2011).

Croft, S. (2012) *Securitizing Islam Identity and the Search for Security*. Cambridge: Cambridge University Press.

Guimaraes, A.S.A. (2003) Racial insult in Brazil. *Discourse & Society*, 14 (2), pp. 133–151.

Havergal, C. (20/10/2015) *Visa refusal fears 'force UK universities out of international markets,'* Times Higher Education. Available from: https://www.timeshighereducation.com/news/visa-refusal-fears-force-uk-universities-out-of-international-markets (Accessed 02/03, 2016).

Kureshi, H. (2011) *Collected Essays*. London: Faber and Faber Ltd.

Mason, R. and Sherwood, H. (18/01/2016a) *Cameron 'stigmatising Muslim women' with English language policy*, The Guardian. Available from http://www.theguardian.com/politics/2016/jan/18/david-cameron-stigmatising-muslim-women-learn-english-language-policy (Accessed, 02/20, 2016).

Mason, R. and Sherwood, H. (18/01/2016b) *Migrant spouses who fail English test may have to leave UK, says Cameron*. The Guardian. Available from http://www.theguardian.com/uk-news/2016/jan/18/pm-migrant-spouses-who-fail-english-test-may-have-to-leave-uk (Accessed, 02/20, 2016).

Moreau, R. (09/04/2010) *Pakistan is the world's most dangerous country*. Newsweek. http://www.newsweek.com/pakistan-worlds-most-dangerous-country-72033 (Accessed 01/03, 2015).

Moreau, R. (20/10/2007) *Pakistan: The most dangerous?* Newsweek. Available from: http://www.newsweek.com/pakistan-most-dangerous-102955 (Accessed 01/03, 2015).

Parekh, B. (2010) What is Multiculturalism? In *The Ethnicity Reader Nationalism, Multiculturalism and Migration*, eds. M. Guibernau and J. Rex, Cambridge: Polity Press, pp. 238–243.

Pearson, G. (1976) Paki-Bashing in a North East Lancashire Cotton Town: A case study and its history. In *Working class youth culture*, eds. G. Mungham and G. Pearson, London: Routledge, pp. 48–81.

Saeed, T. and Johnson, D. (2016) Intelligence, global terrorism and higher education: Neutralising threats or alienating allies? *British Journal of Educational Studies*, 64(1), pp.37–51.

Saunders, F.S. (2016) Where on Earth are you. *London Review of Books*, 38(5), pp.7–12. Available from: http://www.lrb.co.uk/v38/n05/frances-stonorsaunders/where-on-earth-are-you (Accessed 03/03, 2016).

Singh, I. (2004) Language, Thought and Representation. In *Language, Society and Power*, eds. L. Thomas, S. Wareing, I. Singh, J.S. Peccei, J. Thornborrow and J. Jones, Second ed. UK: Routledge, pp. 17–33.

Walsh, D. (24/11/2009) *The mystery of Dr Aafia Siddiqui*. The Guardian. [Online]. Available from: http://www.guardian.co.uk/world/2009/nov/24/aafia-siddiqui-al-qaida (Accessed 11/10, 2012).

6

Challenging Islamophobia and the Security Discourse: Dialogue and the Muslim Activist

In pursuing the discussion on securitization and Islamophobia, this chapter explores how young Muslim women are challenging the dominant discourse that informs their realities as discussed in Chaps. 2, 3, 4, and 5, by the simple act of *answering back*. While they may not change the meta-narrative on Muslims and terrorism, these pockets of dialogue are nonetheless important in altering perceptions at the individual and community levels. Mikhail Bakhtin's discussion on dialogics captures this ability; he observes how '[t]he word, directed toward its object, enters a dialogically agitated and tension-filled environment of alien words, value judgements and accents, weaves in and out of complex interrelationships, merges with some, recoils from others' all of which 'may crucially shape discourse, may leave a trace in all its semantic layers, may complicate its expression and influence its entire stylistic profile' (Bakhtin 1981: 276). Bakhtin's discussion situates human interaction in a historical and political context where individuals may be submerged within socio-historically defined categories laden with value judgments and complex interrelationships. Such 'dialogics' locate individual or community interactions in a meta-narrative about their identities that defines their ability, their language to communicate, to understand and respond. Yet, it is this ability to communicate within an environment that may be restrictive, where the individual voice, although in danger of being consumed by a dominant discourse, still manages to interact with the meta-narrative, to answer back—that is where hope for change is found.

The chapter therefore examines these pockets of resistance and dialogue, between young people in universities and outside, in the university common room and on the streets, as they attempt to take control of a meta-narrative that continues to inform and impact their everyday lives. While the space to engage in such dialogue has become more difficult with legislation such as the Counter Terrorism and Security Act 2015, young Muslims are still successful in changing perceptions in their individual capacities, thereby fulfilling their role as proactive British Muslim citizens.

The Power of Dialogue

In his discussion on dialogue, Bakhtin places the individual 'I' as 'a product of a process of self-creation in interaction or dialogue with the "other" in a historically located world' (Flood 1999: 159–160). It is the location of the individual within a historical and socio-political context where the dialogue can reinforce, but also contradict and challenge, meanings and themes associated with utterances and individuals. Bakhtinian dialogics identify 'the way in which humans encounter one another and enter into a consummating relationship', where this encounter is situated within the wider social discourse, where 'dialogue' takes the form of a 'cognitive-ethical event' (Bernard-Donals 1994: 35). Bakhtin's discussion of the socio-historical position of the individual and this ongoing 'cognitive-ethical event'—i.e. the dialogue—is important in understanding the narratives in this chapter. The narratives are located within the meta-narrative of Islam and radicalization as discussed in the preceding chapters, which is beyond the individual's control, and interrupts and influences the vocabulary of communication that is adopted both by young Muslims and by those with whom they are in dialogue. Roberts (2012), in discussing the Bakhtinian dialogue in relation to other theories—such as Habermas' notion of 'speech-acts'—emphasizes the importance of such contradictions and complexities of real world situations, where human interaction and dialogue permits the possibility of leaving 'a trace', or complicating a dominant 'expression' (Bakhtin 1981: 276). However, the 'other' is central, since 'humans are radically "other" in relation to each other, but it is this relationship that defines human understanding' (Bernard-Donals 1994: 43).

For Gurevitch (1990), dialogue is a 'social act' that is based on an 'ethics of dialogue'. This ethics involves 'the obligation to speak', 'to listen' and 'to respond'; it moves beyond simple everyday conversation to become a recognition of the Other, (1990: 186), where 'a person is then regarded not as power or a resource to be used, but as a person to be seriously recognized' (1990: 194). For Cowan and Arsenault, in their discussion of dialogue in relation to diplomacy, understanding at the international or national level 'begins with dialogue between individuals, whether they are representatives of governments or private citizens' which eventually 'evolve[s]' into 'a broader "dialogue between civilizations"' (2008: 17). Parekh connects the discussion of dialogue to 'multicultural' Britain, 'a way towards understanding, and towards a common framework that conceived of the plurality of perspectives as something positive—not as an impediment but as an opportunity for self-improvement and collective learning' (Parekh 2008, cited by Modood and Dobbernack 2011: 60). Power dynamics, though, are constantly at play, where the recognition of the 'self' and 'other', or understanding 'between civilizations', is located within a power struggle against a dominant discourse, where there is a danger of the dialogue taking the shape of a 'monologue' (see also Cowan and Arsenault 2008), where the missing element is the recognition of the 'other' and their ability to speak, and the 'self's' ability to 'listen'. The Bakhtinian dialogue recognizes this power struggle, yet hope is found in the ability of different narratives to intersect, even though they never reach a concrete conclusion, since meanings are constantly changing through human interaction. The struggle of young Muslims to engage in a dialogue is located within such a context where meanings and narratives external and internal to the dialogue intersect, influence and interrupt the interaction between individuals and communities.

The extent to which Muslim women are submerged in a wider discourse that further influences their interactions and ability to engage in such dialogues is clearly illustrated in the British Prime Minister David

Cameron's call for Muslim women to learn English, as discussed in Chap. 2, where the 'outsider' status of the Muslim immigrant, but also that of other Muslim citizens whose first language is English, is reinforced. It is these meanings and themes around their identity, this securitized discourse, that young Muslims are attempting to challenge so that they may (re)claim their place as equal and valued members of British society.

Individuals and Dialogues: Changing Perceptions

> [S]ometimes you just don't want people to have that bitterness. I would rather build a relationship and even if you know the first five times we meet for coffee and they hate being there and they hate talking to me maybe on the sixth time they might say actually I am going to start thinking about this. I am going to stop making certain comments because sometimes if it is done through the system then yeah they can put on their record that this was addressed and such and such was dealt with but it hasn't actually been dealt with because like it has to be a long term thing.
> —Nadia, West Yorkshire2, 20, Undergraduate (Law), British

The narratives of young Muslim women in this book have highlighted how the security discourse impacts their everyday existence, leaving a sense of insecurity about the Muslim identity in the British social imagination. For young women, their experiences of Islamophobia and Pakophobia are linked to such exaggerated and sensationalist accounts in media reports, with people reacting to Muslims out of ignorance and a misunderstanding about their religious beliefs and practices. In order to remedy this misunderstanding, many of the young people who took part in this study decided to take on the responsibility of changing mindsets themselves, through the basic act of dialogue.

Nadia shared examples of her conversations with individuals who had insulted her, or accused her of being a radical because of her physical appearance. She takes pride in the fact that through these conversations and dialogues these misconceptions were challenged, where individuals ended up apologizing for their Islamophobic behaviour. Farzana also emphasizes the importance of dialogue, which is a 'responsibility' for young Muslims; they need to explain to their friends and colleagues why they practise their religion the way they do. For her, it is important to become 'positive role models', to challenge all the negativity that surrounds Muslims (Farzana, South West1, 20, Undergraduate (Medicine), British; see also Brown and Saeed 2015: 1962). For Farzana, these small steps may go a long way to removing misconceptions, especially for those individuals who are completely ignorant of what Islam or Muslims stand for, those whose only source of information is the media. Tehmina has encountered students in universities who are clueless about Muslims and Islam:

> I think universities are seen as a bizarre place around with some international students, people from different walks of life, many have not had the opportunity of embracing other people's culture, some have, some are quite narrow minded and don't want to […] I know a student who came to see me and didn't know that you don't call someone Islamic you call them Muslim. Islamic is something completely different and she said I haven't met, I don't know any Islamic people […] Again it's little things like that, if they are willing to learn.
> —Tehmina, West Midlands1, 19, Undergraduate (Social Sciences), British

However, Tehmina in her narrative also expresses her frustration at having to engage in such a dialogue, particularly within the same university context where 'ignorance' is not an excuse. This is especially considered problematic in a context where young people are exposed to the Internet, which provides alternative narratives to the dominant discourse on Islam.[1] Yet, Tehmina in her own capacity does not shy away from such engagement. She is more politically active in her student union, while being involved with different youth led initiatives outside the university, in her community. For her, the only way to disrupt the dominant discourse about Muslims and insecurity is to become an active member of society.

Nazia, who is part of a more internationally diverse student group in central London, has also moved beyond the medium of dialogue, taking

---

[1] See The Active Change Foundation (2015) #NotInMyName.

active steps to become more involved with her friends and other students in order to overcome such misconceptions. In a social gathering among colleagues and friends, Nazia was confronted with a fellow student who, on finding out that she was Muslim, declared that 'all Muslims were terrorists', an incident that was upsetting for her. While she debated with the girl, the fact that, in a university context, there were such students who held Islamophobic beliefs was disturbing; something she sought to change.

> I never thought about reporting it. I think it was after this incident that something in my thought process changed. I am not much of a party person […] how many glasses of juice can you have you know […] I am not very keen to go out and hang out with a group who drinks because I don't drink […] for me seeing people get drunk is not my definition of fun but I made an effort to hang out more only because they would understand I am a regular person. I am a Muslim, I don't miss my prayers. I am a practising Muslim as they call me but at the same time I am a girl just like them who wants to have fun. Who wants to go for a movie, go to the dance floor. I will not drink that is fine but I will sit and make fun of you guys when you are drunk […] I would make more effort to stand up and represent myself as a Muslim, female and Pakistani. People don't make that effort to change mindsets because it requires a lot of energy, a lot of effort […] people I would come across would say I don't care. It is unfortunate.
> —Nazia, London3, 28, Graduate (Social Sciences), Overseas

Nazia's efforts did pay off, as many of her colleagues who had previously been hesitant in interacting with her became good friends. However, the level of hesitation that exists, even in multicultural university contexts, is evident from the fact that Nazia did not dress like a Muslim—wearing a hijab, jilbab or niqab—but, rather, wore Western clothes yet confronted such discrimination. As discussed in Chap. 3, Muslim women encounter some form of Islamophobia, but those with the niqab or hijab face the most direct form of Islamophobic abuse. These women who look Muslim are also trying harder to ensure that the barrier of misunderstanding and ignorance is removed between them and others, both inside and outside the university.

> Non-Muslim girls as well will feel that hijab is a barrier. So that is where Muslim women need to make people feel that it shouldn't be a barrier, that

we are no different. For me I was quite involved in activism on campus, talking to people, it doesn't matter if there were Muslims or not but through that interaction people would talk more. I had people tell me that before I met you I wouldn't have approached a girl with a hijab and I realized actually you are no different, you do talk to people. So you do have these misconceptions, more so with the niqab as well.

—FOSIS Representative (2011)

Given media and political discourse about Muslims and their religion, where any attack by a terrorist who abuses the name of Islam results in the Muslim community being dragged into the spotlight, forced to defend their religion and place in Western society, such acts by young people are important in raising awareness within local communities. They may not change the dominant discourse, but even a 'trace' of an alternative point of view (Bakhtin 1981: 276) can go a long way in promoting understanding and dialogue between communities. However, while some practise such individual activism, Amna highlights the frustration that many others face:

the problem with Muslims is also that they get emotional before engaging with someone. So my flat mate had this problem she would defend Islam for no reason. Like at one point […] she was debating with someone that she can't have vinegar because it has trace amounts of alcohol, so that person was debating with her that why are you so fussy, so instead of engaging with her she became all emotional. 'You don't understand my religion, in this country I have to explain myself all the time.' Of course you have to because for them it's a foreign religion, a foreign nationality. So, at least with the public, you should respond differently, you should engage with them more and at the government level your response should be different, you should be lobbying against the government and their laws.[2] With the public it helps to engage and if they say stupid things like your men get married four times, engage with them. Tell them it's true and it's also not true. And the more they interact with Muslim women and Muslim people, the more they realize that these people are not anything less than human, they are just like us.

—Amna, North West1, 28, Graduate (Social Sciences), Overseas

---

[2] Amna is referring to the Terrorism Act 2006 (See HM Government 2006).

While young Muslims are talking back, and trying to influence the wider narrative, many like Amna's friend also feel that the burden of engaging in a dialogue to prove ones normality is unjustly placed on them. Amna's narrative is also important from another perspective. Not only does it highlight the frustration felt by many Muslims who often do not want to engage in a conversation about their beliefs, but it also demonstrates the difference between a non-British Muslim in the UK and a British Muslim. While Amna can dismiss the ignorance of others on the basis of the foreignness of her religion and Pakistani identity, the British Muslim, for whom Britain is her home, where her religion is a part of that home, the excuse of foreignness does not hold true. There is a greater level of frustration felt in the constant need to explain one's own Muslim perspective. While such complexities within individual acts of dialogue remain, young people are nonetheless willing to have such debates. Their voice, their experiences and their success stories need to be highlighted. The need to project such positive images of Muslims is important, both for overcoming Islamophobia and for creating a sense of belonging. Farzana, in her discussion on positive role models, takes the discussion further by suggesting the need to include more members of staff and academics in educational institutions who wear the Islamic signifier:

> I know you can't just hire someone for that but stuff like that to see Muslims in a positive role, that is a nice thing [...] it seems a bit weird but it is a simple thing, you associate certain things with certain things. You see a Muslim person you associate negative things with that, so we need to try and get some positive thinking, educated know what they are talking about is good [...] people here associate things with things.
> —Farzana, South West1, 20, Undergraduate (Medicine), British

Raising awareness is not just confined to individual acts of dialogue; young Muslims are also using social media in an attempt to reclaim the narrative about their identities. The Internet provides a space to challenge the dominant discourse on a much larger scale than individual conversations. Campaigns such as #NotInMyName was launched by Muslims to unite against Isis and the perception that they were 'at risk' of being radicalized. The campaign also talks back to Isis propaganda on the Internet, clearly condemning it for 'abusing the name of Islam with their acts of terrorism'.[3]

While the discussion in this book focuses on Muslim women, their narratives also revealed how Muslim men are engaged in a similar dialogue. The responses to these dialogues vary, based on the level of the religious appearance of men and women; yet, for many young Muslims resisting the meta-narrative through individual acts of dialogue was a way forward. However, such conversations are not only taking place on an individual level, but also students, through ISocs and Pakistani student societies, are trying to promote a positive image of Muslims and Pakistan, and thereby attempting to take control of the wider narrative.

ISocs: Meet a 'Normal' Muslim

> The more normal you seem to people, I know it sounds horrible to say as such but the more as an equal you are seen, you don't segregate, the more involved and loud you are. You have amazing examples of societies who do this making sure that Muslims get involved in mainstream issues not just Muslim issues, also participating on campus, increasing their representation on campus, working with other individuals, interfaith things, also with regards to civil liberties issues and we make sure our services available to Islamic societies [...] We are also campaigning to make sure issues are made public, so we are working continuously.
>
> —FOSIS Representative (2011)

The FOSIS representative's attempt to normalize Muslim student presence highlights the extent to which Muslims, especially British Muslims, have become outsiders in their own country. This normality is placed against an abnormality that was highlighted in Chap. 3, that of being a 'ninja', or a 'lesbian', or 'one of them' against 'one of us'. The conversations that young Muslims are having are unfairly placed against legislation such as the Counter Terrorism and Security Act 2015, which puts them within the 'at risk' category; media and political rhetoric that accuses

---

[3] See The Active Change Foundation (2015) #NotInMyName.

them of being sympathetic to terrorist activities such as the Charlie Hebdo attacks, or the Paris attacks (Milmo 2015; TellMAMA 2015); and politicians that accuse parents of not doing enough to protect their Muslim children in Britain from being radicalized by extremist groups, such as Isis, based in the Middle East. This further results in Muslims and other ethnic groups mostly 'sticking together',

> I think there is a general common theme among campuses they do stick together. I think what forces them to stick together is the events going on, incidents that happen in university, comments made by lecturers or fellow students questioning their faith, how extreme things like that […] they think they are more safer and have a better university experience if they stick together […] but university is about having debate, discussion, dialogue […] students union is about being proactive […] student societies have a responsibility to facilitate this.
> —Tehmina, West Midlands1, 19, Undergraduate (Social Sciences), British

However, student organizations such as ISocs are further tainted within the moderate/extremist spectrum as highlighted in Chap. 4, where their attempts at dialogue are again placed within a wider discourse that constantly informs their place in the university and in society outside. Yet, ISocs and young Muslims are fighting against such odds, a struggle that is marred by obstacles that are often beyond their control. As Zubaida observes:

> If I was standing up for the rights of my culture or religion with all this ruckus around you, I would be scared. Probably I am chicken but I would want to stay out of it because of the impact it might have, be attacked. I think they are really brave when they go out and hand leaflets about Islam, and Islamic awareness and you know on fresher. I wish I could do that but I would be scared.
> —Zubaida, London1, 30, Graduate (Sciences), British Pakistani

ISocs, in their attempt to challenge the meta-narrative and engage in a dialogue with a wider audience, organize Islam Awareness events. The ISoc for a university in the South West England, for instance, organized a Discover Islam Week that started with an event to encourage 'an interactive interfaith discussion' with representatives of other religious communities, and included talks on the Bible and Islam, as well as a special talk dedicated to Coexistence Under Islam. Fliers of the event were given to all students, both Muslim and non-Muslim. The event was nominated by the Student Union for the university's Union awards, which recognizes successful student initiatives. However, while the nomination by the Student Union illustrates how the ISoc successfully connected with other societies and groups in the university, one of the speakers that was invited by the ISoc had been black-listed by the Centre for Social Cohesion in their report 'Radicalism on UK Campuses' (2010a). While the event was successful, the ISoc was nonetheless criticized for this one speaker, which again tainted the efforts of the student organization. In response to the problem of the speaker, the FOSIS representative highlighted how the Centre for Social Cohesion list of problematic speakers was more about its own agenda than the merits or demerits of the speaker in question.

The Islamic Awareness Week demonstrates the capability of Islamic societies to normalize the presence of Muslim students, creating a space for greater interaction amongst student groups. It also demonstrates the limitation of counter extremism initiatives where, instead of working in partnership with organizations that aim to root out extremism on campuses, students are often suspicious of the organizations themselves, viewed as being agenda-driven and biased. Whether there was an agenda or not, under the Counter Terrorism and Security Act 2015 the possibility of debating against such controversial speakers, especially for ISocs, has become next to impossible. This impossibility also means that the ability to present a counter argument to controversial narratives, such as those presented by such speakers, within the safe confines of a university has also become more difficult, thereby removing the most significant characteristic of a higher educational institution—that of debate and critical dialogue. As Tehmina notes:

> Every issue that happens locally or nationally, it makes a difference. Unfortunately, we don't have the room or a platform to debate these issues. Debate is the key thing.
> —Tehmina, West Midlands1, 19, Undergraduate (Social Sciences), British

Despite these constraints, ISocs are attempting to reach out to a wider audience. Other ISocs in West Yorkshire, for instance, publicized their Islamic Awareness Week talks on YouTube for the purposes of greater transparency, and the ability to engage with a larger audience outside the university. Speakers have included public intellectuals, as well as Muslim poets. Publicizing the event on YouTube also led to a greater willingness to interact with a non-Muslim and Muslim audience to challenge misconceptions about Islam. They have also scheduled specific events for the audience to ask questions about Islam. The ISoc, however, does not limit its advocacy to just one event but continues to organize awareness events throughout the academic year, such as a hijab workshop which invited Muslim and non-Muslim students to discuss the importance of the hijab, and provided a platform for asking questions and encouraging debate. While the ISoc continues to struggle with its tainted reputation, a result of its association with students who were later accused of extremism (as highlighted in Chap. 4), they are nonetheless active in challenging this association through dialogue. The use of the Internet by ISocs is important in reaching a wider audience. The ISoc for a university in the North West, for instance, created a Discover Islam website, providing a platform for visitors to ask questions about Islam. The websites also included messages from young Muslims with different degrees of religiosity, spreading their message of Islam as a peaceful religion.

ISocs are further working towards creating a 'safe' environment for Muslim students by encouraging them to come forward and talk about issues of Islamophobia. These conversations are also important in raising awareness and ensuring that young Muslims are not alienated by such experiences. As Tehmina observes:

> I think the Islamic societies, the Pakistani societies, they have a responsibility, that's the whole point of it. I know that there is of course the social experience around it, but I really think it's more about really being there and being a familiar face, so I think they definitely need training around it, something that I am trying to push here. I have worked in the equality and welfare, but I just want to be able to kind of deal with that kind of situation, and you know what would be the procedure through it. Again if it's like a racial incident people I think are quite quick to report racial incidents,

but I feel that when it's about Islamophobic remarks, people don't. They just feel like oh you know you are just making a big deal out of it, or you're paranoid.
—Tehmina, West Midlands1, 19, Undergraduate (Social Sciences), British

The experiences and encounters of the young people discussed in this book allude to such perceptions of paranoia. Often unsure about the intentions of the Islamophobe, young Muslims are quick to dismiss or ignore these incidents, perceiving it to be a result of ignorance or misunderstanding. In situations where students perceive hostility but never directly experience it, this fear of being paranoid or overly sensitive, or 'making a big deal' again, prevents young people from coming forward and complaining. ISocs therefore are instrumental in starting a dialogue on welfare in order to encourage young Muslims to come forward and speak about their experiences.

In order to further normalize Muslim student presence in universities, young Muslims have been successful in nurturing a close relationship with their Student Unions. Ahmed, the anti-racism officer in a university in London, for instance, launched an Islamophobia Awareness Month:

> on campus organized two main initiatives. First week-long exhibition with pictures in terms of headlines from the papers which were demonizing Muslims or portraying Muslims in a negative light. And also like some statistics about how the general British public felt about Muslims in terms of building mosques or Muslim schools or Muslim youth. So we had that exhibition in the Quad which is the hub of the Student Union and a lot of people were looking at that throughout the week. The second initiative was an event, the launch event for the whole month with (academics) and National Union of Students representatives talking about Islamophobia […] one talking about academia and Islamophobia […] other need to counter Islamophobia […] The atheist society was very welcoming of it […] brought everyone together against racism.
> —Ahmed, London3, Student Union Anti-racism Officer

Ahmed's example of an Islamophobia Awareness Month, which was intended to raise awareness about the problem of Islamophobia without targeting any particular student society or group, illustrates the success of such university initiatives. Ahmed's university quad is also open to the public, where the engagement of young Muslims was not just within the university, but also with members of the general public. The fact that all student societies, irrespective of their religious or ideological beliefs, were part of the event also illustrates the power of such dialogue in universities, which has the ability to influence the conversation within the wider community.

However, in cases where such events are not given a more public platform or are not adequately advertised, there is the problem of preaching to the choir, with a greater likelihood of those people attending who are either willing to engage and listen, or are already members or friends of ISocs:

> I think they are trying to raise awareness and I don't know but then when you do raise awareness you only see it with those people who are open-minded and would listen. But people who are more likely to do the discrimination, they wouldn't listen so I don't know, I have no idea how it can actually make a difference. Raising awareness I think is the best way but by raising awareness only some people will listen.
> —Zahra, West Yorkshire2, 19, Undergraduate (Social Sciences), British

The fact that young Muslims and ISocs are aware of such limitations is important, since they are attempting to remedy this problem through online initiatives that target a wider audience. Distributing fliers across and beyond university campuses that would encourage people to join such events is also a practice that continues, but young Muslims are aware of the need to do more:

> there is not enough publicity, it is always at a really small level. For example, when Muslim scholars are invited it is normally Muslims who attend such events. Out of a hundred or one hundred and fifty people only five will be non-Muslim. So we need Muslim students to publicize these events more. Also, it may seem more effective to organize conferences where academics are invited and people tend to participate more, rather than random lectures, since a conference is taken more seriously by students than

one lecture every now and then. I think even if we have a conference once a year, it will have a longer-term impact.
—Rukshanda, London2, 28, Graduate (Science), Overseas

Others, such as Kiran, highlight the possibility of making such religious events more fun to encourage attendance, so non-religious and non-Muslim people would be tempted to participate. FOSIS, for instance, organized a conference that brought academics, students, policy makers and the public together to discuss issues around radicalization and Islamophobia, thereby attracting a wider audience. With ISocs partnering up with Student Unions and other student organizations, as in the case of Ahmed, their outreach has increased. Tasneem's ISoc, for instance, has tried to be involved with the university Student Union, again with the aim of normalizing their presence:

> People do think them to be a little extreme. But I think within the last few years especially how the union functions here they have made a special effort to make sure that people don't get that image and what they have done is started supporting non-Muslim students to be candidates, they have stopped just picking people who are just Pakistani, Muslim or Asian, they are going out of their way to support everybody, giving a chance for people to be associated with them and get to know what they are.
> —Tasneem, North West1, 21, Undergraduate (Social Science), Overseas

Malika, who belongs to the same university as Tasneem, demonstrates how her attitude towards the Islamic society changed as a result of their activism:

> First year got the impression that they were religiously extreme, but when I got to know them, the events they had, got to know about the activities they are involved with, my opinion changed drastically. I realized these people are normal, not out of the world or something like that.
> —Malika, North West1, 22, Undergraduate (Social Science), Overseas

The success of ISocs in normalizing Muslim students, especially those who are stereotyped as extreme because of their religious garb, is important in regard to highlighting how these individual acts of dialogue are influencing the narrative within universities and local communities. The extent to which they can impact the wider discourse remains to be seen, as their activities are still securitized and suspect, as demonstrated in Chap. 4, but these individual acts are permitting an important conversation to take place. Tasneem and Malika, for instance, avoided the ISocs and Muslim students who appeared too religious, only to discover through such initiatives that they were 'normal' young women, 'not out of the world'. However, the space available for such conversations has shrunk because of the Counter Terrorism and Security Act 2015. Yet, the struggle for a counter narrative continues:

> I really believe that the key problem with Islamophobia is about perception, the fear of the unknown and they have particular perception of Muslims, you can't overcome it until you change that perception. How do we change that perception is by making sure Muslims are doing their part, making sure Muslims are involved in societies, making sure they are not given a reason to say they are not integrating doing this or that. So I think that for me is the key focus in what can be done.
> —FOSIS Representative 2011

PakSocs: Celebrating Pakistan

Within universities young Pakistanis, especially overseas Pakistanis, also decided to challenge the wider narrative around their identities, and the resultant Pakophobia, by portraying a positive image of Pakistan. As described in Chap. 5, overseas Pakistanis in particular found themselves caught in a double-bind: the Muslim-Pakistani connection that resulted in a hyper-securitized identity. As Nazia observes:

> One very big factor is obviously the media, where what you see on media becomes reality […] what they see on media becomes reality for them. I try to tell them that what you see on TV is 6–7 per cent of the population. Most of the people are like me. They will pray, they might cover their heads, they may not cover their heads. They are modest people who want

to send their children to school and have good jobs, and have a pension fund, and have electricity and water and security [...] the other reason is that we have just given up, we don't do much to showcase our culture and our country.
—Nazia, London3, 28, Graduate (Social Sciences), Overseas

For Nazia, this showcasing of the 'culture' of her country, Pakistan, was especially important in challenging the meta-narrative, in answering back to the dominant discourse of terrorism and Pakistan. Nazia, with the help of the Pakistan student society (Paksoc) at her university in London, organized events to promote a positive image of Pakistan. Nazia belonged to the same university as Ahmed, which had an open campus where the public could also take part in the events:

I will tell you something that happened, on Monday we just launched Pakistan week at [my university], we are showcasing one event [...] one movie every day ending with a Strings[4] concert. So Monday morning what we did was that we got this typical Pakistan bus with all the decorations on it, there is one in London. So the Pakistan society team came with the bus into the campus, parked the bus on campus and then a *dhol waala*[5] came in and there was a big random *dhol dhamaal*[6] which the Pakistani students did and every single person stepped out of the class to see what was going on and we had put up Pakistani flags and were wearing *shalwar kameez* and the girls and boys were all dancing on the team. Five of my own class fellows came up to me and said we so want to go to Pakistan [...] It was hardly for 10–15 minutes. They parked the bus and the rickshaw and I was like this is what the bus in Pakistan looks like and they were just amazed at me [...] I think just 15 minutes of that effort made people think about Pakistan differently, so we need to showcase Pakistan differently.
—Nazia, London3, 28, Graduate (Social Sciences), Overseas

The 10–15 minutes that Nazia highlights was enough for others to consider Pakistan in a different light, unlike the images in media reports of terrorism. The national Pakistani society in Britain connects Pakistanis

---

[4] A Pakistani music band.
[5] Referring to a person who plays the *dhol*, a local musical instrument that resembles drums.
[6] Dance and music.

with the Pakistani diaspora in order to build networks between Pakistan and Britain. The organization also acknowledged the need to promote a positive image of Pakistan:

> We understand that we are in a privileged position and we understand that that puts us in a particularly responsible position [...] we ought to be helping and nurturing a nation of people who are committed to progressive democratic Pakistan.
> —National Pakistani Society Representative 2010

For this purpose, this organization holds an annual conference that brings together Pakistani and British Pakistani students and young people working in Britain to discuss the political, economic and social problems of Pakistan with the aim of providing solutions. These solutions are not limited to the conference, but are sent to local parliamentarians in Pakistan. Such activism is geared towards using the skills and expertise of students and young Pakistanis abroad to bring change within Pakistan. Given the more academic nature of a conference—which has different panels and a parliamentarian style discussion format—students are less hesitant in attending such events. However, despite such events the efforts of young Pakistanis are often limited, especially in universities which have a small of percentage of Pakistani students and therefore lack Pakistani student organizations. Even in places where such student societies exist, not all are engaged in dealing with political issues related to Pakistan, out of fear of being singled out as highlighted in Chap. 5. Amna, who was trying to organize a protest against General Musharraf in 2007 when he imposed a state of emergency in Pakistan, encountered resistance or apathy from Pakistani student societies:

> When I spoke to the Pakistani society they told me sister we are not political, we aren't religious this is just about partying because we want to show that Pakistanis can also have fun. I was like I am totally with you, for the *halwa purri*[7] parties and the *Eid-ul-fitr*[8] parties, I totally endorse that I am not against it but this is an issue which is relevant to your country, and you can do something and you have a luxury that you can protest over here

---

[7] Local breakfast.
[8] Celebratory event to mark the end of Ramadan, the month of fasting for Muslims.

when our people can't protest in Pakistan so we should really make use of this opportunity
>—Amna, North West1, 28, Graduate (Social Sciences), Overseas

Whether young Pakistanis are political or not, the fact that these pockets of dialogue and the efforts to create a positive image of Pakistan exist is where the possibility of a counter narrative is found, even if the appeal is at a local rather than a national level. For the Paksocs, despite many being apolitical, their efforts are still essential in challenging the negative image of Muslims and Pakistanis. As Tasneem illustrates:

anything that can promote peace, promote a good image of us Muslims and we can get something out of it we are happy to raise our voice for it and stand by it.
>—Tasneem, North West1, 21, Undergraduate (Social Science), Overseas

Furthermore, given the link between Islamophobia and Pakophobia, attempts to promote a positive image of Muslims or Pakistanis will be instrumental in countering both levels of discrimination. It is for this reason that such initiatives need to be supported not only by universities, but also by government agencies that are trying to counter extremism on campuses and in British society at large. Despite the limitations, these initiatives are important in creating a sense of belonging and shared purpose. As Ahmed observes:

On the national level I think the narrative has to change so that Muslims aren't seen as like the fifth pillar in society or people who harbour intentions that are destructive to the rest of society. That kind of narrative which is portrayed now has to change. And that can be changed by engaging in the media, engaging in politics having politicians who are well informed and speak out against Islamophobia when they see it. I think that process is happening and I am quite optimistic about the future in terms of the national picture. I think campuses are just a subset of that national picture, if the national picture changes I think the campuses will also change. So that is why it is important to not just focus on campuses but also be engaged in the national campaign against Islamophobia as well.
>—Ahmed, London3, Student Union Anti-racism Officer

The 'Dialogic' Necessity: Beyond Phobias and (In)securities

'Dialogue is a manifest phenomenon' which 'for schematic purposes [...] can be reduced to a minimum of three elements [...] an utterance, a reply, and a relation between the two', with 'the conviction that what is exchanged has meaning' (Holquist 1990: 38; see also Zavala 1990; Loriggio 1990). It is this meaning in the dialogue between young Muslims and other members of society that has the possibility of having an impact on the local and national narrative about Islam, Pakistan and terrorism. These efforts of young Muslims and Pakistanis in resisting the overarching discourse about their identities through the simple act of dialogue is important to recognize and strengthen in a context where the Muslim identity continues to be securitized. The narratives in this book have highlighted how the dominant discourse has an impact on the everyday lives of young Muslims, especially Muslim women, who are implicated because of their association with a religion or ethnicity. With legislation such as the Counter Terrorism and Security Act 2015, Muslims will continue to be framed within a security discourse which, instead of engaging with them, has created further suspicion and distrust within and outside educational institutions. Yet, the narratives also reveal how young Muslims are moving forward, struggling to ensure that they are not confined by such meta-narratives. Such efforts demonstrate pockets of resistance across and beyond university campuses, with Muslims attempting to alter the narrative that informs their experiences, that determines their realities (Bakhtin 1981, 1986).

While such activism continues at different levels, it is nonetheless limited in its outreach. For the ISocs, the audience is often predominantly Muslim, while the Paksoc is more focused on promoting cultural events that are more likely to attract a South Asian audience. The ISocs may face additional problems concerning their speakers, yet they have been successful in finding a more acceptable place within the broader Student Union body, which is an important starting point in normalizing Muslim student presence in campuses. Furthermore, the limitations of such initiatives as identified in this chapter were often highlighted by students themselves, who are willing to work towards finding more effective solutions to these limitations. As long as Muslims, ISocs and Paksocs are willing to engage with people who may not initially be ready for such a conversation, there is the possibility to promote understanding, and create a space where young Muslims, men and women, can find a sense of belonging. As Ahmed observes:

> For me my personal view is that the only way you tackle extremism is by involving people in a democratic process and allowing them to engage in the mainstream ways of achieving things. When you have far right parties on a national level, if you get them involved in elections they are less likely to espouse radical views. They may still be radical but will not be as bad in terms of something that they will say because they know that by being involved in that process there are certain responsibilities that you take up. When you are not involved in that process at all you have zero responsibilities so for me if you want to tackle extremism on campuses, the government if they are to intervene which is another debate, they have to encourage Muslim students to get involved in their student union, get involved in campus life as opposed to saying no you guys are extremists, you can't bring any of your speakers because they are all extremists, you can't really organize on campus because we have kind of created this image of suspicion because you guys are not necessarily fit to be involved with student union politics or anything to do with campus life. So by setting up the narrative in that sense, you sort of immediately prevent any potential extremist who does exist from moving away from those extremist views or tackling them in the first place.
> —Ahmed, London3, Student Union Anti-racism Officer

Bibliography

Bakhtin, M. (1986) *Speech Genres and Other Late Essays*. C. Emerson and M. Holquist (eds.), Translated by V.E. McGhee. Austin: University of Texas Press.

Bakhtin, M. (1981) *The Dialogic Imagination Four Essays*. M. Holquist (ed.), Translated by C. Emerson and M. Holquist. Austin: University of Texas Press.

Bernard-Donals, M.F. (1994) *Mikhail Bakhtin Between Phenomenology and Marxism.* Cambridge: Cambridge University Press.

Brown, E.K. and Saeed, T. (2015) Radicalization and counter-radicalization at British universities: Muslim encounters and alternatives. *Ethnic and Racial Studies*, 38 (11), pp. 1952–1968.

Cowan, G. and Arsenault, A. (2008) Moving from Monologue to Dialogue to Collaboration: The Three Layers of Public Diplomacy. *The Annals of the American Academy of Political and Social Science*, 616, pp. 10–30.

Flood, G. (1999) *Beyond Phenomenology: Rethinking the Study of Religion.* Continuum.

Gurevitch, Z.D. (1990) The dialogic connection and the ethics of dialogue, *The British Journal of Sociology*, 41(2), pp. 181–196.

Her Majesty's Government (HM Government). (2006) *Terrorism Act 2006.* UK: Crown.

Holquist, M. (1990) *Dialogism Bakhtin and his World.* New York: Routledge.

Loriggio, F. (1990) The Bakhtin Circle and Pragmatist Psychology. In *Mikhail Bakhtin and the Epistemology of Discourse, Critical Studies Vol 2. No. 1/2*, ed. C. Thomson, The Netherlands: Rodopi, pp. 91–110.

Milmo, C. (2015, 23/01) '*British Muslim school children suffering a backlash of abuse following Paris attacks,*' Independent. Available from: http://www.independent.co.uk/news/education/education-news/british-muslim-school-children-suffering-a-backlash-of-abuse-following-paris-attacks-9999393.html (Accessed, 11/15, 2015).

Modood T. and Dobbernack J. (2011) A left communitarianism? What about multiculturalism?, *Soundings* 48, pp. 54–65.

Roberts, J.M. (2012) Discourse or Dialogue? Habermas, the Bakhtin Circle, and the question of concrete utterances, *Theory and Society*, 41(4), pp. 395–419.

TellMAMA. (2015) '*Teacher in Rotherham under police investigation for alleged Anti-Muslim bigotry,*' TellMAMA. Available from: http://tellmamauk.org/teacher-in-rotherham-under-police-investigation-for-alleged-anti-muslim-bigotry (Accessed 10/20, 2015).

The Active Change Foundation. (2015) #NotInMyName. Available from: http://www.activechangefoundation.org/projects/not-in-my-name/ (Accessed 02/01, 2016).

Zavala, I.M. (1990) Bakhtin and Otherness: Social Heterogeneity. In *Mikhail Bakhtin and the Epistemology of Discourse, Critical Studies, Vol. 2 No. 1/2*, ed. C. Thomson, The Netherlands: Rodopi, pp. 77–89.

7

Conclusion: Gender, Islamophobia and the Security Discourse—Future Challenges

In November 2015, a Channel 4 television documentary exposed 'a group of British Muslim women' that were 'filmed urging other women and children to support and join Isis' across 'community centres' in London (Buchanan 2015). The documentary was shocking not only for the fact that British Muslim women were actively propagating and recruiting for Isis, but also that it was happening in the heart of England. The headlines in tabloid newspapers included 'Female British IS supporters preach hate in front of kids in undercover documentary' in *The Sun*, with the sub-heading 'Muslim women call for more Lee Rigby-style terror attacks across UK in shocking programme' (Jones 2015); 'Revealed: Three British women ISIS supporters who are spreading extremist ideology in UK and encouraging young girls to join the jihadists in Syria' in *The Daily Mail* (Tonkin 2015); and 'British women filmed "urging young girls to join Islamic State terrorists in Syria"' in *The Mirror* (Wellman 2015). Photographs of niqabi and hijabi women were splashed across newspapers. The 'unknown unknown' (Jackson 2015) terrorist threat was exposed, reinforcing the belief that the terrorist was hidden in plain sight, thereby validating the intrusive security measures introduced by the British government for the protection of the British public. The British

Muslim female was again placed within the spectrum of the vulnerable-fanatic, where the niqabi clad Muslim emerged as a fanatic, no longer a part of the Orientalist imagination but a real physical threat to the security of British citizens.

The danger posed by such extremists is no doubt real, but the greater danger lies in the demonization of peaceful communities who are pulled into the wider discourse of suspicion and insecurity, where innocent individuals fall victim to a paranoia that can become a catalyst for the radicalization the British government is attempting to prevent. Such a security discourse breeds insecurity, resulting in a vicious cycle that keeps securitizing Muslim communities for the actions of individuals who are as much of a real threat to the Muslim community as they are to the public at large. Ironically, the British government's enthusiasm for securitization has gained momentum in the ten years since the 7 July tragedies, and social institutions, from the family to the university, are all implicated in the security discourse.

This book has illustrated how the securitization agenda after the events of 7 July 2005 has impacted ordinary Muslim women living in Britain, whose everyday lives are placed within the socio-political discourse of insecurity perpetuated by Muslims who do turn to terror, and the sensationalist media and political accounts that follow. The everyday in this book is placed within a historical and political context, informed by a multiplicity of voices and meanings that are constantly in circulation—communicating across, against and within material circumstances and surroundings (Bakhtin 1986; Bernard-Donals 1994; see also Bakhtin 1990). The individual person's 'everyday' is located in a social context that is informed by dominant narratives about her identity, narratives of colonialism and immigration, racism and multiculturalism, the politicization of Islam to the securitization of her different identities. This is the backdrop of the experiences of British Muslim women with a Pakistani heritage and Pakistani Muslims in Britain, as examined in this book.

The book begins with an exploration of Islamophobia that racializes and securitizes the Muslim identity, located within an Orientalist framework. Islamophobia moves beyond physical or verbal attacks; it is embedded in the social psyche where a hijab/niqab clad Muslim woman or a bearded Muslim man become a physical personification of the would-be terrorist.

7 Conclusion: Gender, Islamophobia and the Security...

This insecurity is reinforced by a growing security apparatus wherein the Muslim community is constantly under surveillance, where an existential terrorist threat creates the possibility of an 'unknown unknown' terrorist attack (Jackson 2015), thereby normalizing an Orwellian social order. Islamophobia is defined by this pervasive racializing and securitizing discourse, with the British Muslim always guilty until proven innocent, a potential terrorist hidden in plain sight amongst the mundane (Croft 2012; Meer and Modood 2010).

This Islamophobic status quo is evident in the discussion on the British Muslim Pakistani identity in Chap. 2 which, if media and political rhetoric from the time of the Rushdie affair is to be believed, is a contradiction in terms. Located within the colonialist experience of the British Raj and the Indian subcontinent, the South Asian immigrant enters Britain as a (post-)colonial subject, a 'coloured' immigrant amongst a 'white' populace. The South Asian becomes politicized as a British Muslim after the Rushdie affair, the veracity of his British-Muslim identity being considered suspect. The British Muslim Pakistani male is again portrayed as a 'troublemaker' during the 2001 riots, while the British Muslim Pakistani female is perceived to be a victim of culture and patriarchy, with narratives of forced marriages and honour killings defining her existence. The events of 9/11 and 7/7, however, securitize this politicized British Muslim identity with the emergence of the home-grown terrorist, leading, once again, to the questioning of the nationalistic loyalties of British Muslims because of their religious affiliations. The British identity is representative of freedom and liberal values, while the Muslim and Pakistani are placed within an Orientalist imagination of primitiveness and violence, evident in dress and demeanour, especially for the Muslim woman who physically interrupts the liberal landscape of modern day Britain. The narratives of British Muslim women with a Pakistani heritage in this book, however, challenge such stereotypes of their identity. Far from being in a state of 'crisis' or conflict, British Muslim women balance the different aspects of their identity that only reach disequilibrium in relation to the 'authentic' 'white' British 'self'. Britishness is negotiated not against the different identities of British Muslim Pakistani women but, rather, in relation and 'proximity' to the 'white' non-Muslim community, against the 'outsider' status ascribed to the British Muslim (see Bhabha 1998). The narratives further reveal that there is no one authentic British Muslim Pakistani voice, (see also Contractor 2012) but, rather, a range of associations and identifications with different aspects of an identity, whether religious or ethnic, where being British only becomes a question in relation to the 'white'. Second- or third-generation British Muslim Pakistani citizens are still perceived as precisely that by the white host community—second- or third-generation, pigeonholed as a minority, struggling to be accepted as British against a dominant narrative that equates Britishness with whiteness.

While the question of race and ethnicity determines the level of acceptance of the British Muslim Pakistani identity, the book further focuses on the problematic securitization of the British Muslim female. The book explores the veiled figure, who epitomizes the face of Islam (Tyrer and Ahmed 2006; Zempi and Chakraborti 2014), but also includes Muslim women with different degrees of religiosity from those who wear the niqab, the hijab, the cultural *shalwar kameez*, to those without any physical religious identifiers. The diversity of religiosity amongst believing Muslim women has been constantly overlooked or undermined by the dominant stereotype of the veiled Muslim woman. Everyday accounts of veiled and non-veiled women reveal *how* Islamophobia functions as a socio-psychological discourse, wherein Muslims are forced constantly to prove their normality within a social context that renders them abnormal.

However, added to the problem of the securitized Muslim female is the educated Muslim as a potential terrorist. Stereotypes of the Muslim terrorist also evoke the educated, alienated Muslim citizen, vulnerable to radicalization within educational institutions. For this purpose, universities have continually been drawn into the state's security apparatus (Saeed and Johnson 2016), especially under the Counter-Terrorism and Security Act 2015 which places a 'statutory duty' on universities to inform on students (mostly Muslim) considered at risk of being radicalized (HM Government 2015a sect. 26(1)). Universities were already working with police and Prevent officials to ensure the welfare of all their students by monitoring for signs of radicalization, thereby identifying the would-be terrorist (see Association of Chief Police Officers 2012). Yet, these signs of radicalization are difficult, if not impossible, to determine, working on the flawed assumption that a process of radicalization exists that can be identified and disrupted (Kundnani 2015). The narratives in this book demonstrate how such a misdiagnosis of radicalization has created greater insecurity, implicating innocent Muslim students—in particular, those who are members of Islamic student societies or ISocs. With stereotypes of the moderate or the extremist inundating media and political rhetoric, the ISoc sisters are perceived to be radical and extreme; despite being peaceful citizens, they find themselves having to defend their innocence against the wider discourse of suspicion and guilt.

While the gendered, and racialized educated Muslim is central to the discourse on (in)security that permeates media and political rhetoric, the book further unpacks the Muslim category by examining the securitization and normalization of Islamophobia in the UK. Existing literature on Islamophobia mentions ethnicity and religious observance as factors that result in cultural racism (Meer and Modood 2010; Modood 2005; Sayyid 2010), but the extent to which a problematic ethnic identity existing within a securitized environment contributes to the experience of Islamophobia is often overlooked. Birt (2009: 217) highlights how 'the common experience of Islamophobia creates a unique community of suffering, which conflates ethnically disparate communities as Muslims and creates an assertive Muslim identity politics'. However, what is overlooked in understanding Islamophobia predominantly as an attack on Islam or Muslims are other identities which may reinforce the experience of Islamophobia. This other identity refers to the Pakistani ethnicity and nationality in this book. This nexus complicates a clear understanding of how Islamophobia is experienced, where the troubled nature of the Pakistani identity cannot be easily disentangled from the Muslim identity in a post-7/7 milieu. Hence, the term 'Pakophobia'—a fear of the Pakistani—is linked to a corrupt, violent country in the public's imagination, where children such as Malala Yousafzai are shot by the Taliban for wanting to go to school (Urquhart 2013), where second-generation British Pakistani women such as Shafilea Ahmed are murdered in the name of 'honour' by parents or family members (Carter 2012; *The Huffington Post* 2012b), and the most wanted man in the war against Al Qa'ida—Osama bin Laden—is killed in a covert operation in Pakistan (BBC News 2011b). This is the context in which Muslim Pakistanis enter the UK as students. While their entry is marred by a politics of verification (Saunders 2016) determined by a discriminatory visa process, their everyday experiences are also located within a wider discourse of hyper-securitization and suspicion. As the narratives reveal, such insecurities are translated into self-censorship: experiences of Pakophobia often go unreported; Pakistani students avoid student campaigns such as J4NW10 because of their link to a 'dodgy' country, yet are nonetheless willing to express their Muslim identity within limits.

Despite the narrow space available for young Muslim students to express their identity, whether in a university or beyond, young Muslim women are nonetheless finding simple yet effective ways of talking back to the dominant discourse and trying to change mindsets through the act of dialogue. The book examines how ISocs, Paksocs and British Muslim/Pakistani females in their individual capacity are engaging in dialogue with the sole purpose of removing the ignorance and misunderstanding that has led to Islamophobia. ISocs, especially, are raising awareness about Islam through Islamic Awareness Weeks and by encouraging student political participation across the student body, thereby normalizing a Muslim student presence within universities. The success of ISocs is evident when compared with other studies on universities and Muslim students, especially Tyrer's (2003) doctoral study on institutionalized Islamophobia within universities. Tyrer (2003) highlighted the troubled position of Muslim students within universities, especially the relationship between Islamic societies and the local and national student unions. They were often treated with suspicion, the likes of the National Union of Students (NUS) and the local student body resisting Islamic society requests for religious provisions including *halal* food and prayer rooms (Tyrer 2003). However, as the narratives in this book reveal, the efforts of FOSIS and ISocs to normalize a Muslim student presence in universities has resulted in Muslim students taking on executive positions within the NUS and their local student unions, with the NUS becoming a supporter of ISoc activism. Paksocs and Pakistani students have also been instrumental in challenging Islamophobia and Pakophobia, by presenting a counter narrative to the predominant view of Pakistan as the hub of terrorism and insecurity.

Most accounts of the immigrant community, of Muslims and Islam have been dominated by the troubled male identity. The politicization of the Muslim identity during the Rushdie affair of 1988–1989 also focused on the more outwardly and publicly visible Muslim man. Post-9/11 and

7 July 2005, a similar focus was turned on men as a direct security threat, whereas women were portrayed as victims of religious and cultural practices. British Muslim women became more visible in the discourse on security after the emergence of terrorists such as Roshonara Choudhry, or the more recent 'jihadi brides'; yet, the narratives predominantly focus on a malleable Muslim woman that can be radicalized, but is nonetheless a victim of such radicalization (see Brown 2011). Therefore, the discovery of British Muslim women actively recruiting for Isis or voluntarily travelling to Syria is received with greater shock and horror. However, in sensationalizing the British Muslim female as a victim or fanatic, her perspective, her experience and existence in a post-7/7 context that is predominantly informed by a 'security' discourse is either overlooked or ignored. This book, by focusing on the female British/Muslim/Pakistani, has provided a space for this *female voice* to emerge.

Future Challenges and the Battle of Ideologies

Due to individuals such as Tareena Shakil, the first British Muslim woman to be convicted for supporting Isis, as discussed in the Introduction of this book, British Muslim women actively propagating Isis ideology, as discussed at the beginning of this chapter, continue to pose a threat. This threat is not just in terms of the terrorist ideology they are supporting, but also the emerging Orwellian status quo that, far from protecting British values of individual rights and freedoms, undermines them. From Al Qa'ida to Isis, such terrorist groups have succeeded in promoting a state of paranoia about the Muslim community in Britain, whereby the fundamental values of equality and freedom of religious practice are, without discrimination, compromised. While the 'unknown unknown' terrorist threat persists, the 'unknown' is nonetheless placed within the 'known' Muslim community, securitized as an uncivilized, backward, Western-hating extremist. Britain is not alone in its failing attempts at balancing the fundamental rights of its citizens against its imperative to protect and counter terrorism.

France's Muslims are '7.6 percent of the total population—making the group the largest Muslim minority in Europe' (Safdar 2016).

After the November 2015 attacks, France declared a state of emergency that extended the counter terrorism powers of the police and the Ministry of the Interior, which included raids on 'houses, businesses and places of worship', and imposition of 'assigned residence orders and restrictions on public assemblies' (Amnesty International 2016: 6). These raids and 'assigned residence orders' have indiscriminately targeted the French Muslim population because of their religious affiliation (CCIF 2016). This is evident from the fact that, among France's '3200 raids and some closures of mosques and businesses' there were 'only five terrorism-related investigations' filed by 'the counterterrorism unit of the Paris prosecutor's office' (Safdar 2016). While these indiscriminate practices by the state target the Muslim community, Islamophobia from non-Muslim French citizens has also increased. In fact, after the Charlie Hebdo attacks in January 2015 and the Paris attacks in November 2015, France witnessed an 18.5 per cent increase in Islamophobic attacks against its Muslim community, with 80 per cent of these attacks targeting women (CCIF 2016)—which left Muslim families, including children, traumatized. Samia Hathroubi, a French-Tunisian human rights activist, observes how 'the state emergency is the symbol of France's illness regarding keeping a balance between fighting terrorism, which is a serious question, and keeping our values and sticking to them' (Safdar 2016).

However, this 'illness' is not confined to France or Britain. Countries across Europe, as discussed in the Introduction, have reinforced the idea of a battle between civilizations in its encounter with its Muslim population. According to a 2015 'EU Minorities and Discrimination Survey [...] on average one in three Muslim respondents faced discrimination and prejudice in the past 12 months, and 11 percent experienced a racist crime' (Open Society Foundations 2015). The Muslim problem has also been exacerbated across Europe with the influx of refugees fleeing the war in Syria. According to Human Rights Watch '[b]latant Islamophobia and shameless demonizing of refugees' has 'become the currency of an increasingly assertive politics of intolerance' (Human Rights Watch 2016: 1).

This 'politics of intolerance' is also visible across continents, as witnessed in the USA, where a similar form of blatant Islamophobia persists. The US counter terrorism measures after 9/11 included the controversial Patriot Act, which 'lessened the restrictions on surveillance, allowed various personal records to be obtained by authorities, reduced the privacy of attorney-client conversation, and broadened the definition of terrorism to include "material support," a concept that had "not been fully defined"' (Cesari 2011: 30; see also Goede 2008: 157; Love 2009; Semati 2010). According to the American Civil Liberties Union (ACLU), the New York Police Department (NYPD) has 'engaged in the religious profiling and suspicionless surveillance of Muslims in New York City and beyond'. This has included 'mapping of Muslim communities', 'photo and video surveillance', 'tracking individuals', setting up 'intelligence databases', planting 'Police "Rakers"' that blend into the community and gather information, and 'Police Informants' eerily known as 'mosque crawlers', that employ 'a method called "create and capture,"' starting 'conversations about jihad or terrorism' and capturing and reporting 'the responses to the police' (ACLU 2015). Islamophobic attacks against the Muslim community also increased in 2015 'after a Muslim couple, who reportedly pledged allegiance to ISIL, killed 14 people in a mass shooting in San Bernardino, California' in December 2015 (Dizard 2015). But the extent to which Islamophobia has entered the mainstream and become normalized in the West—and, in particular, the USA—is evident in the virulent hatred spewed by presidential nominees for the Republican party. Not only Donald Trump, but also other candidates have reinforced the paranoia that 'Muslims are inherently untrustworthy people that should be handled very carefully'. According to a New Hampshire poll, 66 per cent of the Republican Party voters supported Trump's ban on Muslims from entering the USA (see Marcotte 2016).

The pervasive Islamophobic rhetoric that has inundated media and political accounts about Muslims and Islam in the West has eroded the fundamentals of a liberal and free society, presenting the greatest challenge that countries in the West, including Britain, have faced. The narratives in this book bring into focus the individuals—in particular, Muslim women—who are located within this wider discourse of insecurity and bigotry, and who face the brunt of such hatred and intolerance. Yes, the terrorist threat is real, but it is equally real for the members of the Muslim population—who are as much British, French, European or American as the non-Muslim; who are as much human beings deserving of the rights guaranteed to any member of a civilized society. The danger in

Britain and the West is an increasing dehumanization and demonization of the Muslim identity under an Orwellian state apparatus where, in the ongoing battle of ideologies between Western countries and terrorist groups such as Isis, the West is building *fortresses of exclusion*, where Islamophobia has increasingly become an unchallenged and acceptable part of the social psyche.

Bibliography

American Civil Liberties Union (ACLU). (2015) Factsheet: The NYPD Muslim Surveillance Program. Available from: https://www.aclu.org/factsheet-nypd-muslim-surveillance-program (Accessed 03/01, 2016).

Amnesty International. (2016) *Upturned Lives. The Disproportionate Impact of France's State of Emergency.* UK: Amnesty International Publications.

Association of Chief Police Officers. (2012) *Prevent, Police and Universities Guidance for Police Officers and Police Staff to Help Higher Education Institutions Contribute to the Prevention of Terrorism.* UK: Office of National Coordinator Prevent.

Bakhtin, M. (1986) *Speech Genres and Other Late Essays.* C. Emerson and M. Holquist (*eds.*), Translated by V.E. McGhee. Austin: University of Texas Press.

Bakhtin, M.M. (1990) *Art and Answerability: Early Philosophical Essays.* Austin: University of Texas Press.

BBC News. (23/07/2011b) *Belgian ban on full veils comes into force.* Accessed from BBC News. [Online]. Available from: http://www.bbc.co.uk/news/world-europe-14261921 (Accessed 09/15, 2012).

Bernard-Donals, M.F. (1994) *Mikhail Bakhtin Between Phenomenology and Marxism.* Cambridge: Cambridge University Press.

Bhabha, H.K. (1998) Anxiety in the Midst of Difference. APLA Distinguished Lecture 1996, *PoLAR*, 21(1), pp. 123–137.

Birt, Y. (2009) Islamophobia in the Construction of British Muslim Identity Politics. In *Muslims in Britain Race, Place and Identities*, eds. P. Hopkins and R. Gale, Edinburgh: Edinburgh University Press, pp. 210–227.

Brown, K.E. (2011) *Gender matters, soundings policy matters for Muslims in Britain.* Muslim Council of Britain. [Online]. Available from: http://soundings.mcb.org.uk/?p=44 (Accessed 08/03, 2012).

Buchanan, R.T. (24/11/2015) *British Muslim women filmed glorifying Isis and urging Muslims to 'reject democracy' in undercover investigation*, Independent. Available from: http://www.independent.co.uk/news/uk/home-news/british-muslim-women-filmed-glorifying-isis-and-urging-muslims-to-reject-democracy-in-undercover-a6746226.html (Accessed 01/02, 2016).

Carter, H. (03/08/2012) *Shafilea Ahmed: the murder that tore her family apart*. The Guardian. [Online]. Available from: http://www.guardian.co.uk/uk/2012/aug/03/shafilea-ahmed-murder-background?intcmp=239 (Accessed 02/03, 2013).

Cesari, J. (2011) Islamophobia in the West: A Comparison Between Europe and the United States. In *Islamophobia: The Challenge of Pluralism in the 21st Century: The Challenge of Pluralism in the 21st Century*, eds. J.L. Esposito and I. Kalin, USA: Oxford University Press, pp. 21–43.

Collective Against Islamophobia in France (CCIF). (2016) *Report 2016*. Available from: http://www.islamophobie.net/sites/default/files/CCIF-Annual-Report-2016_0.pdf (Accessed 03/01, 2016).

Contractor, S. (2012) *Muslim Women in Britain: De-mystifying the Muslimah*. Routledge.

Croft, S. (2012) *Securitizing Islam Identity and the Search for Security*. Cambridge: Cambridge University Press.

Goede, M. De. (2008) Beyond risk: Premediation and the post-9/11 security imagination. *Security Dialogue*, 39 (2–3), pp. 155–176.

Dizard, W. (09/12/2015) *US Muslims experience rise in Islamophobia*, Al Jazeera America. Available from: http://america.aljazeera.com/articles/2015/12/9/us-muslims-experience-surge-in-islamophobic-attacks.html (Accessed 03/01, 2016).

Human Rights Watch. (2016) *World Report 2016*. USA: Human Rights Watch.

Jackson, R. (2015) The epistemological crisis of counterterrorism, *Critical Studies on Terrorism*, 8:1, pp. 33–54.

Jones, A. (25/11/2015) Female British IS supporters preach hate in front of kids in undercover documentary, *The Sun*. Available from http://www.thesun.co.uk/sol/homepage/features/6762859/Female-British-IS-supporters-preach-hate-in-front-of-children-in-undercover-documentary.html (Accessed 02/01, 2016).

Kundnani, A. (2015) *A Decade Lost. Rethinking Radicalisation and Extremism*. UK: Claystone.

Love, E. (2009) Confronting Islamophobia in the United States: Framing civil rights activism among Middle Eastern Americans. *Patterns of Prejudice*, 43 (3–4), pp. 401–425.

Marcotte, A. (10/02/2016) GOP Islamophobia: Two-thirds of New Hampshire Republican primary voters want to ban Muslims from entering U.S, *Salon*. Available from: http://www.salon.com/2016/02/09/gop_islamophobia_two_thirds_of_new_hampshire_republican_primary_voters_want_to_ban_muslims_from_entering_u_s/ (Accessed 03/01, 2016).

Meer, N. and Modood, T. (2010) The Racialisation of Muslims. In *Thinking through Islamophobia: Global Perspectives*, eds. S. Sayyid and A. Vakil, London: Hurst and Co. (Publishers) Ltd., pp. 69–84.

Modood, T. (2005) *Multicultural Politics Racism, Ethnicity, and Muslims in Britain*. Minneapolis: University of Minnesota Press.

Open Society Foundations. (2015) *Islamophobia in Europe*. Available from: https://www.opensocietyfoundations.org/explainers/islamophobia-europe (Accessed 03/01, 2016).

Saeed, T. and Johnson, D. (2016) Intelligence, global terrorism and higher education: Neutralising threats or alienating allies? *British Journal of Educational Studies*, 64(1), pp.37–51.

Safdar A. (18/02/2016) France state of emergency 'extended on slim evidence.' *Al Jazeera*. Available from: http://www.aljazeera.com/news/2016/02/france-state-emergency-extended-slim-evidence-160217174759408.html (Accessed 03/01, 2016).

Saunders, F.S. (2016) Where on Earth are you. *London Review of Books*, 38(5), pp. 7–12. Available from: http://www.lrb.co.uk/v38/n05/frances-stonorsaunders/where-on-earth-are-you (Accessed 03/03, 2016).

Sayyid, S. (2010) Out of the Devil's Dictionary. In *Thinking Through Islamophobia: Global Perspectives*, eds. S. Sayyid and A. Vakil, London: Hurst & Co. (Publishers) Ltd, pp. 5–18.

Semati, M. (2010) Islamophobia, culture and race in the age of empire. *Cultural Studies*, 24 (2), pp. 256–275.

The Huffington Post. (13/04/2012b) *Pakistani students made to take face-to-face interviews for UK study visa*. The Huffington Post. [Online]. Available from: http://www.huffingtonpost.co.uk/2012/04/13/pakistani-students-interview-uk-study-visa_n_1422884.html (Accessed 02/04, 2013).

Tonkin, S. (23/11/2015) *Revealed: Three British women ISIS supporters who are spreading extremist ideology in UK and encouraging young girls to join the jihadists in Syria*, The Daily Mail. Available from: http://www.dailymail.co.uk/news/article-3330855/Three-British-women-exposed-ISIS-supporters-spreading-extremist-ideology-UK-encouraging-young-girls-join-terrorist-group-Syria.html (Accessed 03/02, 2016).

Tyrer, D. (2003) *Institutionalized Islamophobia in British Universities. Degree of Doctor of Philosophy.* Institute of Social Research, University of Salford.

Tyrer, D. and Ahmad, F. (2006) *Muslim Women and Higher Education: Identities, Experiences and Prospects. A Summary Report. Liverpool John Moores University and European Social Fund.* Oxford: Oxuniprint.

Urquhart, C. (27/03/2013) *Malala Yousafzai sells life story for a reported £2m.* The Guardian. [Online]. Available from: http://www.guardian.co.uk/world/2013/mar/27/malala-yousafzai-life-story-2m (Accessed 04/01, 2013).

Wellman, A. (23/11/2015) "*British women filmed 'urging young girls to join Islamic State terrorists in Syria*" The Mirror. Available from: http://www.mirror.co.uk/news/uk-news/british-women-filmed-urging-young-6887691 (Accessed 03/01, 2016).

Zempi, I. and Chakraborti, N. (2014) *Islamophobia, Victimisation and the Veil.* London: Palgrave Macmillan.

Appendix 1A

University Profiles

West Yorkshire1

The West Yorkshire region has a high percentage of Muslims, with 11 per cent of the entire Muslim population in Britain located in this area, according to the 2001 census (Hussain 2008: 46; see also Peach 2006a: 650). However, this percentage is likely to have increased, with a growth in the population of Muslims in Britain to 2.7 million, as illustrated in the 2011 census (Office for National Statistics 2012: 1).

According to the same census, specific areas within West Yorkshire continue to have a high percentage of Muslims (Office for National Statistics 2012). Within this region, West Yorkshire1 is located in a culturally and religiously diverse neighbourhood. The university itself has a relatively small proportion of Muslim and Pakistani students. The Students Union consists of a welfare officer, who deals with all students and their welfare concerns, together with a black and ethnic minority student officer and an international student officer, who support and encourage greater participation of students from different backgrounds.

The university also provides support in the form of counselling services. These services are aimed at the general student body and cover a wide range of issues from harassment or discrimination to emotional and psychological health. However, as outlined by the participants, while services may be available for student support, including Muslim students in the university in general, students remain unsure about whom to contact to report a specific form of discrimination, such as Islamophobia. To meet the needs of its Muslim students, there is provision of both halal food and prayer rooms. The university has an Islamic society but encountered problems establishing a Pakistani society, with opposition from British students with a Pakistani heritage. This problem is further explained in light of the association between this university and Islamist terrorists involved in acts of terrorism in the UK. These terrorists (of Pakistani heritage) were part of the university alumni.

West Yorkshire2

The university is located in a town with a large South Asian community. This is also represented in the student population, consisting of a large Pakistani student body. The university's welfare provision includes faith advisors for different religious groups, with three in particular allocated for Muslim students, where one advisor is a member of staff. The contact information for these advisors is clearly available on the university's welfare website. A university Welfare member was also interviewed for this research, who further highlighted the nature of such provisions, which provide religious, intellectual, psychological and emotional support. However, the biggest problem for Muslim students—especially women at this university, as outlined in the interview—related to issues of forced and arranged marriages, as well as problems more directly related to academic underperformance, with no cases of Islamophobia being reported.

Information about such welfare provisions, particularly for issues relating to forced marriages, were publicized not only on notice boards across the university, but also in female toilets. Welfare provisions were further provided by the Students Union through the welfare officer, a part-time black and minorities officer and a part-time international students officer. The university also provides halal food options and prayer room facilities.

The university has a large Islamic society but, despite having a large presence of students with a Pakistani heritage, the university does not have a Pakistani society. The number of overseas Pakistani students is also quite small, which was evident from the fact that, for many, the researcher was the first Pakistani they had met. The university was in the news over the arrest of some of its students on charges of terrorism.

North West1

The North West region is also reported to have a strong Muslim community, with a large Pakistani presence (Hussain 2008: 46; Office for National Statistics 2012: 8). The region has also been highlighted in the news due to Pakistani students from universities in this region being arrested on charges of terrorism. This led to the Justice for North West 10 Campaign, which is discussed in Chap. 5. North West1 in the sample has a large population of Pakistani students compared with other universities in this region, as indicated in the HESA dataset.

The university also has a strong Pakistani student society and an Islamic society. In providing support to students against hate crime, which includes racism and religious discrimination, the Students Union is working together with the local police authorities so that crimes can be easily reported through the Union.

The Union also provides welfare support through a wellbeing officer, as well as a diversity officer, in order to guarantee support to all students relating to problems of health, as well as issues concerning discrimination. The university itself provides counselling services, as well as personal tutors that look after the academic and other welfare needs of the students. There is also provision of prayer rooms and halal food.

South East England1

This university town has a small population of Muslims and Pakistanis, both in the region and within the university. It has an active Islamic society and a Pakistani student society.

The university provides a race equality platform to discuss issues relating to race and inequality, as well as religious discrimination, with the aim of finding solutions and facilitating both staff and students. The university is also in the process of addressing student concerns regarding prayer facilities, as highlighted by a survey undertaken by the Equality division, though a temporary prayer facility was provided to students. Halal food can be found in shops around the university campus. The race and equality officer for the university was also interviewed, and highlighted the support given to students facing discrimination in terms of counselling services; but this officer also underlined the disconnect between students and university welfare provisions, which are seldom utilized. The Students Union also has a welfare officer and an international students' officer, as well as providing peer support across the university.

South East England2

Located in the same town as South East England1, this university has a small population of Muslim students. The university provides a platform for multi-faith dialogue, as well as provisions such as prayer rooms and halal food for Muslim students. The Students Union comprises of an ethnic minorities student officer, an international officer and a full-time 'student experience officer', with all three positions aimed at assisting students' diverse welfare needs. The university's race and welfare officer was interviewed for this research; as in South East England1, the officer mentioned how miscommunication was often the biggest problem facing Muslim students in their relationship with the university.

South West England1

This area has a small percentage of Muslims. A university town, South West England1 has an Islamic society but, given the small population of Muslim and Pakistani students, it does not have a Pakistani society. However, to cater to the religious needs of its students, the university provides a multi-faith chaplaincy. It also has a prayer room, and halal food is available in the Students Union store.

The university further provides counselling services to students in general. The Students Union also has a welfare officer, who deals with issues relating to both welfare and equality. It further provides part-time officers, especially the international student officer and a part-time widening participation officer, to cater to the diverse needs of students, encouraging greater participation of students from various backgrounds across the student body.

West Midlands1

The West Midlands—in particular, the area of Birmingham—has a strong presence of Muslims and Pakistanis (Peach 2006a; Hussain 2008; Office for National Statistics 2012). However, West Midlands1 is located in an area with a small proportion of Muslims, and the university itself has a small population of Muslim and Pakistani students. It is for this reason that the university does not have a Muslim or Pakistani student society.

The university is included in this list of profiles because of Tehmina, who is a student at West Midlands1 but was interviewed for her involvement not only with her Students Union, but also at the national level, and for her insights and experiences with Muslim students across the West Midlands area.

The university provides a multi-faith prayer room, with a multi-faith chaplain who can direct students to facilities outside the university. There is no provision of halal food within the university campus. The university provides counselling services for the wellbeing of its students. The Students Union welfare support comprises of diversity, representation and international officers, to encourage and support students from all backgrounds.

North East England1

A university town, North East England1 has a small population of Pakistani and Muslim students. Students are given support through personal and academic tutors, as well as a counselling service. It has an Islamic society but, given the small population of Pakistani students, there is no Pakistani student society. The university provides a Muslim chaplain, as well as a prayer room. However, the prayer room is located behind a public house, which proved problematic for students—particularly for young women who encountered drunk individuals on their way to prayer. The university does not provide halal food on campus.

London

According to the 2011 Census, London is the most diverse city with a large presence of Muslims (Office for National Statistics 2012: 1). The student sample from universities across London varied, depending on student response and accessibility. The universities themselves had a diverse distribution of Muslim students, as the following profiles illustrate.

London1: This University of London Higher Educational institution is dedicated to research relating to health and wellbeing. It has a small population of Muslim and Pakistani students, with no Islamic or Pakistani society. The main source of support for students is their student adviser, as well as a counsellor to provide academic and non-academic welfare support. London1 is affiliated with the University of London Union which provides further student support in the form of the black students' officer. As students' narratives demonstrated, London1 does not have prayer room facilities on campus; neither is there any provision of halal food on campus.

London2: Also affiliated with the University of London, London2 has a large presence of Pakistani and Muslim students. The Students Union provides support in the form of a welfare officer and an international students' officer, and has been supportive of the Islamic society. The university also has a vibrant Pakistani society. The university provides a Muslim chaplain, as well as counselling services for Muslim students. There are prayer room provisions and halal options are available for students in the Students' Union store.

London3: This university also has a vibrant Muslim and Pakistani student body. While it has an active Pakistani and Islamic student society, the Students Union, under the anti-racism officer, is quite active in raising awareness about Islamophobia and counter terrorism. The Students

Union organized an Islamophobia Awareness Month, as well as a conference on security and student extremism on campuses. The Union also took a stance against Islamophobia and anti-Semitism, and implemented a no tolerance policy on all forms of religious discrimination, including Islamophobia, for all student societies. The university provides prayer room facilities, and halal food on campus. As with other universities in the sample, it also provides welfare support such as counselling services. While the provision of a prayer room exists, students have recourse to a multi-faith chaplain, who directs them to the relevant authority.

London4: While located in an area with a strong South Asian presence, this university has a small percentage of Pakistani students compared with the other three London-based universities. However, the Students Union has a large network of welfare officers, including individuals dealing with multi-culturalism and international students. London4 has both an Islamic society and a Pakistani society. The university makes welfare provisions, including counselling, with a multi-faith chaplain. Students are also provided prayer room facilities, and halal food on campus.

Appendix 1B

Narrator Profiles

Salma, North West1, 28, Graduate (Business), Overseas

Salma was born in Lahore, Pakistan. Her mother is a homemaker and her father is a businessman and a landlord. She has two sisters. She went to a single-sex missionary school in Lahore, and a single-sex private high school. She attended a mixed-sex liberal arts university in Lahore, where she studied Social Sciences, with an emphasis on political science and history, and a took minor in Economics. She also worked in the university, a requirement of a scholarship she was awarded as an undergraduate. Her work entailed interacting with potential students and their parents, as well as managing other students who worked under her. She was never inclined towards extra-curricular activities, as she would rather spend her spare time reading books. She would have liked to pursue creative writing and literature as a career. However, describing herself as a practical person who wants to be financially independent, for a graduate degree she chose business school instead, something 'she is good at'.

She read for a Masters in Business at a university in Coventry, and then worked as a research assistant at a business school in West Yorkshire. She joined another business school in West Yorkshire to pursue a PhD. She had visited England before on family vacations, and the transition from Pakistan to England was quite easy for her, despite having doubts about being away from her family. She made friends easily, although it was often people who befriended her, rather than her approaching other students, as she does not mind being on her own. However, she is more inclined towards being friends with women rather than men, as it takes her more time to trust men. On her PhD course, she now has more male friends than females, after having known them for four years. She moved to a big city for her PhD as she felt a PhD degree would have been an isolating experience, especially in a small campus town, whereas a big city would be more busy with more to do. While she goes to clubs and pubs, she does not drink alcohol for religious reasons, which she feels limits her friendship with British students, as there is a drinking culture of which she cannot be a part. Despite avoiding extra-curricular activities, she has been voted as the class representative for both her Masters and PhD degree courses. She believes people chose her because she is approachable and she consciously tries not to be judgemental, 'like people in Pakistan'.

While a practising Muslim, she does not wear the hijab.

Zebunnisa, North West1, 21, Undergraduate (Law), Overseas

Zebunissa comes from the city of Karachi, Pakistan. Her father works for the government and her mother is a teacher. Her parents sold a piece of property they had inherited from her grandfather to finance her studies. Her father was a little hesitant about sending her abroad. In school, she was both studious and active in her debating club. When she won a local debating competition and was selected to go abroad for another competition, she was accompanied by her mother and grandmother. When she won international competitions, her father 'was over the moon' and felt confident enough to send her abroad for her studies. Zebunissa also has an older sister and a younger brother. Her sister got married at a young age, she 'had a love marriage', and she is happy and settled. However, her sister regretted not going abroad for further studies, a factor that further influenced her parents' decision in letting her go to England. Her brother is still in school but will soon be also applying for undergraduate degrees abroad.

Zebunissa chose North West1 because it was located in a town with a strong Muslim population, so she felt she would not have any issues with halal food. She is active in her university's Pakistani society, and is passionate about portraying a positive image of her country. She wants to be a lawyer and serve Pakistan. In her narrative, she also highlighted the problem of Pakistani women being less politically active, even in their student Pakistani societies. She believes women need to be more involved in student politics, and tries to encourage others. She also co-founded' a charitable organization based in Pakistan that promotes education for the underprivileged. She runs the organization while studying for her undergraduate degree in North West1.

She is a practising Muslim but was not wearing the hijab or a religious signifier.

Hafiza, London, 25, Alumna, British

Hafiza lives in London. Her father is from Lahore and her mother is from elsewhere in the Punjab. Her father came to England to study. She has five other siblings, two sisters and three brothers. While all her sisters, like her, wear the niqab, the youngest does not strictly observe this. Her mother is unwell. Her father always encouraged the sisters to wear a hijab and *shalwar kameez*, and they were allowed to wear long loose skirts but never anything tight. Her father also gives the Friday sermons at their local mosque. She describes her father as 'religious but his religion is tainted by culture', and gives the example of 'celebrating the Prophet's birthday' which for her 'is a cultural practice, not Islamic'.

She started thinking about religion after a course on philosophy, media and politics that she took in her A-levels; this confused her and made her question God's existence. She was in an accident, being hit by a car when she was in college, and describes how she 'had a strange vision' and she 'didn't feel any pain'. She was just grateful that she had said her morning prayers that day. Having survived, that accident made her even more religious. She wanted to use philosophy to prove that Islam was right. That is when she started studying about Islam, since she did not want to believe what she was told.

She tried attending a regular university but felt 'that university life compromises a Muslim woman's modesty'. She felt she stood out because of her clothes. It was also the time she started wearing the niqab, which she describes as the hardest thing she has ever done. Her father discouraged her, since he was afraid that she might be targeted. Since she was still learning about the niqab and did not realize whether it was mandatory in Islam or not, for her father's sake she only wore it within the university, since her father was afraid of her travelling with the niqab on. Outside the university, she would take it off. Soon, she dropped out of university and, instead, joined an online university programme, since she felt more secure. She wanted to marry a man who would support her decision to wear the niqab and, in her last year at her university, she got married and feels more confident wearing the niqab since she now has the support.

Hafiza has travelled to Pakistan but she feels that she does not fit in. She also has never been to a protest because she believes 'going to protest is against Islamic ethics' and 'modesty'. She does, however, have a website through which she creates awareness about Islam, and has a separate section about the causes and campaigns she endorses.

In the interview she asked not to be audio recorded, as she was uncomfortable with being recorded.

Faiza, West Yorkshire2, 22, Undergraduate (Humanities), British

Faiza was born in a predominantly South Asian town in West Yorkshire, where she has lived all her life. Her mother is a homemaker. Her father is a salesperson, or so she thinks, since she is not sure about exactly what he does. Both her parents are from a small village in Northern Punjab, Pakistan, and her ethnic background is Pathan. She has six sisters, four older than her and two younger. She went to a state-sponsored primary school and then attended a faith school, which received state patronage while she was a student there. She then attended a Muslim girls' college and, after sixth form, taught at a Muslim girls primary school for one year. She is reading for an undergraduate degree in Humanities at West Yorkshire3. She is repeating her first year for the second time, as she failed her qualifying exams.

She does not take part in extra-curricular activities, and has described herself as someone who lacks self-confidence. Her biggest highlight of her school years was 'getting something that you didn't think you could do'. She enjoys watching cricket, though she does not know how to play the game. Her idea of fun is to go to theme parks with her family. She does not go to the cinema to watch films and, while she sometimes spends time with her friends, she does not enjoy it as much as spending time with her family.

She wears a niqab, which she started wearing at the age of 19 when she attended evening classes on Islamic theology. Her mother also wears the niqab. She started wearing the jilbab at age 18, since it was part of her sixth form uniform. She has continued with the hijab since school, where it was part of the school uniform.

She has never been on a plane and has never travelled to Pakistan. She imagines Pakistan as a place with 'open air, close to nature' having 'a lot more freedom to do things than you do here', since, for her, England feels 'quite closed'.

Hafsa, North East1, 22, Graduate (Law), Overseas

Hafsa was born in England but mostly grew up in Karachi, Pakistan. She has a dual British-Pakistani nationality. While growing up in Karachi, she used to visit England during the summer. Her father is a businessman and her mother is a lawyer. She has an elder brother and a younger sister. She studied in a single-sex missionary school in Karachi and attended a mixed-sex private high school. She hated her high school experience, as she was not used to boys and 'that kind of attention'. She came for her undergraduate degree in law at a North East university in England, after which she continued to pursue law in England. She has always been involved in extra-curricular activities throughout her academic life. From sports and student politics in school, to becoming involved with the Islamic society and the student council at her university, she now volunteers for a pro bono legal advice organization in England.

She started wearing the hijab as an undergraduate. She had always wanted to wear one in Pakistan but her parents were not supportive of the idea. Her mother was especially against the idea of her wearing a hijab in England, as she was afraid her daughter might encounter discrimination. When she started wearing it in England, she did not tell her parents for a month. Despite wearing the hijab for three years, her father and brother still have a difficult time accepting the hijab. Her mother, inspired by her, started wearing the *dupatta* [a piece of cloth in the form of a sash, part of Pakistani traditional dress] in Pakistan.

Aliya, South West1, 20, Undergraduate (Sciences), British

Aliya was born in a town in the West Midlands which has a large Pakistani diaspora. Her mother was born in the same town but her father immigrated from Mirpur in Pakistan. Her father has a hearing disability. She has one younger brother. She is studying in a university in South West England, She is in her second year of an undergraduate degree in audiology. She went to a mixed-sex primary and secondary school, and went to a grammar school for the sixth form. She visited Pakistan when she was aged five. She has been active in extracurricular activities from primary school to her university, becoming involved in the student council, entering writing competitions, as well as playing hockey. She is also a member of her university's sign language society and is learning sign language. She has also joined the photography club and a pottery club, though she feels she is not that 'good at making pottery'. She has volunteered at a Red Cross shop, as well. She is a member of the Islamic society, though not part of the committee, and helps out with society events. She feels that she is an organized person, which is why she can be involved in extracurricular activities and study at the same time, though her course is not that demanding.

She describes herself as a British Muslim first and a Pakistani last, while her grandparents keep telling her that she is a British-Pakistani and then a Muslim. She disagrees, since she has only been to Pakistan once, does not speak the language and her 'Mirpuri is like that of a 7-year-old, it is that bad'. She also does not feel as though she is a 'typical Pakistani girl', since Pakistani girls are either into 'boys, Bollywood films and songs', or try to 'be white'. She has never been in either category, and believes that 'having boyfriends' is not allowed in Islam. She has had friends from different backgrounds, since she makes friends based on the person not their background. Her sixth form best friend, though, was of a Pakistani background.

She wears the hijab, but her mother discouraged her from wearing it in the beginning. Her mother felt that she should wear the hijab for the right reasons, rather than changing her mind later on and taking it off. Her mother also wears the hijab. She started wearing the hijab whenever she would go out while still in school. However, she would never wear it to school. She and her friends also used to wear it during Ramadan. She realized the importance of the hijab when she read the Quran in English and has been wearing it ever since.

Amna, North West1, 28, Graduate (Social Sciences), Overseas

Amna was born in Lahore, Pakistan. Her deceased father was a doctor; she has a stepfather who is a businessman. Her mother used to be a beautician but now is a full-time homemaker. She has two sisters and three brothers. She went to a single-sex missionary school in Lahore, and a single-sex private high school. She completed her undergraduate degree from a liberal arts university in Lahore.

She travelled to West Yorkshire to study part-time for a Masters in Social Sciences at West Yorkshire1. At the time of the interview, she had returned to Pakistan after completing her Masters and was working for an NGO related to education. She was involved in sports in school and became 'politically aware' during her undergraduate degree course. As a graduate student at West Yorkshire1, she was politically involved in the Justice for North West 10 campaign. She also initiated a political campaign in West Yorkshire against General Musharraf in September 2007, when he declared an emergency in Pakistan. She became politically active in West Yorkshire because she was frustrated by the lack of student activism for Pakistan, and felt the need to take initiative. She continued her political activism on returning to Pakistan, attending street protests and organizing discussion groups on current affairs in Pakistan.

While a practising Muslim, she does not wear the hijab.

Aisha, London4, 22, Undergraduate (German), British

Aisha was born in an Asian neighbourhood in Lancashire. Her mother is a community worker and was the first woman in her community to start teaching in the local mosque. Her father is a pharmacist. She has one sister and one brother. Relatives on her father's side are from both Lahore and England, as her grandparents moved to England from Lahore. Her relatives on her mother's side are from Lahore. She went to a predominantly white primary school. She then joined a state secondary school, which was really bad so her parents moved her to a private high school. Her school was located in a vastly Asian neighbourhood. In her high school, there were not many Pakistanis. She was in a class of 70, in which one in four were girls. She soon realized she was 'different' from the other girls, when she used to show up at school wearing long skirts while the other girls wore short skirts. She also spoke Urdu and Punjabi fluently, in which the others could not communicate. She described her mother 'as the driving force behind her education'.

She is studying German for her undergraduate degree course. She feels Pakistani and that German people find it strange that she is pursuing German. She wanted to be a pilot but her father's friend advised her parents against it, as he was a pilot and felt that such a profession was not good for a woman, especially when she is married. Her father tried to make her take up pharmacy but she was not interested. She thought about what she enjoyed and realized it was German, so she pursued it in her undergraduate studies. Her undergraduate course has a big Asian population, with a strong Bengali community. She used to be involved in extra-curricular activities growing up. However, since coming to university, she describes herself as an introvert. She mostly kept to herself. It was difficult for her because she came from a protective environment, even though her mother encouraged her a great deal. She has now moved to a big city and has to deal with financial issues as well as other problems on her own. She also felt that she has been involved in many extra-curricular activities while at school so, whilst at university, she just wanted to focus on her work. She tried to join student societies but never felt like attending their events. She feels the university is in a 'very Asian area'.

She does not 'like the way it looks'. She also feels there needs to be more interaction amongst students from various backgrounds in the university, as students have a tendency to stick with their 'own people'.

She has become more religious in recent years, though she is neither part of any student society, nor does she wear the hijab.

Mehreen, South East England1, 28, Graduate (Science), Overseas

Mehreen describes herself as a true 'Lahori'. She was born in Lahore, Pakistan. Her father used to be an engineer in the army. As a consequence of his job, they moved around Pakistan a great deal when she was growing up. Her father now teaches in a university and her mother teaches at a government college. She describes herself as coming from a family whose 'fifth generation' is in education. Her grandparents were doctors. She has two sisters. She went to an army school growing up. She talks highly of her father. People also believe she has a mind like her father's. Her father was supportive of her education. She applied to both the USA and Britain but felt that, in Britain, there were 'more human rights', as her friends did not have good experiences at the airports in the USA. She is pursuing a PhD in the sciences in a university with a small Muslim and Pakistani population. She describes herself as a 'very friendly person', yet she has had trouble making non-Muslim friends as she feels they don't talk to her because of her scarf. However, her circle of close friends, while mostly Muslims, also includes a German who is in her course and was also her flatmate. She is involved in extra-curricular activities with the Pakistani and Islamic societies.

She wears the hijab and the Pakistani dress, *shalwar kameez*, in her university. She is very proud of her Muslim and Pakistani identity. She started wearing the hijab when she was aged nine or ten. At first, inspired by her sister who wore the *dupatta* [a piece of cloth in the form of a sash, part of the Pakistani traditional dress], she started wearing the *dupatta* but soon felt that she should cover her entire head. Despite negative experiences, she confidently asserts her Muslim and Pakistani identity.

In the interview she asked not to be audio-recorded, as she was uncomfortable with being recorded.

Nadia, West Yorkshire2, 20, Undergraduate (Law), British

Nadia was born in Germany and came to Britain before her GCSEs. Her mother is a civil servant and her father runs a shop. Her mother's family is originally from Lahore, though her mother moved to England. Her father's family is originally from Kyrgyzstan and then her grandfather moved to Pakistan. Her father eventually moved to Germany. Her mother's side of the family is mixed because of the area in which she grew up. They include non-Muslims, mainly Afro-Caribbean. She has two sisters and lives in a predominantly Pakistani neighbourhood in West Yorkshire.

She is reading for an undergraduate degree in Law at West Yorkshire3. She has always been involved in extra-curricular activities, learning martial arts and drumming, and becoming involved in the student council. However, having grown up in Germany and then having moved to the UK, she has a keen interest in anti-fascist student politics, and has been active in the university as well as in the community, doing youth work and tackling racism. She was also involved with the National Union of Students. She is the head sister of her university's Islamic society, and was previously the head of the United for Palestine society. She describes her purpose in coming to university as being not simply to gain an education, but also to become involved in student activism. For her, this activism means standing up for what you believe in. During her own freshers' week, she organized a stall for Palestine and anti-fascism. However, she has moved away from socialist societies towards Islamic societies, though it was 'not an easy transition' for her to realize that socialism was not the answer.

She wears the hijab and jilbab. She started wearing the hijab one year after joining her university. She had thought about wearing it, but it was quite a shock for her parents as she used to have dreadlocks before. She considered wearing the hijab after she cut her hair but 'did not want to do it for the wrong reasons'. However, one day she wore it and never took it off. She put more thought into the jilbab. She read the Quran, researched it, felt there was a 'rational thought process' behind it and realized that she should wear it. She also had supportive friends in her university. Her family, however, was not supportive initially. They were a little shocked, especially after she wore the jilbab, as none of them wear a hijab. Her father has 'come around' to the jilbab though, in the beginning, they were all 'against it' as they felt 'it was a bit too much'. She feels that she looks like an 'adopted child' whenever she goes out with her family, as she is the only one wearing both the hijab and the jilbab.

Abida, West Yorkshire1, 21, Undergraduate (Law), Overseas

Abida describes herself as being from all over Pakistan. While her father is from Muzafarahbad, a town in Azad Kashmir, and her mother from Quetta in Baluchistan. She has grown up in different cities in Pakistan because of her father's job in the army. She attended mostly army public schools. She moved to England on her own to study for her A-levels when she was 16, and has been in England for five years. She came to England because she did not want to 'regret missing an opportunity' to study abroad. She chose England over the USA because she prefers the British education system, believing that the British are 'more cultured' and more 'informed about the world' than the US population. Before pursuing an undergraduate law degree at West Yorkshire2, she took one year to study an international business foundation course.

She has been involved in extra-curricular activities since she was in kindergarten—debating, swimming and heading her school basketball, cricket and netball teams. She was also involved in the English literature society and the school literary society, and was the head prefect in school. She felt that there was 'no group' that existed without her. In England, she did not pay much attention to extra-curricular activities, though 'she did stand in elections for the international student representative in her college'. She is now trying to create a Pakistan society at her university, though she has faced opposition from British Pakistani students.

She does not wear the hijab. In fact, people have a hard time believing she is Muslim. This is because 'she does not really hang it by the neck'. People are also often surprised to see her in the Islamic society.

At the time this student profile was being created, Abida had successfully founded the Pakistan society at her university despite opposition from some British Pakistani students.

Farzana, South West1, 20, Undergraduate (Medicine), British

Farzana was born and lived most of her life in Leicestershire. Her father was born in a place called Sangla Hill in Pakistan but lived most of his life in Lahore. He had a business in Lahore and moved to England much later in his life. Her mother is from Africa, though originally from Pakistan. Her parents are cousins but they 'had a love marriage', as she describes it. Farzana has never travelled to Pakistan. She attended 'normal state schools' and a single-sex madrassa before starting her undergraduate degree in medicine. She is now in her second year.

She has always been involved in extra-curricular activities. She used to take karate lessons in junior school and 'French lessons now and then'. She was part of the netball team in her secondary school, participated in Christmas productions at school and helped with school activities such as parents evenings. She has not been as active during her undergraduate degree course. She helps with a charity for the homeless and is a member of the Islamic society and the marketing society. At her university, she has come across students who have never met a Muslim before. For her flatmate, she was the first Muslim friend. She often engages in conversations with her to clarify any misconceptions about Muslims. She often gets asked 'What are you?' in the Islamic society. People are confused about her identity since, for many, she doesn't look Pakistani.

She used to wear the hijab but stopped wearing it. She felt she was wearing it for the wrong reasons. She started because her friends wore it. However, she soon reached an age where she realized she was not praying five times a day and, despite 'being good' by not having boyfriends, not smoking or drinking, and not going to clubs, she still felt that she needed to 'work on the praying thing'. Her parents have been supportive of her decision. Her mother does not wear the hijab and 'has short hair'.

Kiran, London1, 22, Graduate (Science), British

Kiran had been married for almost three years at the time of the interview, living in an area South West of central London. Her grandfather worked for the Pakistani government but was based in England. According to Kiran, the British government invited his entire family to live in England. Her mother at that time was six-years-old. Her father, who is also her mother's cousin, moved from Pakistan; her parents fell in love, got married and moved to a district in South West London. Her father has severe arthritis and 'was made redundant' because of his illness. He has had five hip replacement operations. She looks up to her father, who she describes as the 'bravest man' she knows, who 'never complains about his pain ever'. Her mother works at a 'company taking care of training for people'. Her husband has just completed his degree in politics and will start work.

Kiran wears the hijab, but started wearing it properly a year before she got married. She had tried wearing it before but, at that time, she 'wore it' for the 'wrong' reason, as more of 'a fashion accessory'. She felt disgusted with herself for treating it like that and also feels that she should not have taken it off, but explains it as being part of the process. She feels that the hijab keeps away unwanted attention from men. Her mother does not wear the hijab, her elder sister wore it 'for a year or two' but then she stopped. Now she only wears it when she goes out with her husband, as he wants her to. Her younger sister, however, wears the hijab. Her mother, on first seeing her in a hijab, told her that it was her choice but she did not have to wear it as 'Allah looks at your heart more than anything'. Her father was pleased, though he also told her that he would not mind her not wearing it. However, as a father, he does not like it when his daughters wear tight jeans so he was happy to see her in a hijab, as was her husband. While she wears the hijab, it has not stopped her from dressing up, which she enjoys doing.

She is quite critical of the new generation in Pakistan. When she went to visit her relatives in Pakistan, wearing the hijab for the first time, she felt people treated her differently, assuming that she had changed. She also feels the new generation does not have good role models. 'There is a lot of materialism and a lot of people [...] think wrongly of religion [...]

They think that if somebody prays five times a day they are a big *aalam* [religious authority] or something', an 'impression' she got from her 'cousins'. As for the Pakistani female students who come to the UK, 'a lot of them have gone off the rail. A lot of them are making an effort with their education which is really admirable', people like the researcher as she points out, who 'will go back to' her 'community and become a role model and give back …'

Zubaida, London1, 30, Graduate (Science), British

Zubaida comes from a town north of Manchester, which she describes as 'a racist little town'. Her grandfather was a sea merchant who lived in Egypt but then moved to England, where he met her mother's grandfather. She sarcastically calls the marriage between her parents as 'doing business', when her maternal grandfather invited her father and paternal grandfather to his place to choose which daughter he wanted in marriage. Her mother, who was unaware of this arrangement, was initially quite upset but 'it worked out in the end'. Her father was recently made redundant and her mother is a housewife. Her mother comes from a small village in Afghanistan, while she describes her father as being of 'Mongol-like' origin from the north of Pakistan and a little Libyan. She has six sisters and a brother, with her being the second eldest. She describes herself as still under her mother's influence, unlike the 'younger generation' in her house; one sister lives away from home with her boyfriend, without her parents' knowledge, and another lives at home and constantly gets drunk in front of the mother. She, on the other hand, cannot conceive of ever upsetting her mother, a sort of influence which she thinks will last till the age of 60. She also believes that, while her mother wants her to be happy, secretly she is hoping that Zubaida would marry one of her cousins. The idea that she would choose someone in her present university would completely 'destroy' her mother, something she could never do.

Zubaida went to a 'racist school' which was predominantly white and where she was continuously bullied. Her high school was also full of bullies. The fact that her mother made her wear a headscarf from a young age and also stitched clothes for her to wear, as she was not allowed to wear Western clothing such as skirts or trousers, made the bullying worse. She would be beaten up, called 'Paki' and often returned home with bruises. Her father was always busy with work but her mother tried to talk to the teachers. However, the mother could not speak English, having basically taught herself while watching *Sesame Street*, which is why, when she would try to talk to the teachers, they would dismiss her by telling her they could not understand what she was saying. The teachers were also often complicit in the bullying, looking the other way or telling Zubaida off for making up stories, ignoring her bruises. A teacher in high school also once physically assaulted her. Zubaida, in her narrative, constantly mentions how she carries this trauma with her, even at the age of 30; now, she reacts if anyone is rude to her and often answers back with anger. She has also struggled with religion, removing the hijab as a teenager without her mother's knowledge, since she pretended to wear it but removed it after leaving home so as not to get bullied. She does not wear the hijab now. She also mentioned how she tried her first drink while at university but, because of getting 'alcohol poisoning', did not drink for almost 'two-and-a-half years' after that incident and felt guilty for lying to her mother.

Mehnaz, West Yorkshire2, 22, Undergraduate (Law), British

'Born and bred in Britain'. She is a third-year law student who lives in a town with a high percentage of Pakistanis, attending a university that also has a high proportion of Pakistani students. Her father is a taxi driver, born in Pakistan but 'bred in the UK'. Her mother is a 'housewife' born in Pakistan who only came to the UK after her marriage. Her family comes from a small village near Lahore, and she describes herself as Punjabi. The last time she visited her village was in 2007 (i.e. four years ago at the time of the interview). She has three brothers, and she is the second child. She mentions how all her brothers are overprotective. If someone said anything to her or swore at her 'they would actually go' and 'beat the hell out of them'. She finds Pakistanis outside of Pakistan, particularly overseas female students, really 'modern'. She believes that by going abroad they have already 'taken a step' forward, which is described as something 'fantastic'. In further elaborating her observation, she points to the researcher, indicating 'how the only way' she could tell the researcher was not British was from the accent.

She studied in an Asian populated school, but her nursery was in an English populated locality. Her high school was very Asian, with only four English people in her class. Sixth form comprised a majority of white students. She recounts how, while in the sixth form, she removed her hijab once in class because her hair had become loose. Since she was sitting at the back of the classroom, she thought no one would notice. But on seeing her hair, all her classmates including her teacher were in shock. They were shocked because they thought she was bald and did not realize she had hair underneath her scarf. However, she doesn't think she has 'experienced any form of racism' because she describes herself as a 'volatile person'; her motto is 'if you push me I will make sure you fall'. She believes that it is the attitude of the person that also influences experiences; if anyone messes with her she will 'mess' with them. However, the fact that she has grown up in an Asian community is one of the main reasons why she feels she hasn't encountered Islamophobia. She started wearing the hijab at the age of eight because her mother was wearing it and she has continued to wear it ever since. She did not struggle in taking on the hijab since it felt natural to her. Her mother wears the jilbab and has advised her to wear that but, for the moment, she feels the hijab is more than sufficient'

Rukshanda, London2, 28, Graduate (Science), Overseas

Rukshanda originally comes from the city of Peshawar but her family moved to Lahore. Her father is retired and used to work in Saudi Arabia as a health professional, while her mother is a retired social worker. She has one brother who is a businessman. She chose to study in England as opposed to Australia, which is the other option she was considering, since the universities in England had a higher ranking. When she came to England for her doctoral research, she suffered a 'cultural shock' since she had never lived away from her family, or been in a non-Muslim country. It took her a while to adjust which, in the beginning, was emotionally difficult. She also had trouble in her laboratory since the research in her British university was quite advanced, compared with Pakistani universities where she had previously been based. It therefore took her time to adjust to the new university environment.

While a practising Muslim, she does not wear a hijab or any religious markers. She had problems with her supervisor because of her Pakistani identity, as her supervisor—a British citizen of an Indian heritage—often brought up issues of insecurity and terrorism in Pakistan in their discussions, which she found upsetting. She also claimed to be a proud Pakistani and planned on going back after her PhD to help her country.

Zahra, West Yorkshire2, 19, Undergraduate (Social Sciences), British

Zahra is in her second year of undergraduate studies in sociology. Her parents are from Mirpur in Pakistan. She lives in West Yorkshire with her family. She grew up in an area in West Yorkshire with a large percentage of Pakistanis and Asians, even her school had a large South Asian presence. She did not experience any discrimination in school, as she felt everyone was more or less the same. She started wearing the hijab in primary school; her sister does not wear it, but her mother does. She started wearing the jilbab in the sixth form. At first, she was not sure whether the jilbab was an Islamic requirement, but soon learnt at 'a madrassa where' she 'was studying' that 'in Islam it says you should wear it'. For her, a Muslim is someone who recites the *Kalima*, making a pledge to God and His Prophet, and someone who practises—i.e. follows the fundamentals of Islam which include, which include praying; fasting; giving *Zakat* or alms; and, if possible, going for pilgrimage to the *Ka'aba* in Mecca. She also includes wearing the scarf as an act that may be part of being a Muslim, as well as following the *Quran* and *Sunnah*. However, she is uncertain about the niqab and can understand people who do not like the niqab since 'you can't see their face' and there are problems in communication as a result of that restriction. Zahra visited Pakistan when she was in grade 8. That was also the last time she left her home town.

Areesha, West Yorkshire2, 20, Undergraduate (Social Sciences), Overseas

Areesha is an overseas Pakistani student studying at a university in West Yorkshire which has a large presence of British-Pakistani students. She lives with her relatives and chose this university because she had been rejected from universities in Pakistan and the others to which she had applied. She is studying psychology and feels that her university provides strong academic support. She used to live in Saudi Arabia but moved back to Pakistan and lived mostly in Islamabad. Since she studied in an American high school in Saudi Arabia, she has had no difficulty in making friends from different religious groups and nationalities. However, she did have trouble adjusting to a different lifestyle in Britain.

She wears the hijab and the jilbab. However, in her interview she was quite critical of the British Muslim students with a Pakistani heritage. She felt they were confused, living in Britain but trying to keep a Pakistani culture. She also felt that Pakistan was more modernized than the people she met understood, as they 'have a perception ... that in Pakistan no one wears English clothes and no one goes out'. She feels that since people come 'from villages ... they have mixed their culture and religion with the British lifestyle' which is why 'it is quite messed up'. She also believes that British-Pakistani women are more restricted, and is further critical of young girls who pretend to be religious in front of their parents but remove their hijabs the moment they enter the university.

Fatima, West Yorkshire2, 21, Undergraduate (Law), British

Fatima was born in West Yorkshire, where she grew up. Her parents are from Mirpur in Pakistan. She studied in a local primary school, attended an Islamic high school followed by a Catholic college, and is now studying Law at West Yorkshire2. At high school, she was a head girl and prefect, while mostly she did not participate in extra-curricular activities. At university, she is active in the Islamic society.

Fatima wears both the *shalwar kameez* and a hijab. She stood out in her university campus, which had a small percentage of Pakistani and Muslim students. This was also obvious when she was taking the researcher to a seminar room for the interview, since other students would stare at her and her clothes, though she would just ignore them and stare elsewhere.

Fatima is the first girl in her 'whole generation to actually go as far as university'. No other girl in her 'generation has even gone to college. They just did a high school education and are sitting at home', are either getting married or waiting. Since her family is living away from her extended family because of family problems, with her mother's encouragement, she pursued an education. Her mother thought that she 'was doing pretty well in' her high school and her teachers thought that she should go to college as it was pointless staying at home in this age, so she went to college and was successful enough to get admission into West Yorkshire1.

She looks up to her mother who is the first woman in their whole generation to start driving. She described the rest of her extended family as living 'in the stone age', with many of them having problems with her coming to university. Her father, while somewhat reluctant at the beginning, has also gradually accepted the fact that she is studying.

Nargis, South West1, 25, Graduate (Sciences), Overseas

Nargis was born in Dubai and lived there for 18 years, after which time her family moved back to Pakistan. She did her undergraduate and graduate degrees in Pakistan in a top research university in Islamabad. She came as a doctoral candidate to South West1, because of their research facilities and financial aid. She had trouble finding friends in the beginning, since she had never previously lived in a non-Muslim country and could not find someone who understood or shared her culture. However, she felt the Islamic society was useful in helping her settle in.

She is an active volunteer in science related projects at the university, which she enjoys. She does not wear the hijab, though she wore it when she was in Pakistan. Before coming to the UK, she decided to remove the hijab out of fear of experiencing discrimination. Her family was also hesitant about her wearing the hijab. She believes her family is really paranoid about Muslim groups in the UK, which is why she did not tell her parents about the Islamic society at first, when she started attending their events. Her parents think that the Islamic society is extremist, so she was afraid that her parents might think that their daughter is at risk of being radicalised. Even though her mother wears the *dupatta*, she would not encourage her daughter to wear the hijab. Her graduate course supervisor in Pakistan also warned her about Muslim groups in the UK who may try to recruit her. Her supervisor advised her to stay away from Muslim groups and avoid Islamic events, as those are the places where young students are targeted. She believes that such reactions from her loved ones back home further add to the paranoia, since she felt the Islamic society in her university was an ordinary student society and people were friendly. She finds her laboratory colleagues also supportive; she prays in an office next to the laboratory, and all her colleagues and her supervisor respect her and often give her the space to pray.

She is still considering wearing the hijab and has asked several of her friends at her university about their experiences, getting a mixed reaction from some who faced discrimination and decided to remove it, while others have had a good experience. However, what prevents her from taking on the hijab is the number of questions that she will have to answer from colleagues and other people if she makes that decision, not to mention her family who would be concerned about her safety.

Rehma, South West1, 29, Graduate (Sciences), Overseas

Rehma is originally from the Swat Valley but her family moved to Peshawar. She comes from a traditional Pathan family, with seven other siblings, three brothers and four sisters. She is the first girl in her family to go to a university and to go abroad. Her father, described as a strict individual, has always been supportive of his children's education, encouraging his sons and his daughters to pursue higher studies. He was the one who also encouraged her to apply for a PhD programme within Pakistan and, when she secured a scholarship, was happy to send her abroad. Two of her brothers also supported her ambitions. Her mother, however, was hesitant at the idea of her daughter living alone in a foreign country, but she kept quiet and never discouraged her. She also has a fiancé in

Pakistan. She got engaged before she came for her PhD. Her fiancé was the son of a family friend who was recommended by her mother, and she agreed. Before the proposal, however, her relatives had voiced their concern about her eligibility for marriage on getting a PhD degree.

She describes herself as *gharailu*—i.e. more domestic, being interested in housework. In Pakistan, she would attend university and be busy at home helping her mother, which is why she faced problems in getting a bank account and sorting out the official details when she came to England, as she was unfamiliar with the procedure, never having dealt with such official business. She never participated in any extra-curricular activities while at school or during her undergraduate course, describing herself as always the 'quiet and unnoticed' one. While she was interested in sports, she never had the confidence to pursue them. In England, since she is getting used to a new system, she does not have the time for extra-curricular activities. It is for this reason that she has not joined the Islamic society.

She used to wear the niqab in Pakistan, as she felt more comfortable wearing it in Peshawar. However, she decided to only wear the hijab in England, because she felt she would stand out otherwise. In Peshawar, there is a culture of women wearing the niqab and people are still familiar with each other, whereas in England she felt people would not be able to recognize her and it would cause unnecessary problems. Her decision to remove the niqab was based on the realization that, in Islam, veiling is for the purpose of modesty and 'looking Muslim', which she believed could still be achieved with the hijab. Her Muslim appearance due to wearing the hijab also ensures that people know their limits in interacting with her.

Since she was more comfortable with the Urdu language, the interview took place predominantly in Urdu, with some phrases from English included in the conversation.

Shaista, South West1, 27, Graduate (Sciences), Overseas

Shaista is in her second year of a PhD course. She is from Multan in Pakistan. She undertook her undergraduate course from Pakistan. This is her first time in the UK and she is the first girl in her family to go to a university, or even to go abroad. She is married. Her husband is in

Pakistan, where he is doing his PhD. In university, she is mostly busy with her academic work and is not involved in any extra-curricular activities—though she does interact with the Islamic society, as her friends are members. She did not join the Islamic society as she does not have time and, being a 'disorganized person', she felt she would not be able to participate fully in the society, which would make her feel guilty for doing something half-heartedly.

She describes herself as a quick learner, which is evident from her pronounced British accent, which she picked up when she moved to England. She feels she has the ability to pick up accents without realizing it. She wears the hijab and the jilbab. While her supervisor has always been supportive, she had problems with some of her laboratory colleagues and fellow students, including a female from Pakistan, who were not supportive of her Muslim appearance. However, she believes it was the result of miscommunication, as people often misunderstood her. She also never complained about it to her supervisor. She further believes that she is a positive person, who does not realize when someone is behaving in a negative manner towards her, which surprises people.

While the conversation took place in English, towards the end of the exchange she switched to the Urdu language.

Sanam, South East England1, 25, Graduate (Social Science), Overseas

Sanam grew up in Saudi Arabia but her family moved back to Lahore, in 2003. Her father is an academic; her mother has been unwell. She has a brother and a sister, being the youngest in her family. She studied in an American school in Saudi Arabia, moved to a British school as her parents wanted her to take the GCSE exams, but then returned to her American high school when she realized that she did not want to take A-levels. On moving back to Pakistan, she went to a public university, rather than a private one, for the experience of being in the Pakistani system. She has always been involved in extra-curricular activities from debating, amateur dramatics and sports, especially basketball, to becoming the editor of her school magazine. She chose England because of her scholarship, and her university was well-known in Pakistan.

She is active in her English university, attending talks and participating in debating and sports. She also attends ISoc events. While she believes the ISoc is welcoming, she does not spend too much time with them as she feels there is a strand in the ISoc that expects students to dress a certain way, especially if one gets involved with ISoc events. She used to wear a scarf when she was 15 or 16, but only wore it for a few months. All her friends wore the scarf; her elder sister also started wearing it, as did her cousins, and she was part of the Islamic society in her school where she felt inadequate for not wearing it. However, she soon realized that she did not like it and felt like she was 'two different people'. Overnight, she had to behave in a certain way with her male friends, who had always been close friends, and was different at home. She could not take it and decided to remove the hijab. While some of her friends were not happy with her decision, as the hijab for them was not a light matter, she nonetheless felt she was being honest in removing it. She visited the UK with her father when she went through that phase and, while she stayed within a university, she recounts how she wandered off on her own to explore the countryside and asked an Englishman for directions to a town. While he gave her directions, he warned her not to go there alone as she would face discrimination because of her scarf. However, since coming to the UK for her graduate degree she has not worn the scarf; neither does she feel the need to wear it.

Dalia, South East England1, 21, Undergraduate (Social Sciences), Overseas

Dalia is from Karachi, where she attended a private English medium school. She has one younger brother, who will be applying for his undergraduate degree. She has always been involved in extra-curricular activities. At her undergraduate university in England, she is also quite active in student societies, from acting to politics. She describes her family background as liberal in terms of religious practice, and she does not wear any religious symbols or signifiers. However, she faced problems settling in because of the drinking culture at her university. During her first week, she attended a student event; she was put off by students getting 'drunk and hitting on each other', which discouraged her from attending any of the other events. She felt a bit scared at the beginning, not having any close friends, and did not know how to handle such situations. She also did not fit into the Islamic society, described as being too 'conservative', while the Pakistani society for her was also too insular, as they did not encourage students to mingle outside their group. However, gradually she made other friends, especially on her course, which she describes as 'multi-cultural', and found a place for herself.

In her discussion about the Islamic society, she shared the experience of a friend who became an active member of the ISoc. However, her friend started wearing the hijab because everyone in the society wore a hijab and she felt left out. Only later did she realize that she was wearing the hijab for the wrong reasons and stopped. While the ISoc for Dalia is friendly, she tends to go to their events during Ramadan, when she can eat free food for Iftar (the time when Muslims break their fast). She has met British-Pakistanis and, in her description, divides them into two groups: those who are completely assimilated, and those who are still stuck in 1950s Pakistan. Only a small minority for her have found a place in between.

Dalia, in discussing Islamophobia, highlighted the discrimination faced by Pakistani students when applying for student visas. She personally knows friends who could not join British universities because of visa issues. She feels students are discriminated against because of their Pakistani identity.

Tehmina, West Midlands1, 19, Undergraduate (Social Sciences), British

Tehmina was born in a multi-cultural town in the West Midlands, where she grew up. Her father is from Pakistan but her mother was born in Britain. While studying for an undergraduate degree related to youth work, Tehmina has been involved in youth projects within and outside her university. She has been active in community projects relating to young people focusing on integration. She has also received several national and local awards for her activism. One of the reasons why she was invited to participate in this research was her involvement in student activism inside and beyond her university. Having been active in the national and regional student organizations, she was familiar with the problem of Islamophobia across universities in her region. She highlighted the issue of non-reporting of Islamophobia by students and, on several occasions, intervened on behalf of students. She is also active as an equality officer within her university.

Tehmina wears a hijab and has been verbally attacked because of her political views, which she believes is a result of the nature of the work she does as a youth activist, having debated with workers from the British National Party. She also started an online radio station and a magazine for young people. She disagrees with terms such as 'minority' since she feels she is British and not part of some minority community—a term that 'was made popular by middle-class politicians'. She also believes that Muslim women and men need to become more involved in mainstream politics, where they can change negative perceptions about their community. For her, the problems faced by the British community with a Pakistani heritage is a consequence of a culture which is confused with religion, and hence misunderstood.

Sehrish, North West1, 21, Graduate (Social Sciences), Overseas

Sehrish is from Sialkot, in the Punjab province of Pakistan. She went to a private English medium school. She came to England to pursue an undergraduate degree, but stayed for her Masters. Her university has a strong presence of Pakistani students. While she has never been involved in extra-curricular activities, she is part of her university's Islamic society. She feels more comfortable with Asian students and has friends from East Asia, but cannot feel the same level of connection with English people. She has been to England before on a family vacation. While she has not experienced Islamophobia herself, she is familiar with friends who have experienced it in public. She also knows of a family friend who wears the niqab and encountered Islamophobia on the street, being called a 'terrorist'. She believes that if she suffered Islamophobia, she would go and report it to the Islamic society.

She wears a loose *duppata* with Western clothes.

Bano, North West1, 22, Graduate (Sciences), British

Bano was born in England in a town that has a strong presence of South Asian Muslims. Her father is from Faisalabad and her mother is from Sahiwal in Pakistan. Her father had a cloth manufacturing business, but he is now retired. Her mother is a housewife. She has three siblings, two brothers and a sister. She is the youngest. Her parents always encouraged their children to excel in school and have continued to be supportive, letting them study whatever they want to study. Her parents themselves are not educated, since their families could not afford their education. However, her father's brothers are doctors; their education was supported financially by her father when he started working. She speaks Urdu fluently and is also well-versed in Punjabi. All her siblings speak Punjabi, but she was the 'guinea pig' who was taught Urdu by her parents at home, instead of Punjabi. As a rule, she and her siblings can only speak in Urdu or Punjabi with their parents, but they speak in English amongst themselves.

Bano went to a primary school with a strong Pakistani student community. However, her parents moved and, at the age of ten, she joined another school where she was the only 'brown person'. She struggled at her new school and often came home crying. In explaining her experience, she describes how it was difficult for the 'all white' students to have a 'brown' person in their midst, since they were not used to seeing someone like that. They used to ask her all sorts of questions about her eating habits, and her culture and religion which, at times, were asked just to annoy her. However, soon, through group projects, she managed to make friends. Her high school and college was quite multi-cultural, which also prepared her for university.

Bano has always been involved in extra-curricular activities. She learnt how to play the piano and the guitar, and she writes poetry and plays badminton. She also teaches 'Bollywood dancing'. She does charity work and has raised funds for Pakistani flood victims. She is a member of the Islamic society and is active in her university's Pakistan society. She feels a greater affinity with Pakistan, which she illustrated through an anecdote. When she was aged ten, she filled in a form and ticked the Pakistani box in response to a question on identity. This created a problem, as her father was contacted to check whether his daughter was of a Pakistani nationality. She was lectured by her father and was told that she was Pakistani within the house but was a British citizen outside. She could not understand since she always felt Pakistani. She also wants to go to Pakistan and contribute, since she feels she can be of more use there than in England.

While a practising Muslim, she does not wear the hijab.

Malika, North West1, 22, Undergraduate (Social Sciences), Overseas

Malika grew up in Canada and Pakistan. She chose England to pursue a law degree as it would have taken longer in Canada. She has been involved in extra-curricular activities such as debating and activities related to her degree. She was also involved with her college Paksoc in her first year. However, she is not that active with the Islamic society, which she felt was 'extreme' initially, until she interacted with them and saw 'their events', and 'realized they' were 'normal'.

While brought up in Canada, her father was very strict about her speaking in Urdu at home, because he was afraid that she might lose touch with her culture. She spoke in English outside, but at home she always conversed in Urdu, which is the reason why she is in touch with her Pakistani culture. She believes the problems concerning Muslims and Pakistanis in Britain are more related to the media, which create a 'paranoia around Muslim students'.

While a practising Muslim, she does not wear the hijab.

Tasneem, North West1, 21, Undergraduate (Social Sciences), Overseas

Tasneem is from Karachi. She chose England in which to pursue her studies as it was closer to home compared with the USA and Canada, and she already had her brother studying in North West1. Her parents therefore felt more comfortable sending her to North West1. She went to a private school in Karachi and has always been involved in extra-curricular activities. At her university, she was involved with her Students Union and was also active in the Pakistani society. She did not have trouble adjusting because of her brother and her friends from Pakistan, who also chose North West1.

She is a practising Muslim who does not wear the hijab. She has worked closely with the Islamic society as a member of the Students Union and believes that the ISoc is misunderstood. She never felt she was treated differently, despite not wearing the hijab, and believes that the members are 'normal' people. She feels that the problem of Muslims in Britain was exaggerated after the events of 9/11, as Muslims had 'been around' before those events, dressed in the same way; while they may have experienced discrimination, they became more visible after the events of 9/11 and 7/7.

Noor, North West1, 19, Undergraduate (Social Sciences), Overseas

Noor is from Islamabad, though she has travelled a great deal within and outside Pakistan because of her father's job; he works for a tobacco company. She chose North West1 because she was rejected from the top universities of her choice in Pakistan and, within the time she had left to apply, North West1 was one of the few good ones in the UK that was still accepting applications. She felt other countries, such as the USA, were too far away from home.

She has always been involved in extra-curricular activities in her school from amateur dramatics and debating to the student council and sports. However, during her undergraduate course she 'slacked' and was only involved 'in a few charities'. She is not involved in the Pakistan society, as she just never got around to it. However, she is also not involved in the Islamic society, which she describes as 'too religious for her'.

She recounts an anecdote about her first experience with the ISoc. In her first week, she went to their stall and was talking 'to a boy, who was fine with her' but then a 'girl' came up to her and told her that if she 'had a question she should ask a sister'. She was a little taken aback and simply apologised. She does not understand why, on their fliers, they have separate contact information for men and women, which is why she never joined the ISoc. She has suffered discrimination outside the university in a well-known store in the area when a woman, who was being friendly, admired a necklace she was wearing. On asking her what it was and being told that it meant 'Allah', the name of God in Arabic, the woman just walked away without saying anything.

While a practising Muslim, she does not wear the hijab.

Natasha, North West1, 34, Graduate (Social Sciences), Overseas

Natasha is from Pakistan. She mostly grew up in different cities across Pakistan, but also lived in the USA for over three years, where she enrolled in an American high school. The rest of her education was in Pakistan. The reason why she moved a a great deal was because of her father's job; he was a government servant but is now retired. She has also travelled to the UK sporadically and, as a child, 'attended one year of kindergarten' in the UK. She has always been drawn to the social sciences. She has been involved in sports and amateur dramatics in school, but was not particularly involved in extra-curricular activities at her undergraduate university, which was small and did not offer many facilities in that regard. She is also not involved in extra-curricular activities at her present university because of the demands of her degree.

When she came to the UK for her graduate studies, she had problems adjusting—more so because she came from a working-class background and was not used to just studying. She worked in the education sector for a couple of years before she came to North West1. She has a closer circle of Muslim friends, since she feels that the requirements of her religion do not permit her to participate fully in the culture of non-Muslim class fellows. For her, 'friendship is something that you develop when you have commonalities'. She does not blame the non-Muslim students but feels that she did not 'feel comfortable' with them, since she could not join in the drinking culture, and so preferred to mingle with people with whom she had more in common.

While a practising Muslim, she does not wear the hijab.

Lyyla, North West 1, Activist, Alumna, British

Lyyla has been politically active on university campuses locally and nationally, being involved in leftist organizations but, in particular, in campaigns such as the Stop the War Coalition and United Against Fascism. Her parents are from Pakistan; her father is from a town near Islamabad and her mother is from the Azad Kashmir region. While she graduated from her university some time ago and was not politically active as a student, after graduation and working in different parts of England, she came back to the area where her university was located, and joined the anti-war movements.

She calls herself a 'radical' and believes that the problem with Islamophobia is related to the 'war on terror, media' and Muslims themselves who 'refuse to fight back'. In working with Muslim students and ISocs on university campuses, she felt that the Islamic societies reinforce the stereotype of a non-political Muslim, particularly for Muslim women. She shares her own experience, after she started wearing the hijab recently. A male Muslim student, also a leftist, was surprised when she told him she was going to go pray. He explained how he felt there were two kinds of Muslim women who wear the hijab, the ones who do it for religious reasons, as found in the ISoc, and people like her who are trying to make a political statement but are not religious. She feels frustrated at the idea that such external judgements and categories exist about Muslim women, though she also feels that Muslim women themselves reinforce it. For her, the Islamic societies in universities provide a safe environment for students who are away from home where 'no one pushes their' boundaries.

Lyyla has also encountered discrimination within national leftist parties, with a fellow activist questioning her loyalty to a leftist cause because of her Islamic belief. She is a strong believer in being politically active in the community and blames the leaders of the Muslim community for not setting an example of activism. She gives the example of an English Defence League (EDL) protest when the Muslim community was asked by the police to stay inside that day, being told that their 'safety' could 'not be guaranteed'. What upset her the most was the announcement by the local police that, if they saw 'Asian men' out on the streets that day, they would arrest them on counter terrorism charges, accusing them of creating mischief. The fact that the EDL was allowed to protest whereas Muslim citizens were told to stay inside, which they quietly did, reflects the lack of political will on the part of the community and the institutional problems that exist within the government, as well as the British leadership. A similar lack of activism is also present in the Muslim student community in universities.

While an active member of leftist groups within and outside the university, she also works for an IT company.

Nazia, London3, 28, Graduate (Social Sciences), Overseas

Nazia has grown up all over Pakistan. Since her father was a government servant posted across Pakistan, the family moved around with him, though her main schooling was in the city of Islamabad. While her father comes from a conservative region in north Punjab, he was always supportive of her education, and encouraged her and her sister to pursue a higher degree. She believes that she is successful because of the support of her parents. She was married but divorced her husband despite 'social pressures'. She worked in the banking sector but joined the graduate programme at London3, since she wanted to change her career path. She wants to be in academia and is a strong advocate of education for girls. She was the first girl in her family to receive an education because of her father's support and 'knows how education can change a girl's life', as it gave her the strength to be where she is today. She wants to contribute in the field of education for this reason.

She is also patriotic about her country, having been involved in Pakistan society events. She believes there is a need to promote a positive image of the country, which she has been doing at an individual and group capacity. She feels things are changing for women in her country, which is evident by the number of Pakistani women she has met at her university compared with men. However, she highlighted how this presence of women might also be the result of racism from the immigration and visa services. She has heard accounts of young Pakistani women getting visas and scholarships, while Pakistani men have faced more issues by being denied a student visa. She believes the reason for this is discrimination and the idea that Pakistani men would be a greater 'security' risk and inclined to join terrorist activities; Pakistani women do not pose such a threat.

She is a practising Muslim, particular about praying, fasting and halal food, and does not drink alcohol either. She does not wear the hijab or any Islamic symbols or signifiers.

Rubab, London1, 29, Graduate (Science), Overseas

Rubab is from the city of Karachi. Her father is a retired banker. She has two brothers and a sister. She is married and lives with her husband in England, who works as an export sales engineer. She wears the hijab and has experienced Islamophobia from her laboratory colleagues. She described one such incident, where her laboratory colleague told her how she felt 'scared' when Rubab would go to pray in a separate room. She believes that she is not a 'weak person', neither is she 'afraid'—but she does not want to create issues in her laboratory by reporting such remarks. She wants to 'leave a good impression', which is why she ignored her colleagues at first, but soon decided to talk to them. While she believes that the talking has helped, it was difficult for her in the beginning.

She started wearing the hijab at the age of 20. No one in her immediate family wore the hijab and her mother was a little apprehensive when she started wearing it. She was influenced by her cousins and realized that she 'felt comfortable' with it. She has worn it since then. She was married while enrolled in her graduate degree. It was an arranged marriage, which she was happy about, though she constantly had to defend her decision to her laboratory colleagues, who kept asking her if she was being 'forced' to marry.

Zunera, London3, 24, Social Science Alumna, Overseas

Zunera is from a town near Islamabad. She went to a private school in her town and an undergraduate college in Lahore. She did not have any problems adjusting to her programme in England. Her 'university is very international' and has a strong and active Islamic society, so she never felt any form of discrimination during her time there. She did witness Islamophobia while she was waiting in a tube station, where a man was being shouted at for looking 'Pakistani' and 'Muslim'. She feels Muslims themselves can also be Islamophobic and gives the example of her sister, who is studying in the USA. Her sister was quite ashamed of herself when she looked at a man with a 'Muslim' and 'Pakistani' appearance, with a turban, beard and *shalwar kameez*, boarding a train and found herself afraid that he might be 'a terrorist'. In narrating this incident to Zunera, her sister explained how she was shocked by her own reaction.

Zunera has participated in one protest against General Musharraf's self-imposed coup in 2007, outside the Pakistani High Commission in London but believes that Pakistani students in general are less inclined to be politically active. The reason for this is the protective environment in which they have grown up, since they do not know anything about political activism and the most they would do is sign petitions.

She does not wear the hijab but is a practising Muslim. She does not think that wearing the hijab or a religious symbol is the only thing that makes a Muslim stand out. She believes that she dresses conservatively, especially in summer, and people can tell that she is Muslim, since Muslims 'look a certain way' despite the lack of any prominent religious signifier.

Sabahat, West Yorkshire2, 25, Alumna, Teacher, British

Sabahat was born in West Yorkshire, where she grew up. Her parents are from Pakistan. She has a big family, three brothers and three sisters, and nieces and nephews, all of whom live in West Yorkshire. After graduating from West Yorkshire2, she joined a teaching degree course and taught in primary schools for two-and-a-half years. During her undergraduate studies, she only started making friends outside her Pakistani circle in her second year. Throughout her life, she had always had close Pakistani friends but was happy to interact and get to know non-Pakistani British students. In her school, they never encouraged students to go beyond their small, close-knit groups, which she felt was the reason why she was never confident enough to become friends with a non-South Asian or Pakistani. She also suffered racism at secondary school, when 'white kids used to throw sticks and stones at' the South Asian kids when they were walking back from school. She never told anyone, not even her parents, because she felt it would be too difficult for her parents to handle when they were already struggling with 'bringing up their children in a Western society'. She did not mention it to any of her teachers either, which she regrets.

She has also suffered racism on her teaching degree course from fellow students. She narrates one incident in which classmates who were part of her group came into the classroom and, instead of sitting at her table—where there was plenty of space, and no other table available—they fetched a separate table, found chairs at the back of the classroom and created a separate corner. 'That moment' made her feel 'horrendous'. She mentions how frustrating the situation was for her, especially knowing that the same people who kept ignoring her existence will become teachers and teach in multi-cultural schools.

She started wearing the hijab four weeks before the interview and has already noticed a change in people's behaviour. Her colleagues at school look at her differently, and those who do not know her are often surprised when they hear her speak English. However, she feels that she has the confidence now to answer back to anyone who is Islamophobic or racist towards her.

Sana, London1, 23, Graduate (Medicine), Overseas

Sana is from Lahore in Pakistan. She comes from an industrial and feudal background. She attended a private English medium school school in Lahore and was involved in extra-curricular activities in school. She further attended a University of London institute for her undergraduate degree and came to London1 for her graduate programme. She chose England because she was familiar with the British system as well as London, since her family used to spend their summer vacations in London.

In discussing Pakistanis and Islamophobia, she believes that the family background and geographical location of students who come from

Pakistan is an important factor in how they interact with people in Britain. In trying to understand the difficulties some of her more religious classmates have faced in adjusting to a Western context, she believes that if she did not have the kind of exposure she had growing up in a city such as Lahore and, instead, had come from a less diverse city or village, she would also have a different attitude to Western countries. For her, the problem of Islamophobia is two-sided; Muslims need to explain themselves to people who do not know their religion to prevent discrimination from happening. This need for Muslims to explain themselves is particularly important in today's environment.

Sana is a practising Muslim and does not wear the hijab.

Maqsooda, West Yorkshire2, 24, Alumna (Social Sciences), British

Maqsooda attended West Yorkshire2 for her undergraduate degree course. Her father is from Lahore while her mother is half-British and half-Polish. Her father's family lives in Pakistan, which she visited quite frequently until the security situation worsened. She went to a private school and a girls' public secondary school. She wanted to appear for her A-level examinations but was not allowed to take A-levels because her school's headmistress told her she would not get good grades. Instead, she ended up attending a sixth form college. She does not know of anyone else who was discouraged from taking their A-level exams, but she felt greatly discouraged by that incident. However she liked her undergraduate university, as she was given the space to develop her thinking and express her opinions.

She understands the British-Pakistani dilemma that young people face, though she believes it should not be a problem, as identity is something subjective. Some people feel they are British, others do not. She does not mind being called either, but she does feel like she 'identifies' with her Pakistani background more. Her mother, being half-Polish, faced discrimination in England, so she never formed a strong English connection.

Maqsooda feels that, in today's climate of suspicion and apprehension, people 'have a responsibility to find out' about things that they are afraid of, rather than accept that fear without question.

She is a practising Muslim but does not wear the hijab.

Tamana, West Yorkshire2, 19, Undergraduate (Social Sciences) British

Tamana was born and brought up in West Yorkshire. Her parents are from Pakistan's North West Frontier Province (now known as Khyber Pukhtunkhwa) 'but her grandmother was Indonesian who reverted to Islam'. She has three sisters and one brother. She is the youngest. She is also an *alima*, described as someone who 'is an Islamic scholar'. She graduated from a madrassa a year before the interview.

She started wearing the hijab when she was in high school. She 'used to wear it loosely then' but now wears it 'properly', after her 'mom explained 'the importance of the hijab. Her mother also wears the hijab 'and a coat' with it. Her sisters also wear 'the coat' and one of them wears the niqab. She felt her family was ignorant about Islam, confusing it 'with culture' but, gradually, her mother learnt more about the hijab and started wearing it. She 'hates the word "Paki"', which she finds offensive. For her, it was used against her 'forefathers' when they were employed doing work that 'the English people didn't want to' do. It was a word that was used for people such as her grandfather and she hates it, especially when Pakistanis use it with each other. She also mentioned an incident with her sister who wears the niqab; she was called 'a ninja' on the street, which shocked both of them. She believes the nature of discrimination depends on where Muslims live, as in some areas no one would ever experience Islamophobia whereas in other places one would.

She also does not understand the British-Pakistani identity question. When she goes to Pakistan, her relatives call her *walaity*, meaning 'foreigner'; when she is in Britain, people question her Britishness. She does not understand this obsession, as British history is filled with 'Roman' invasions, 'the Vikings' and other foreigners that have defined British identity. For her, there is no contradiction or dilemma in being British, Pakistani and Muslim.

Romeena, South East2, Alumna, University Welfare and Islamic Society Executive

Romeena is an alumna of South East2. She also works full-time at the university with their welfare services and manages the Islamic society. She is also on the board of an organization that is in charge of madrassas in South East England. While she has encountered problems amongst student and staff—the result of misunderstanding and miscommunication—she believes her university is proactive in protecting the rights and welfare of their Muslim students. Being active in different Islamic organizations, she mentions how she is used to receiving interview requests from researchers working on Muslims in England.

Romeena is a practising Muslim with a Pakistani heritage. She also wears the hijab.

Tabussum, South East1, Racism and Equality Advisor

Tabussum works with both staff and students in ensuring the welfare of university members. Her work concerns a 'mixture of policy [...] keeping up with the legislation but also doing project work and responding to students' needs'. She also 'facilitates' a working group on race and religion, focusing on multi-faith dialogue. She is further exploring the impact of university policies on religious groups. She believes that the problem of Islamophobia is primarily because of misunderstanding and miscommunication in universities. This can be overcome by creating greater dialogue within the university, and also encouraging students to step forward when they experience any kind of discrimination.

She is a practising Muslim of a Pakistani heritage. She does not wear the hijab.

Diane, West Yorkshire2, University Welfare, 2011

Diane is part of the University's welfare programme, which is specifically concerned with diversity and widening participation. Her university provides mandatory training to all its staff members regarding equality and diversity. Since her university has a diverse student body, with a 'large proportion of non-white British applicants' and 'international students', she believes they have an 'ethical requirement to be aware of the "cultural" and "religious" preferences of their students'. Her university has a clearly defined no tolerance policy on discrimination, which she thinks is not a problem at West Yorkshire2. For her, the greater problems are to do with 'family issues', 'forced' and 'arranged' marriages and general academic related stress, which she believes the university is dealing with successfully.

Ahmed, London3, Students Union Anti-racism Officer

Ahmed is the anti-racism officer of his Students Union. He is active in spreading awareness about Islam through student led conferences on Islamophobia and terrorism. He has worked closely with the Islamic society and the National Union of Students society in his capacity as an officer of his Students Union, and believes that Muslim students are making a difference by becoming more politically proactive in student politics within and beyond the university campus.

He is a practising Muslim.

FOSIS Representative, 2011

The Federation of Students Islamic Society (FOSIS) was established in 1962, and is claimed by the FOSIS representative to be the 'oldest Muslim organization in Britain.' It serves Muslim students in higher and further educational institutions in the UK and Ireland. 'It is the representative, umbrella organization' of Islamic student societies. Their 'work revolves around reporting and representing the interest of Muslim students across the country, whether' related to 'welfare,' politics, 'or training Muslim students in leadership' (FOSIS).

The representative of FOSIS interviewed for this research is part of the National Executive Committee. She is also a practising Muslim who wears the hijab and jilbab.

National Pakistani Student Representative, 2010

The National Pakistani Student Association (a pseudonym) is an organization that aims to build a network between Pakistani students and alumni, as well as encourage greater cooperation between British students with a Pakistani heritage and overseas Pakistani students in the UK. It further aims to encourage a positive image of Pakistan, for which purpose it organizes an annual Pakistani student conference to discuss the social, economic and political problems in Pakistan with the aim of providing workable solutions. These solutions are sent to the Pakistani parliament.

The representative interviewed for this research is the media spokesperson, who is also an overseas Pakistani student.

Bibliography

Hussain, S. (2008) *Muslims on the Map A National Survey of Social Trends in Britain*. London: Tauris Academic Studies.

Office for National Statistics. (2012) *Religion in England and Wales 2011*. UK: Crown.

Peach, C. (2006a) Muslims in the 2001 Census of England and Wales: Gender and economic disadvantage. *Ethnic and Racial Studies*, 29 (4), pp. 629–655.

Index

A
Abdulmutallab, U.F., 2, 15, 85, 94
agency, 10, 36, 39, 44, 48, 49, 58, 59, 70, 91
alienation, 45, 62, 67, 71, 72, 78, 87, 95
alterity, 10, 11
assimilated, 25, 213
assimilation, 25, 26, 38, 49

B
Bakhtin, M., 147
Belgium, 8
belonging, 6, 8, 25–49, 62, 87, 102, 111, 120, 154, 165
Bin Laden, O., 12, 16, 27, 73, 118, 122, 131, 173
British Muslim, 122, 123, 125, 127, 142, 148, 154, 155, 169–72, 174, 175, 195, 207
Britishness, 44–6, 48, 49, 58, 78, 171, 172, 225
British Pakistani, 130, 131, 138, 139, 142, 156, 164, 173, 194, 195, 200, 201, 207, 213, 224, 225
British values, 2, 31, 35, 37, 42, 46, 58, 60, 72, 143, 175

C
Cameron, D., 37, 60, 65, 66, 130, 140
CHANNEL, 36, 169. *See also* counter terrorism

© The Author(s) 2016
T. Saeed, *Islamophobia and Securitization*, Palgrave Politics of Identity and Citizenship Series, DOI 10.1007/978-3-319-32680-1

Chaudhry, R., 15, 111
citizenship, 37, 41, 87
clash of civilization, 7, 59
colonialism, 6, 48, 170
Commonwealth, 26, 48
CONTEST, 34, 35. *See also* counter terrorism
counter terrorism, 34–7, 85, 90, 94, 95, 100, 110, 118, 121, 131, 141, 148, 155, 157, 162, 166, 172, 175, 176, 188, 220
Counter Terrorism Act 2006, 34
Counter Terrorism and Security Act 2015, 3, 15, 35, 85, 90, 94, 95, 110, 121, 141, 148, 155, 157, 162, 166, 172
cultural racism, 9, 10, 173

D

Daish, *See* Islamic State of Iraq or the Levant (Isil or Isis)
degrees of religiosity, 3, 15, 76, 85, 158, 172
dialectic, 13
dialogics, 147, 148
dialogue, 4, 13, 16, 17, 62, 91, 109, 147–67, 174, 186, 226
discrimination, 143, 152, 160, 165, 175, 176, 184–6, 189, 195, 206, 208, 209, 213, 217–19, 221, 222, 224–7

E

ethnicity, 4, 14, 15, 26, 27, 29, 40, 44, 47, 119, 126, 141, 166, 172, 173
European, 5, 7–9, 177

everyday, 3, 13–17, 33, 58, 63, 64, 69, 72, 94, 102, 133, 148–50, 166, 170, 172, 174
extremist, 3, 8, 15, 27, 35, 36, 58, 59, 61, 64–7, 72, 75–8, 85, 89, 90, 93–5, 98, 100, 104, 106–11, 120, 142, 156, 167, 169, 170, 173, 175, 209

F

fanatic, 2, 38, 60, 62, 64, 65, 67, 77, 85, 94, 101, 102, 132, 133, 170, 175
fatwa, 28, 29, 33
forced marriages, 38, 39, 60, 171, 184
FOSIS, 69, 73, 89, 90, 94–6, 101, 102, 105, 107–11, 135, 153, 155, 157, 161, 162, 174, 227
France, 7, 8, 119, 175, 176

G

Germany, 8, 199
Ground Zero mosque, 7

H

Hebdo, C., 7, 156, 176
hijab, 3, 10, 40, 58, 65, 67, 68, 70, 72–6, 78, 97, 100, 101, 124, 126, 127, 142, 152, 153, 158, 169, 170, 172, 191, 192, 194–6, 198–202, 204–14, 216–19, 221–7

honour, 14, 27, 38, 39, 49, 60, 171, 173
hyper-securitization, 4, 16, 117–19, 127, 141, 174. *See also* security

I

Imperialism, 6, 7
(in)security, 2–4, 48, 143
Islamic State of Iraq or the Levant (Isil or Isis), 1, 2, 6, 7, 10, 17, 36, 38, 60, 62, 66, 67, 77, 78, 85, 86, 102, 111, 143, 154, 156, 169, 175, 177, 178
Islamic student societies (ISocs). *See* ISoc sisters
Islamist, 2, 6, 27, 34, 88, 184
Islamophobia, 1, 5, 49, 57, 58, 63, 64, 68, 71, 72, 74, 76, 78, 85, 97, 100, 101, 117, 119–21, 127, 131, 133, 139–41, 143, 147, 150, 152, 154, 158, 159, 161, 162, 165, 169–74, 176, 184, 188, 189, 205, 213–15, 219, 221–7
ISoc sisters, 3, 13, 16, 86, 94–111, 135, 141, 155–62, 166, 167, 173, 174, 220

J

jihadi brides, 1, 15, 58, 62, 72, 78, 175
Jihadi John, 1, 15, 85, 111
jilbab, 3, 70, 100, 152, 194, 199, 200, 205–7, 211, 227
Justice for North West, 12, 133, 185, 196

K

Khan, S., 58, 60, 61

L

lesbian, 72–3, 78, 155
liberal feminists, 59, 73

M

Malik, S., 2, 15, 58, 60
minority, 13, 26, 42–4, 48, 71, 77, 87, 104, 119, 172, 175, 183, 213, 214
moderate, 3, 10, 15, 16, 27, 58, 59, 64–7, 72, 75–8, 85, 98, 99, 156, 173
multiculturalism, 26, 32, 37, 47, 170

N

niqab, 3, 8, 10, 45, 57, 58, 60, 67–73, 78, 100, 124, 152, 153, 169, 170, 172, 192–4, 206, 210, 214, 225

O

Orientalism, 5–12
outsider, 25, 42, 44–7, 69, 72, 103, 118, 121, 124, 125, 130, 150, 155, 171

P

Paki, 42, 46, 70, 121–4, 204, 225
Pakistani student societies (Paksocs), 13
Pakophobia, 4, 16, 117–43, 150, 162, 165, 173, 174

Prevent, 27, 34–6, 89–91, 95, 96, 100, 108, 110, 159, 167, 170, 172, 209, 224

R

race riots, 32
racialization, 5
racialized, 4, 9, 10, 173
racism, 9, 10, 13, 30, 31, 45, 49, 76, 107, 124, 128, 159, 165, 167, 170, 173, 185, 188, 199, 205, 220, 223, 226, 227
radical, 12, 15, 16, 36, 64, 85–7, 89–96, 99, 102, 104, 105, 110–11, 142, 149, 150, 167, 173, 219
radicalization, 2–4, 15, 16, 34, 37, 38, 65, 72, 77, 85–112, 148, 161, 170, 172, 173, 175
radicalized, 2, 36, 61, 90, 91, 106, 107, 154, 156, 172, 175
Ramadan, T., 25
Runnymede Trust, 6
Rushdie affair, 28–31, 33, 38, 45, 48, 59, 171, 174

S

scarf affair, 38
securitization, 2–5, 12, 14–16, 33, 47, 58, 63–9, 71, 72, 74, 78, 90, 117, 118, 141, 147, 170, 172, 173
securitizing, 12, 16, 17, 37, 57–79, 85–111, 117–43, 170, 171

security, 1–17, 23–49, 60, 63–5, 67–73, 76–8, 85, 86, 89, 90, 94, 95, 105, 107–11, 117, 118, 121, 125, 126, 129, 133, 135, 136, 141, 142, 147–67, 169–78, 189, 206, 221, 224
Shakil, T., 1, 62, 175
South Asian, 14, 25–49, 60, 122–7, 130, 166, 171, 184, 189, 193, 206, 215, 223
surveillance, 3, 15, 17, 91, 99, 109–11, 119, 134, 171, 176, 177
suspect, 4, 27, 35–7, 74, 76, 77, 86, 89–91, 95, 98, 104, 108, 111, 118, 119, 126, 137, 141, 162, 171
Switzerland, 8

T

Tebbit test, 44, 45
terrorism, 2–4, 11, 12, 14–17, 27, 34–7, 60, 64, 71, 73, 75, 85, 88–91, 94, 95, 98, 100, 110, 118, 120, 121, 128, 131, 132, 137, 138, 141, 142, 147, 148, 153, 155, 157, 162, 163, 166, 172, 174–7, 184, 185, 188, 206, 220, 227
Terrorism Act 2000, 2, 34, 60
terrorist, 1–4, 7, 9, 15, 17, 27, 33–5, 37, 47, 49, 57–78, 88, 90, 92, 100, 101, 104, 107, 110, 111, 127, 128, 131–5, 137, 152, 153,

156, 169–72, 175, 177, 178, 184, 215, 221, 222
Trump, D., 7, 177

U

United States of America (USA), 2, 3, 6, 7, 9, 17, 85, 94, 138, 176, 177, 199, 201, 217–19, 223

V

veil, 15, 58, 59, 62, 67, 68, 71, 73, 76, 78, 172, 210

W

welfare, 3, 90, 96, 98, 99, 102–4, 109, 111, 158, 159, 172, 183–9, 226, 227

Wells, H.G., 28

The manufacturer's authorised representative in the EU is Springer Nature Customer Service Centre GmbH, Europaplatz 3, 69115 Heidelberg, Germany. If you have any concerns regarding our products, please contact ProductSafety@springernature.com

Printed and bound by CPI Group (UK) Ltd, Croydon, CR0 4YY

23/03/2026

02076662-0007